# BRAVE CROSSING

## A Journey In-Between

## Maria Alvarez Stroud

**LITTLE CREEK PRESS**
AND BOOK DESIGN

MINERAL POINT, WISCONSIN

Little Creek Press®
A Division of Kristin Mitchell Design, Inc.
5341 Sunny Ridge Road
Mineral Point, Wisconsin 53565

Book Design and Project Coordination:
Little Creek Press and Book Design

First Printing
August 2021

Printed in Wisconsin, United States of America

For more information or to order books,
www.littlecreekpress.com

Library of Congress Control Number: 2021911055

ISBN-13: 978-1-955656-01-6

Dedicated to
Leah & Sawyer

# Author's Note

When people read historical fiction, it is common to have questions about fact and sources. These notes are being provided to give some answers and shed light on the research that was conducted to make the story as historically accurate as possible.

Because the story is based on a true story about my father, the historical figures and events are as real as I could render them according to recorded history. I relied on memories of my relatives, both in the Philippines and in the United States, for specific family events and consulted articles from the *Chicago Tribune* for events taking place in and around Chicago. Numerous sources were used for historical events taking place in the Philippines, although I'd like to give special mention to the *Casa Ordoveza—The Story of an Illustrious Filipino Clan* history book, including its extensive family tree. This book was my go-to source for both big picture and important insights about the times, culture, and events during and after the Philippine-American War.

Other sources were acquired through the Newberry Library and Harold Washington Library Center in Chicago, as well as the Milwaukee Public Library and Medical School of Wisconsin Libraries. In addition, the following universities provided factual information: the University of Chicago, the Lewis Institute (now the Illinois Institute of Technology in Chicago), the Medical School of Champagne-Urbana, the Jefferson College of Philadelphia's Medical School, and the Medical School of Wisconsin (now Marquette Medical School) in Milwaukee, Wisconsin.

The description of the ship is based on written descriptions and pictures. However, other than Ricardo, all passengers are fictional.

Similarly, other than family, most of the characters are completely fictitious with the exception of the physician and judge in Galesville, Wisconsin.

# Table of Contents

Three Years Later

**PART SIX**

# Praise for *Brave Crossing*

*Brave Crossing* is the best kind of historical fiction, a novel that makes you care for the characters and keep turning the pages. I was hooked from Ricardo's early ocean crossing to the United States as an uncertain Spanish-Filipino immigrant to his reflections near the end of his life in a small western Wisconsin city. It's a wonder, and some might say only in America. I say only in the hands of a gifted storyteller like Maria Alvarez Stroud.

Doug Moe, Writer at Large

.·········.

This is a wonderful immigrant story. With impressive research and "what's going to happen next" writing, Maria Alvarez Stroud tells the tale of young Ricardo Alvarez, who, traveling alone, makes his way from the Philippines to the United States in 1916. He faces racism of the worst kind. But he keeps picking himself up and continues to pursue his dream of becoming a medical doctor, a fascinating story.

Jerry Apps, Author of *The Wild Oak*

.·········.

This epistolary tale provides fresh and compelling insight into the immigrant experience. Readers travel vicariously with young Ricardo on a physical and emotional journey that presents unending challenges. Ricardo is a complex character who struggles with injustices and sometimes makes mistakes, but never loses his compassion, determination, and dream of becoming a doctor. Maria Alvarez Stroud vividly evokes the journey, from the Philippine Islands' church bells and cockatoos to Chicago's squalid boardinghouses to rural Wisconsin's peaceful beauty. *Brave Crossing* will enlighten you, wrench your heart, and ultimately lift your spirits.

Kathleen Ernst, Author

One of the most difficult writing genres is the historical novel. That a first-time author chooses to write in this genre is a reflection of great self-confidence. Maria Alvarez Stroud's first book, *Brave Crossing*, is a tribute to her father, clothed in fiction. It is the story of a young man's dream of adventure and a different if not a better life in another country.

While most migrant stories are of men running from a life of poverty and a hopeless future, the hero in *Brave Crossing*, Ricardo Alvarez was none of these. He was a young Filipino belonging to an upper-class family in the province of Laguna, Philippines. That he decides to leave the comforts of a privileged life and go to America, albeit as a first-class passenger on the ship Tanyu Maru, is an unusual story.

The book covers several decades from 1912-1972. Maria Alvarez Stroud writes with a passion for details and an authenticity to historical events that cannot be questioned. Read the book and learn a bit of Philippine history and culture through the letters of Ricardo to his family. Discover the mixed bag of kindnesses, great opportunities, as well as ugly racism Ricardo encountered in his early days in America. *Brave Crossing* is a story of victory over mindless discrimination, great pride in a dream fulfilled, and the triumph of enculturation. If we have the story of Everyman, then this graced narrative is the story of Every Migrant.

Merle O. Basco, Author, Philippines

.·········.

Through letters, notes, journaling, and telegrams, *Brave Crossing* is a deeply personal look into the desire, the doubt, and the decision of one man to leave everyone and everything dear behind and embrace the unknown in search of the promise of America—a promise both earned and kept.

Rodney Nelsestuen, MFA, Author, Book Critic

Ang mahabang paglalakbay ay nanggaling sa Isang hakbang.

**A long voyage begins with just one step.**

# The Beginning

I don't look like many Filipinos. With my wide nose and bigger frame, I stand out. I know I do. Well, not as much as my papa. He was a beanpole, at least a foot taller than the typical Filipino. But then he was a full-blooded Spaniard, not even a drop of Filipino. Everyone called him "The Captain"—not because he was one, although he did come over on a ship from Spain. Because he was so much bigger, I guess they thought it fit.

While my papa was big and commanding, my mama was anything but. She was a Filipina beauty, tiny like a flower in constant bloom. My sister took after her. Me—I'm much more like my father. I used to take such pride in that fact. I know I walked around as if the world were in the palm of my hand. Not so once the Americans took us over. I was only a niño pequeño, barely old enough to blow my own nose, and I didn't understand until years later what their presence meant for me and my family, for Filipinos.

How many years it has taken me to know our twisted history. How first the Americans fought with us against Spain. Then once the Spaniards were defeated, the Americans fought against us when we wanted to claim our independence. I remember learning this in one of my first history classes, and I couldn't stop scratching my head. Apparently both times, we had to hide away in the hills. Seeing I was only in my fifth year, I have bits and pieces of memories of the second time we hid. Then a disease struck that killed thousands right when we became America's colony to do with as they pleased. By then, death had become as natural as drinking water. You couldn't escape it. That, I remember.

And now, my Lola is dead. After all she had lived through, how could a simple fall from her horse-drawn carriage cause death?

"She was too young to die." That's what everyone whispers as they parade past her casket, looking as if she is in deep slumber. Women I've never seen before whimper, others wail. Men of all ages hold her hand while children are lifted up to bow their heads. So many seem to need to touch her. My Lola, my grandmother, who wrapped me in her world of kindness, held me when my mother suffered, wiped my tears away when my father was no longer with us, and promised she would always be there for me. A promise I know she wanted to keep but couldn't.

"Remember, Ricardo," she said to me the day before she died. "Remember all I have taught you: to pray with your whole heart, and to take that prayer into what you do in kindness." She paused and squeezed my hand until I wanted to pull away.

"And remember to find your own path, even though it lies elsewhere. *Oye*, we've talked about this. I know you will not forget." I flashed on memories I didn't want to recall. Neighborhood friends whispering behind my back, some no longer friends. Did their parents tell them to stay away? In Manila, standing alone at parties, busying myself at home when I wasn't invited, teachers no longer calling on me first, sometimes not at all. I shook my head, willing the images to go away.

"Lola, I do remember most but not all of the reasons why you think I must leave and set my sights on America. I'm only seventeen. I'm not ready," I told her. Her smile was a drop of rain mixed with sunshine. It almost made me give in to tears and laugh at the same time.

"No, my dear boy, not yet. You will know when the time is right, and you'll remember all of the reasons why it is for the best. Now I need to close my eyes."

I held her hand as she floated into slumber. I hoped she was right about remembering. But so much of my childhood is hidden behind a murkiness I can't make out or even touch. Growing up, I so often felt half-blind to what was and what wasn't.

Now, eight days later, half of Santa Cruz is here to honor her, to say goodbye to the woman who brought life back to this church after the Americans almost destroyed it—and her home, steps away. And here she lays lifeless, her cries for peaceful negotiations long ago drowned out by bombs and bullets.

I've heard countless stories of her efforts: how her days were full, tending to the needs of the church as if its very structure was part of our family. She told me once that what she loved most about La Iglesia de la Concepción was its ability to create community for everyone, even the old men who lived on the streets, the families who looked like they had everything but were lost to each other, and the little boys like me who wondered where they belonged.

Today hundreds stand in line to bid her farewell. Some are here to honor, others to watch, to listen, and to lay eyes on my grandmother who some think to be a saint, a miracle maker, a woman who gave herself to the church and the people of Santa Cruz up until her final days.

My legs have fallen asleep from standing so long, my cheeks are almost raw from kisses, and my hands are sore from shaking. I'm ready for this day to be over.

Finally, the casket lid is lowered and sealed. Family and close friends form a circle around her one last time, and we bow our heads in prayer. Her face is perfectly framed below the casket's window. For a moment, I can't breathe. I want to stop everything and drag her out. She can't really be dead, can she? In my short life, there are too many who have been taken away. And then I hear a sound so desperate and mortally sad, and I realize it is coming from me. I bite my tongue trying to contain what is escaping. My sister, Nena, squeezes my hand. Tito Juan gently grabs my other, as if to say he understands how hard it is to say goodbye.

When we finally escape to Lola's house and her grand parlor, where dancing and frivolity were once commonplace, I slink into a corner chair, away from prying eyes. As wine and beer begin to flow, the stories roll out, mostly about Lola Brigida, the war between the Philippines and the United States. In that war, Lola Brigida knew both sides. American soldiers she once cheered on, only to become enemies a short time later. Tonight I listen intently, hoping something will be said to help me truly remember.

As they talk, more fragments of memories flash before me: an American soldier striding into Lola's home and picking up a ball I had dropped, him getting down to my eye level to ask me my name. He had a round face covered in hair. I hid behind my mother. People arguing, pounding fists on the table. Sleeping under a tree next to Papa with a sea of stars overhead and being jolted awake to what I thought was a storm.

Tonight I learn there was no storm—only the roar of guns killing. I hear how much has changed for many of our clan since the Americans have come to stay, especially those who, like me, look more Spanish than Filipino. Rafael announces he will no longer be the city administrator for MajaMaja, and Cousin Domingo is contemplating studying law in the United States, "so he can find his way in this new place," he says. Other cousins complain of new American teachers who can't speak a word of Spanish or Tagalog, forcing their children to learn English. Although the night is warm, I'm shivering.

Not far away sits my dear sister, Nena, with Vicente, whom I'm sure will be her husband. At twenty-one, she's perfect. She catches me watching and waves me away with eyes twinkling. How many times today was I asked, "What will you do without your grandmother?"

Each time, all I can say is, "I don't know."

Ang taong hindi lumingon sa pinanggalingan
ay hindi makakarating sa paroroonan.

**A person who does not remember where he came
from will never reach his destination.**

# PART ONE
# On The Boat

**June 2, 1916: Leaving the Port of Manila, Philippines**

Where are they? With so many carriages zigzagging their way through masses of people and wagons filled to the brim, I can't see them. I push my way to the upper deck railing and wave in hopes they see me. I'm encircled by passengers, boat hands trying to clear passageways, and families attempting to stay together, as they, too, look for their loved ones far below.

And then I catch sight of Nena leaning heavily on Vicente, surrounded by my aunts, uncles, and cousins. Invisible string ties them together, with their heads shifting in unison from right to left, scanning the upper decks for me. And yet, they can't see me even when I wave my arms wildly over my head.

My legs tremble, and suddenly I want to run to them. What am I doing, leaving my homeland, the people who care about me, my sister? As tears of worry roll down Nena's cheeks, mine begin to flow in concert. Soon I'll be looking like I'm having a seizure, as I can't stop my body from shaking as if I'm draped in slabs of ice.

Could I still get off the ship? The only thing that stops me is a silent whisper in my ear: "This is what you're meant to do." I freeze, no longer aware of the noise or the people pushing and shoving around me. Lola, I hear you. Without warning, I can hardly breathe. I thought I would feel detached, finally free of burden. Instead, I'm plagued with doubt.

Still, I know this journey is something I have to do. Years and years ago, my father set out from Spain, found a new home, happiness, wealth beyond most Filipinos' dreams, a family. And yet, this wasn't enough for him.

What is *my* enough? I have to find out.

Ako ay dudulog sa Diyos. (I go with God).

**JOURNAL ENTRY**
10:00 a.m., June 3, 1916
Aboard the Tenyo Maru

I have to keep reminding myself why I'm here. Lola Brigida was the only one to tell me what I had guessed for some time—being more Spanish than Filipino was no longer a blessing. "More of a curse, especially without parents," she said more than once. I didn't tell anyone what she told me. Slowly, though, I came to believe she was right. Oh, but Lola, others didn't make me getting on this ship easy. I can still hear them:

"Ricardo, I think you should stay and become a pharmacist like your father was."

"Ricardo, have you ever thought of starting your own business?"

"Ricardo, you have the life. Why change it?"

Of course, they thought my life was grand. I lived in one of the nicest houses in Santa Cruz, owned a motorcar, went to the best university, looked like I had the means to never go hungry and always be well cared for.

But ...

They don't know I live on my grandmother's kindness.

They don't know whereas once I could go anywhere and be greeted by Spaniards and Filipinos, now most Spaniards are long gone, and some Filipinos no longer are friendly.

They don't know.

*Kaya ko ito.* (I can do this).

**JOURNAL ENTRY**
June 6, 1916

Today, I learned there are 300 of us in first-class quarters. So few are Filipinos. This morning at breakfast, I counted thirty-two. I thought there would be more of us—more passengers who spoke Spanish, at least. They're here but hidden, far below in steerage. At home, I got by with the English I knew, but not here. Why didn't I think to learn more before I left? Why was I so lazy? I wouldn't want to hear my sister's answers to these questions. She would not be gentle.

I should have known better about skin color as well. *Kung paano tanga ako* (how stupid of me), like I didn't learn those lessons in the Philippines. How Papa would yell at us to stay out of the sun! I didn't understand why until I got a bit older and finally noticed those with darker skin were darker because they weren't able to stay out of the sun. Until then, I hadn't noticed they were the ones who worked in fields, on top of buildings, in the streets—anywhere they could to put food on the table. I never noticed or thought about it. There, I always was on the lighter side. To be the darker one on this ship has given me a knot in my stomach whenever I leave the safety of my stateroom. How sheltered I was.

Yesterday when I heard a little American girl say, "I'm scared, Mommy. Why is that man so dark?" I wanted to scream. I've heard so many indistinguishable languages the past several days, and no one flinches. Unusual styles of dress, and no one is afraid. Why is skin color any different? Do the Americans assume that I have earned this color by laboring under the hot sun?

As the Americans examine me, I observe them. The women seem exotic, like porcelain dolls my sister collected, the men a mix of everything. Some look unhealthy; they're so fair, almost gray, like their time of parting is not far away. Men have marks, almost like little craters. Not something you see on the faces of Filipinos.

What do they see when they look at me? They have no idea who I am and how I came to be here. Have no idea of my family's position back in the Philippines, how influential and widespread we are. My hand curls into a fist as I write this.

I want to hide in my quarters, but I won't. I need to do more than look and listen. I need to be with them, if I hope to live amongst them. I write this and have no idea what living amongst them even means.

### Letter to Anuncian (Nena)
8:30 p.m., June 7, 1916

Dearest Nena,

First, I have to tell you about this remarkable ship. Do you remember when Lola Brigida took us to Hotel de Oriente in Manila? You must, as I recall you commenting on the hallways that looked like they were encased in gold and stairways that seemed to go into the heavens. I'm sure you remember the ballroom where we dined was twice as big as our house. Walls were covered with paintings of important people we were supposed to know. There are rooms like that on this ship.

One room I know you would love is the Reading Room with bookshelves from floor to ceiling, ornate loungers, and cozy chairs to sit on and enjoy a hardcover treasure. If I lost you on this ship, that is where I would find you. I can imagine you spending hours in an attempt to explore every corner.

The Promenade is where passengers walk relentlessly around the ship, not so much to look at the ocean but to look at each other. Some lounge in the sun. Others quietly chat with each other. I've strolled, although I have found few to chat with along the way. Another space you'd love is right off the Promenade, a lounge with clusters of chairs to gaze out windows on either side of the ship. When the weather is questionable, this is where everyone will likely come to watch while remaining safe and warm.

The room I am most taken with is the ballroom. Picture me, Sister, dressed in my favorite suit in which you say I look so—what's the word you used?—refined. Or was it dashing? Thinking back on it, I'm not sure if you were serious or not. Either way, I did look good, didn't I? Having been seen by all of these people that I spied on throughout the day, I wanted to appear dashing.

So off I went to dine. All I needed to do was follow the melodies that floated throughout the ship, as they were our calling card: sweet notes encouraging you to walk faster to hear more. As I fought the urge to run down the winding stairway, I noticed it was wide enough for two dozen people to walk side by side. Even the bannisters looked like they would support an army of strong men. I descended alone. I wasn't prepared for the spectacle that lied before me.

I dropped into an affair fit for kings and queens—this even more elegant than our finest celebrations. With over fifty tables adorned with white linen sparkling from the light of candelabras and reflected in enormous windows looking out on the sea landscape, I found myself staring in awe. Others did the same, all of us in a trance. In that moment, we were all royalty.

Of course, Sister, the moment passed as I began to look at the sea of faces. Never before had I been with such a large group of non-Filipinos. I was one of no more than three dozen in the room. Broken English and all, I had intended to regale them with my infectious personality. If I can win over Filipinos, I thought, I could win over Americans and all the others as well. Once seated, however, I remained quiet, jolted into a world engulfed by English. When I tried to talk, my tongue seemed to get twisted in the middle of a thought. Words in English tripped out of my mouth, greeted with polite smiles and obvious confusion.

And so my journey begins, Sister. Lord in heaven, I pray I am ready for what is to come.

Warmest wishes to you,

*Lyong kapatid na lalaki* (Your brother),

Ricardo

### *Letter to Tito (Uncle) Juan*
June 8, 1916

Dearest Uncle,

And so here I am, on a massive ship in the middle of a deserted ocean. You told me it wouldn't take me long to get a sense of how different the world outside of our country is, and it hasn't. I can't seem to go anywhere without hearing English, something I managed to avoid quite well at home. My brain is taxed from trying to recall as much as I can. Otherwise, I'll be destined to become a mute. Today I pushed myself by trying to converse with a young man around my age standing near me on the Promenade.

The only reason he talked with me was because my hat flew off, almost into the sea. As he grabbed it, he said something I didn't understand. I nodded and said, "Thank you." At least I knew how to say that in English. I knew instantly I had said the wrong thing as he repeated what he said. All I could say was, "Sorry, I don't understand." In hopes our conversation would continue, I quickly added, "You American, yes?"

He looked amused.

"I am, and you are not," he said.

I didn't like the way he tilted his head back and laughed a little too long. I half-heartedly joined in because I was desperate to talk. He asked where I was from. When I answered the Philippines, he looked surprised. He took a half-step away from me to have a better look. I felt like an oxen on bid at the market as he studied me from head to foot. His manners were atrocious. Uncle, who does such a thing?

"You are here alone?"

"Yes," I said.

He looked at me and around us at the Promenade like something was amiss. Was it me? Did he think I didn't belong? Before I could think of anything further to say, he nodded and simply walked away. No "Good day." No "Pleasure to make your acquaintance." No nothing. Uncle, is this what you were implying when you said I would learn quickly about Americans? I pray not. My attempts will continue, hopefully with more positive results.

I look forward to any counsel you have to share.

Your reverent nephew,

Ricardo

*Letter from Nena*
Found June 11, 1916

My dearest Brother,

My hope is you find this letter several days into your trip. Although knowing you, your discovery will be at least a week or two later. Putting things in their proper place was never something you thought to do. I wonder, do they have people who pick up after you in your room? I do hope so. Oh, where to start, little Brother? I have so much to say, I don't know where to begin—I miss you, and you're not even gone.

What will I do without you? You have always been the person who makes me smile, even when it was the last thing I thought possible. And, yes, more than anyone, you know how to calm me and help me through those mysterious moments of quiet hysteria when I'm quite sure I'm about to run screaming from the room. Then there you are. Ready to take my hand, give a subtle nod, and I'm right again.

The last time was at Christmas several years ago. Do you remember, Ricardo? We were at Lola Brigida's, and the gifts were piled so high you couldn't see out the windows to the patio. At sixteen, I felt ancient next to many of our cousins. They couldn't sit still, running about like little demons, waiting for their gifts.

"Let's go family to family," someone said. "Parents can hand their gifts to their children, one by one."

I began to panic, afraid of how we were going to handle once again not having parents at our side. You looked at me from across the room and could tell I was on the verge of running out of the room. Suddenly you were by my side, your arm around mine, reassuring me we would be fine. You calmed me, quietly, so others wouldn't notice.

We have always done this for each other. So you'll need to imagine me next to you when things look bleak as they may when you feel all alone. We haven't seen each other as much as we once did, but to know you were near always brought such comfort. Whether you were nearby in Santa Cruz or hours away in Manila, I knew you were there. Now I will learn to hold you deeply in my prayers. You are family, no matter how far away you choose to be.

I won't lie. I don't completely understand why you had to leave. Yes, of course, there are opportunities for you because America has finally opened its doors to Filipinos. I do know that you long to do something and find your place in the world, as you have put it. I only wish it weren't in America. I worry; you know I do. What will you face with no family at your side? Will there even be other Filipinos to converse with? The Americans have taken over our country; will they take you over as well? Please, Ricardo, don't become one of them. Do keep your promise to write and let me know of your many adventures. I, too, will be dutiful in writing back, boring you with our daily goings-on.

About your future, Ricardo, I have great faith in you and trust that success will find you. Patience and prudence need be posts for you to lean on in the months ahead. Remember, *ang dios ay malapit na malapit*. (God is always close at hand.)

I will write as soon as you give me the details of where you are. My prayers are with you, Brother.

Nena

❧

## Letter to Nena
### 8:00 a.m., June 12, 1916

Sister, what a surprise!

Finding your letter suddenly made the first sunless day a bit brighter (and yes, it was over a week when I decided to really go through my trunk and try to put things in place). I've read and re-read your letter countless times, and I am sure it will be read more in the days ahead.

Life abroad the Tanyo Maru is difficult to describe. My days are spent wandering through this massive ship, or lounging on the Promenade or in the library. I spend too much of my time alone, still struggling to open my mouth for fear of embarrassing myself. I've taken up reading, sometimes even in English.

I miss simple things I never much gave a thought to, like the early morning songs of cockatoos, dogs barking, people haggling, the church bells ringing. On this huge ship, the quiet is deafening, even with little ones all around.

The other day, I retrieved a ball that had gotten away from a little boy. I was about to chat with him when his mother appeared. Without a look in my direction, she grabbed his hand, her eyes burrowing into the poor boy. She scurried him away. I ached for the boy whose only friend was a ball he couldn't play with.

Thank goodness I have met a fellow Filipino couple, Jaime and Esperanza Rodriguez. For the last several evenings, we've dined together. They both are more than proficient in English. I am grateful for that. I, too, get a reprieve from the constant English. We go back and forth between Spanish and Tagalog. Although they are quick to remind me, "Ricardo, the more English you speak, the better it will be for you."

They're maybe fifteen years older than me. Mr. Rodriguez looks Filipino: small, lean, wiry, hair black with hints of gray, and that Filipino nose—narrow yet refined. He dresses impeccably, every day another tailored suit or embroidered *camisa* with tailored pants. He tells me he comes from humble beginnings but looks like a man now who has plenty. He finds friends like Tita Josephina finds stray dogs. No matter what language they speak, they seem to like him. The man exudes confidence.

Mrs. Rodriguez is like a small flower, her face delicate with deep brown eyes, her body small but solid, almost robust. When she enters a room, you notice her. Although quieter than her husband, she too exudes friendliness. You would like them both. They live in a city called Chicago, somewhere in the middle of the country, reachable by train from San Francisco, which is where we arrive.

Several nights ago, they witnessed my initial attempt at dinner conversation in English and have taken it upon themselves to teach me more words so I might sound more like an adult rather than, as they stated, "a boy of about seven or eight." More importantly, they have taught me the words to properly ask someone to dance. With their coaching, last night I did.

My first challenge was to find a young woman who would say "yes." I noticed one young woman looking longingly at the dance floor. Her face, the color of ivory, was framed with long golden curls. I felt destined for a "yes," but when I approached her table, her father held his hand up and denied me before I even opened my mouth. I did notice, however, her being tossed about by several other white fellows a short time later. One I recognized—a young man who wanted nothing to do with me when I previously attempted to engage him in conversation. He could use some help on the dance floor. The poor girl's feet were sure to be bloody.

I had almost given up when I noticed an American family with a daughter close to my age. She wasn't simply watching dancers; she was transfixed with all their moves. I approached their table, addressing both her and her parents. They seemed pleased. With encouragement from her mother, she agreed. Margaret is her name. She is timid, has a pleasant face, big moon-shaped eyes, and untamed sunlit hair. She has the tiniest of hands, with skin the color of cream. During our first dance, I thought she was merely waiting for the song to be finished. But she relaxed finally.

We danced again. This is when I realized eyes were upon us. Small groups of men and women were covering their mouths, like what they were saying shouldn't be heard by anyone nearby. Several women pointed in our direction. Apparently this is not common—a young American girl on the dance floor with … what am I? A foreigner? To them, I guess I am. At first, I was self-conscious, like a child being caught doing something wrong. But then knowing we were being watched, I danced with a bit more flare, swooping Margaret with more finesse. She laughed, looking like she was enjoying herself, and didn't notice their stares.

I miss you, Sister. How is your work with the children at the orphanage? Are you still managing to help Uncle Victor with his history project? Honestly, I'm hungry for most any news: silly sagas of family, secrets about friends, or even details about your time at market. Yes, I am lonely, but do not worry for me.

Thank you for your trust, dear Sister. I appreciate every kind word you wrote, and I do pray for you every night. Blessings to Vicente, who hopefully hasn't grown tired of your musing for me.

*Mahal ka sa akin.* (You are dear to me.)

Ricardo

### JOURNAL ENTRY
June 12, 1916

I can't tell Nena the truth. How every morning I make myself rise to face another day of frustration. How I try not to search for a fellow Filipino to relax with each day. How some Filipinos are not interested in talking with a needy boy who wants to speak to them in Spanish. Probably afraid their daughters might be interested in me instead of an American.

Thank God I've met Jaime and Esperanza Rodriquez. They have their feet already planted in America, and I want to learn from them as much as I can. They seem comfortable with whom they are and what they look like. They stride into a room without worry, shaking hands, willingly sharing stories. I watch them from a distance as they chat with Americans as if they are best of friends. I'm like a stray dog in need of training.

### JOURNAL ENTRY
#### 11:00 p.m., June 17, 1916

I haven't dreamt of Papa in years. And now this dream—before I forget, I have to write it down. Running after him over dimly lit cobblestone streets, streets I don't recall surrounded by worn-out buildings. At first not even knowing it was he. All I knew was someone was there, someone moving through the shadows with ease, almost gliding. I sensed there were secrets there, and I had to find out what they were. Secrets, always secrets.

I didn't recognize him. He was dressed in such formal attire, and his shadow loomed over him, his top hat and scarf of red-speckled gray tied loosely around his collar. They stood together, his shadow and him— unmoving, one looking meek, the other menacing.

Not until he bowed, crossed himself, and lifted his hands to his lips did I know it was Papa. I flew after him. It was so real that my legs still feel as if I've actually run. One minute, he's there, and the next gone, swallowed by shadows. I remember a clock chiming—one, two, three times. Then there he was again. "Papa, Papa, stop! I want to talk to you. Come back!" I yelled. I was close enough now to touch him, but my arms wouldn't move. He turned, and with his full-faced smile, I heard the voice I once knew, "Ricardo, my son." And then he vanished. It felt as real as the bed I lie on or the journal I write in. For a moment, we were together.

Papa, I miss you, and Mama, too. Sometimes I can't remember what she looks like. Her features are blurred, faded like the photograph I carry with me of the two of you. Maybe I shouldn't be surprised I dreamt of you, but I am. Why now? Is it because I'm doing what you did? Leaving home for a new world? In the dream, there were secrets I was chasing after that you must hold. What are they, Papa? If I knew, I might be braver. Every night, I pray for strength. If I could only get words of wisdom from you or even a simple nod, I might get closer to knowing if this journey is truly for the best.

## Letter to Nena
June 21, 1916

Nena,

Today while I walked the Promenade, I witnessed a most disturbing event: an older gentleman and a young Filipino engaged in what initially looked like a rough game of sorts. But as I watched more, I realized this wasn't a game. The older gentleman, definitely an American, was determined to catch the lad, who was not much older than fourteen. He looked terrified of being caught.

They flew down the Promenade, the older gentleman doing a good job of keeping up, even though he carried an extra twenty pounds around his middle. He was issuing a string of commands as he moved.

"Stop!" he yelled. "Stop this instant! I saw what you took! You can't get away!"

"*Mangyaring*, sir, *huwag saktan ako. Kinuha ko ang wala sa halaga.* (Please, sir, do not hurt me. I took nothing of value.)"

I knew the boy's words were not understood. He continued to sprint in and out of people and furniture, hiding himself and then again jumping into a gallop. He truly was alarmed. The gentleman who chased him was persistent, yelling at others to grab the boy. I'd seen this gentleman before. Recently. The encounter wasn't pleasant. He was the man who watched with a look of disgust as I walked away from Margaret and her family the other evening. How could I forget his face, embroiled in distaste the way it was?

Sister, the Filipino boy needed help, I knew it. But for a moment I stood still as a statue. The young man was from steerage—you could tell by his dress and his desperation. What would fellow first-class passengers think about my intervention? What would this man who chased him do to me as a result? I knew I already stood out. Would my helping make it even worse?

I broke into a run after them. The race ended when someone reached out and grabbed the boy so hard he fell to the floor. Within minutes, others had their hands on him to hold him down. I wasn't far behind. I squeezed my way into the group.

"Thank you, sir, for stopping this thief. I witnessed it with my own eyes," the gentleman shouted through gasps of air. "He took my wife's ring right off the table next to us!"

"Let's search his pockets," someone hollered.

The Filipino kept repeating, "Please, I meant no harm" in Tagalog, but I was the only one who knew what he was saying.

I stepped forward before it went any further, saying as politely as I could and in the best English I knew, "Excuse me, pero the boy does not know what he did wrong." I could have been the priest stepping up to the pulpit to start Mass, as suddenly no one spoke or moved. All eyes were on me.

The man who had chased the boy scowled, his nostrils dilated, his breath fast, reeking of pork. I stepped back.

"I have often seen you on the first-class Promenade and dining room," he said. "You say you can understand him?"

"Yes. He is from my country, the Philippine Islands."

"Do you know him?"

"No, sir, but I can help. Please, I tell him what you think he did," I said trying hard to pronounce each word as best I could.

"He took my wife's ring. I saw it with my own eyes."

"Please, sir," I said. "My English is not good. I speak Tagalog, what the boy speaks. What did he take?"

"My wife's ring," he said. Looking annoyed, he pointed to the ring on his hand. I nodded.

I proceeded to softly tell the young man in Tagalog what the man had said.

"No, no!" he said, looking around with pleading eyes directed to the older gentleman. "I did not take a ring. I only took half a sandwich that had been sitting there for a long time."

I asked him if he knew any English, and he said, "No."

"*Ano po ang pangalan nila?*" I asked.

"Eduardo Lorenzo."

"Ricardo Alvarez," I said, shaking his hand. The men holding him down grumbled about my kindness.

The older gentleman stood as a ringmaster would—hands placed on his wide hips, chest puffed out. "Well, what does he say for himself other than denying he took it?"

"He says he took food, no ring."

"Let's find out." He bent down to reach into Eduardo's pockets. He pulled out a photo; a well-weathered letter; a small knife, which brought gasps from the growing crowd of passengers now gathered around us; and half a sandwich wrapped in paper. There was nothing else.

My distaste for this man grew. He liked being the center of everyone's attention and showed no sign of empathy for the lad.

"The scoundrel has hidden it somewhere. Take his clothes off," yelled the pompous beast, now looking more like a crazed bloodhound.

As I started to protest and the buttons started to fly, a distraught heavyset woman ran into the group.

"Hubert, here is my ring. It simply fell off the table." She held the ring high in the air for everyone to see. "Remember? I took it off. Please, Hubert, let the young man go." She looked from her husband to Eduardo, then to me with imploring eyes. I could tell she was embarrassed by what was taking place.

Well, Nena, it was a sad scene. Hubert stood there in disbelief. He stared at the ring, then back at his wife. What he did next was the most upsetting. He grabbed his wife and marched away, bumping into me without a word of apology to Eduardo. He strutted off. All I could do was have pity for his wife who had to sleep in the same room with the brute. *Crazy darn fool.*

There sat Eduardo, now with his shirt half torn off and his few possessions splayed around him. He looked like a little boy lost, bewildered about what had happened. One by one, people silently slipped away. One gentleman was kind enough to pick up Eduardo's knife and hand it to him. Another gave him a short pat on the back.

Then they were gone.

I helped Eduardo stand up and collect his things. Few as they were, they were his. His shirt was torn, and he was roughed up, beaten by the experience. I took him to the parlor as my guest to get something to eat. I must have had a look of defiance because no one questioned me when I ordered food for both of us. We sat and had lunch together in silence. Neither one of us knew what to say. He refused to eat all of his food, saying he would rather have it later and wrapped it up to take it with him. I walked him back to the third-class entrance. I was unable to say much as I was still so alarmed by what had happened.

Eduardo thanked me so many times that I told him to stop.

"Why did you take the sandwich? Don't they give you enough food in third-class?"

"They do, but I worry about my mother. She is having a baby, and the food isn't the best. She needs more." He looked away, sadness written all over his face.

I nodded, trying to imagine what his time in steerage was like. In Manila, how many times have we seen boys like Eduardo being scooted away? But never have I witnessed such ugliness perpetrated against them.

Nena, who are these people who think you can treat someone like an animal? This man, Hubert, he didn't care about Eduardo, only his ring. No one should be treated this way, steerage or not. I wonder if there will be any repercussions because I helped. Pray for me, Nena, and for Eduardo, too.

Your brother,

Ricardo

## Thank-you note from Eduardo–in Tagalog
### June 22, 1916

Señor Alvarez,

Thank you again for helping me. I don't know what would have happened if you weren't there. Even when they knew I hadn't taken the ring, some of them looked like they still wanted to hurt me. It makes me scared of Americans.

My family would like to meet you. Please come visit. We have simple quarters we share with many others, but we are a happy community down below.

Eduardo Lorenzo

## Note from Mr. Rodriguez
### June 24, 1916

Ricardo, I've been meaning to talk with you, but there simply hasn't been the right time. I know you're upset about what happened with the boy from steerage. As you described it, I can only guess how difficult it was to witness. Now you often talk about what you're missing back home, how wonderful our country is. The picture you paint is perhaps one you hold onto from years ago. As you know, I hadn't been there for many years until this last month. I think it had been over seven years ago since we had visited family.

Much had changed. Seven years ago, I knew Filipinos who filled high posts. Now, Americans sit in their place with only the wealthiest of Filipinos involved. Most speak little Spanish; fewer yet, Tagalog. For many Filipinos, life has not improved. If anything, they are more desperate. When we were there, I felt their unrest, Ricardo, and I was shocked to see even more people living on the streets, without shelter or food.

Maybe you felt some of this before you left. I share these thoughts with you so you remember there is both good and bad about our homeland. What happened to the lad here on the ship could very well happen back in Manila, in American neighborhoods. As our homeland changes, so must we.

As my father would have said to me, "Ang kalakasan ng loob ay bunga ng pag-asa". (Boldness is the fruit of hope.). I'm proud you stood up for the boy.

Your friend,

Mr. Rodriguez

### Invitation from parents of Miss Margaret
#### 10:00 a.m., June 26, 1916

Mr. Ricardo Alvarez,

It would be our pleasure to dine with you this evening. Would you be so kind as to meet us for a cocktail at 6:00 p.m., and we could proceed to dinner together?

We look forward to formally making your acquaintance.

Respectfully,

Mr. & Mrs. Arthur Johnson

### JOURNAL ENTRY
#### 12:00 p.m., June 26, 1916

Mr. Rodriguez tells me it would be an insult if I were to decline the invitation to dine with Margaret and her parents. "Make the most of it," he says. "Explain as best you can that you speak limited English."

But how uncomfortable will I be? How uncomfortable will we all be? In two weeks, I can speak and understand much more. Thanks to the Rodriguezes and Margaret, I can now utter questions and understand most answers. I can manage simple conversations, but not much more.

Mr. Rodriguez says, "Don't be embarrassed. See your evening with them as an opportunity!"

As he said, I do like to dance with Margaret. Wish he wouldn't have said this with a smirk. I need to give them a written response soon or this, too, is an insult. In English! *Masyado ito.* (This is too much.)

### Note to Mr. & Mrs. Arthur Johnson
1:30 p.m., June 26, 1916

Thank you. I am happy to dine with you this evening.
Respectfully,
Ricardo Alvarez

### JOURNAL ENTRY
June 27, 1916

Margaret must think me a buffoon. My conversation with her father unburied opinions I hadn't expressed before. Even while Margaret and I danced later, I wasn't able to stop replaying what we had said to each other. *Dios mio*, I made the man apologize for not knowing my background or Philippine history. I'm the one who should apologize.

How did it come to that? The evening had started out well. I remember telling them about my family, how I grew up in Santa Cruz, and about Lola's many banana plantations. That's when Mr. Johnson talked of his business of buying abaca—hemp is what he called it. Yes, that's right, he imitated peeling a banana as banana and hemp plants look much alike. I finally understood, and we all chuckled. Inside, my heart was in my stomach, and I felt as slow as a banana bug working his way to the fruit.

Mrs. Johnson asked me if I planned on attending a university and what I hoped to learn. "English," I said and laughed. Thank goodness they joined me. I felt a rush of blood running to my head.

We all settled into eating, and I recall thinking our conversation was nice. We were talking, even laughing together. Margaret, sweet Margaret—how kind she was, occasionally reaching for my hand for a short squeeze. I should have known by now to feel this way is only a prelude to the bad about to happen.

Mr. Johnson wanted me to know how well versed he was on Filipino history. His opinion about Spain was where it started. How did he put it? Oh, yes, something like, "Spain did little— *un poco*—for your people. The country is not ready to rule itself, don't you think?"

He didn't know my father was a peninsular—Spanish-born and raised in Spain. He didn't know how, for over 300 years, Spaniards and Filipinos had intermixed through marriage. Marry a Spaniard, and a Filipino family was rewarded with property, as my mother's family and many others had been, revered as mestizos. I tried to not sound surprised or, worse yet, angry, but I'm sure my words felt unkind to him.

When I said, "I am Spanish, I am Filipino, and was taught to be proud of both," I'm sure I spoke too loudly. Then I broke into Spanish. I couldn't stop myself. By the look on Mr. Johnson's face, he understood some, about America breaking its promise to give "independence," a word I said in English.

At first, he was silent. We all were. Tension, so much tension. My hands were wet with it. After that came his apology and admission he hadn't realized the complexity of our history or of mine.

His admission felt like suddenly a window was opened, with much needed fresh air blown in. I knew his lack of understanding wasn't his fault, but I said nothing. I responded only with a nod. How long we sat in awkward silence.

When Mrs. Johnson suggested Margaret and I dance, we both leapt to the floor. To have Margaret in my arms helped the pounding in my head go away. Margaret quietly mumbled apologies for her father. I shook my head and said nothing more. I knew I was in the wrong but couldn't say it.

I had thought they were going to be difficult to be with, and they weren't. Mr. Johnson with his square chin and balding hairline likes to discuss issues at hand. The issue of Filipino independence was simply too close to home for me. And Mrs. Johnson showed such grace throughout the entire evening. Like Margaret, she isn't stunning but more alluring with her kind eyes, ready smile, and simple dress. I write this and know I need to apologize to Mr. and Mrs. Johnson and to Margaret, too.

Ricardo, let me again apologize to you for the statement I made during our dinner this past evening. Of course, your country's history is more complicated than I would realize, and how foolish of me to not see how personal as well. How easy it is to make broad-stroke assumptions without seeing the ramifications.

I do hope this won't change your opinion of me or of Margaret. This past year has been a rather unpleasant one for her, and you have become a much-needed companion. I know she has great admiration for you. And we would very much like to further acquaint ourselves as well. Elizabeth and I look forward to dining with you again.

With sincerity,

Mr. Arthur Johnson

# JULY

## Letter to Tita (Aunt) Carmen
July 1, 1916

Dearest Tita Carmen,

I have thought of you often the past few days. I've had ample time to stew—too much really. We've been in the middle of a tropical storm, a mild one, the captain tells us. God forbid if I were to experience anything more than mild. I have spent much of my time in my quarters, feeling like I'd rather die than spend another day with pail in hand, ready for another outburst.

How many times you helped me when I was ill as a child. You were always such a help to my mother. I recall one time in particular when I was no more than five years old. You and Mama had tried everything to make me feel better: cod liver oil, cold baths, baked apples, anything to settle my tumultuous stomach and to stop my body from burning up. You sat with me all night long, giving me sips of something warm with hints of cinnamon and vanilla. In the morning, I felt more myself. I hugged you with all of my might, probably more like an attack than anything. You let me stay that way for a long time. You whispered, "Hush, child, I would do anything for you, anything." Tita, I hold that memory dearly. I always will.

Before I left, you encouraged me to write to you if I needed a friend. How did you put it? You'd be a person to share your doubts and fears with, without judgment. I write because I do need this.

I had no idea how difficult this journey would be—how different, strange, exhausting. At times, I have wanted to become that little boy you knew and scream at the myriad of impatient Americans: "Stop! Stop treating me like I'm an idiot. How dare you. I'm not stupid."

Of course, I haven't. What good would my ranting do? The Americans would only look at me with even more angst. I didn't know we are so different from Americans. Did you?

I try hard to be friendly to everyone on board, especially the Americans. In first-class quarters, they seem to be everywhere. They're boisterous, confident, and showy. They don't walk. They strut. They want to be seen–yet some don't see me. Some only talk to me when I speak to them. Others don't even try.

How can we dress so much alike yet be so very different? Our clothes are made of similar fine cloth, our shoes of superb leather, and our families are of high standings. To think my brown skin and imperfect English keep them from interacting with me no longer shocks me. I find it sickening, truly maddening.

I hope I have never shunned anyone for his or her skin color or lack of status. But then I fear I have and had no idea. You would tell me if I have, would you not? Like you, I've never had to worry if I would eat the next day or not. Or where I would sleep. In Manila and even in Santa

Cruz, we saw people go hungry, living in homes we wouldn't consider fit for our pet dog. Those circumstances were what we were accustomed to, comfortable with. Their situations were a reality I never questioned.

But in Santa Cruz, we lived among those in need of help. We interacted with the poorest, and with the help of Lola Brigida, we always helped others when we could. In school, the poor and wealthy were classmates. At celebrations, we were neighbors. We interacted with each other.

Here on the ship, rich and poor are separated, much more like Manila, although I know I never thought about how separate we were while attending the university. Without effort, we don't even see each other. I know on this ship, two floors down, are people who have spent every peso they have to be here. I've seen firsthand how they are treated—with contempt, distrust, without respect when they dare to be seen in first-class areas.

Sometimes I wonder if I would feel more comfortable with the passengers in steerage. Then again, I'd be miserable without all the comforts of first-class, and I don't imagine I'd really fit in. But then my fit in first-class is questionable as well. At times, I wish I could turn around and go home to what I know, to the comforts of our clan, to feel a sense of belonging. In my letters, I tell only so much of this to Nena. I fear to write how I truly feel, even in my journal—afraid to make what I feel too real. But all of this is real. I don't fit in, and I'm afraid of what I am going to experience once we reach America. I shudder to think I will be treated differently, seen as less, when I may have more. How can I become more accepted? And if I was, would I, too, become inflated, unable to accept others who aren't what I see in the mirror?

Thank you for giving me a safe place to express my fears. I clearly have painted a picture of despair, which isn't fully accurate. Many days have been pleasant. I have made acquaintance with several fellow Filipinos, both in first-class and in steerage. I'm even friendly with several Americans, regardless of limitations with language.

You know me, Tita. I do not give up easily. I will persevere, especially with your willingness to listen to me sputter and spew. I feel remarkably better, and this time you didn't even need to give me medicine.

I'll mail this when I get to Honolulu. And when I have an address, I will send it to you. Here I am, twenty-one years old, and you are still taking care of me. I hear your voice still: *"Hush, child, I would do anything for you, anything."* And I would for you, my dear Tita.

With deepest regards,

*Ako po ay taos-pusong nagpapasalamat.* (I am sincerely thankful.)

Ricardo

## Letter to Tito Juan
### 10:00 p.m., July 4, 1916

My esteemed Uncle,

I trust this letter finds you well. Tonight, I write to you about a topic I believe you know well. Today is July 4, a day Americans celebrate. I didn't know this until this evening at dinner when an American at my table proposed a toast to the United States for being independent for 140 years. He called this day Independence Day. I recall reading about it in my studies in school, but at the time, it meant little. At my table were several Americans, a couple each from France and Japan, and two men from Great Britain.

The gentleman who proposed the toast jumped up from his chair and stood before us. He asked us to raise our glasses to the United States.

"To the best country in the world," he said.

I reluctantly tipped my glass, while he proceeded to recite a poem. He said it was written in the 1800s, when America was at war with Great Britain. I understood only bits, only pieces of the poem, but the other Americans at the table nodded their approval and gave encouragement when words were momentarily lost.

The poem ended, and the American again raised his glass of wine: "To a successful and peaceful future for us all. God bless America."

Tito Juan, here it is. They call it "The Star Spangled Banner."

*O say can you see, by the dawn's early light,*

*What so proudly we hail'd at the twilight's last gleaming,*

*Whose broad stripes and bright stars through the perilous fight*
*O'er the ramparts we watch'd were so gallantly streaming?*
*And the rocket's red glare, the bombs bursting in air,*
*Gave proof through the night that our flag was still there,*
*O say does that star-spangled banner yet wave*
*O'er the land of the free and the home of the brave?*

Have you heard this poem before? I was glad the gentleman from Japan asked what war the poem was about and who they fought to gain their independence. Another American explained the battle took place during the War of 1812 with Great Britain. "The Brits had just burned the American colonies' first White House and Capitol Building," he said, "but our flag was still flying. The war was not lost."

When the topic of war came up, one Brit spoke up. "We may have fought against each other in the past, but Britain could sure use your help right now." He looked around the table to see the response he was getting. The French couple nodded in agreement. One American nodded, the other crossed his arms over his protruding stomach.

The other Brit added, "Those Germans are savagely attacking us, and it doesn't look like they will stop until Britain is no longer." He paused. "Doesn't America realize they are part of the bigger world who fight for freedom, just as you once did?"

Well, it was dead quiet for a bit until the American who had recited the poem shook his head. "Our country is in turmoil about your war. We have people who have come to America from all over Europe—many from Germany, many from the countries being attacked. The war isn't a simple matter for us."

The French man whispered: "What war is simple?" I nodded my head. I certainly know the wars we have fought in the Philippines weren't, especially the one we fought with the Americans.

Tito Juan, the conversation brought up memories of that war. All the stories I heard, the killings, the betrayals, the devastation. *¿Estoy loco por dirigirme allí?* (Am I crazy to be on my way there?) The country that holds our independence in the palm of their hands, the country that some believe betrayed us? What will happen if America does join this war? Will

I suddenly be a soldier, off to Europe?

I don't expect you to answer these questions. I am simply grateful to be able to pose them. I do have doubts about my decision to be on this journey. Not every day. But with this evening's event, how could I not?

I look forward to any thoughts you might have after you receive this letter, even though I know I won't receive letters for months.

Respectfully yours,

Ricardo

## Invitation
### 9:00 a.m., July 7, 1916

Ricardo,

I invite you to have drinks with me following dinner this evening. There is something I would like to discuss with you. It is a matter of importance and could make our remaining time aboard this traveling prison a bit jollier. We do need to do something to add some spice to our days, don't you think?

I hope you are able to join me, as I have tried to pique your interest! Has it worked?

Kindly,

Jaime Rodriguez

## Response to Mr. Rodriguez
### 10:30 a.m., July 7, 1916

Mr. Rodriguez,

Yes, you have my attention. Neither bulls nor dancing women would prevent me from joining you. Perhaps you could continue to help me become more familiar with the American cocktails I have seen you cradle as well.

Always the student,

Ricardo

## JOURNAL ENTRY
### 9:00 p.m. July 7, 1916

I can't stop chuckling. Mr. Rodriguez continues to amaze me. I would never have guessed the man played poker, and here he is organizing a group to play every week, and for money, with the Americans. The man has *cojones*.

Should I have told him I knew the game? But his offer to have a practice session with me sounded fun. Why not play through several hands and walk through the rules? I might pick up something new. He always watches out for me.

With my English being what it is, I'm a little uneasy about playing cards with Americans. Even though I speak much better now and am able to converse with anyone willing to talk to me, poker is another matter. If I can't tell what they're thinking, what good will my speaking be? I guess I'll have to trust Mr. Rodriguez. They must be decent fellows if they're friends with him. The truth is I'd like to show the Americans I'm no fool, and I'd like to take their money.

When my childhood friends and I started playing poker, none of us knew what we were doing. Oh, to think of those loyal friends who stayed at my side even when others walked away. They didn't care. We grew up together, and I think we all needed each other. Ramon never did fully learn how to play, while Mario often couldn't seem to lose. Mario. I miss him. But then there was Wally: He was the worst. He couldn't stop himself from continually trying to get away with one thing or another. To think he even accused us of cheating!

Will there be a Wally in this group? Or will I find all of the Americans to be like him? The thought of losing even the smallest amount of money to an American right now makes my heart beat faster. I want to win, to feel I can beat them at something. If one person makes fun of my limited English, I leave.

## Letter to Mario Garcia Lopez
July 8, 1916

Mario,

My friend, you have been on my mind enough that I finally decided to write. Are you wondering why? Well, this won't be a shock—poker, my friend!

I can almost hear your heehaw of a laugh. Just when you think it's about to end, you roll it out even louder. You know you still owe me from the last game, and I do plan on collecting one way or another.

You won't believe this, but I've started playing poker aboard our ship. In fact, yesterday evening was our first game. It was quite different from our five-card stud, but the principles are still the same. We play with seven cards, which gives you a better chance to hit a hand. I think you'd like it. Only here, I'm more determined to win—not for the money but for the pleasure of beating the three Americans I play with.

There are six of us, and we could not be more different. Most are older than I am, and a couple of them look like they may not only have children but even grandchildren. Of the three Americans, one is in business, a man of solid means, and another is on holiday with his family. (Can you imagine? They came to Manila on holiday?) The third American is a quiet chap who says he is at work and at play. I'm not sure what that even means. The fourth player is a fellow Filipino, who was back home visiting family but has lived in America for the past five or so years. I have gotten to know him quite well and am thankful that he is on board. He is the sort of fella who gets along with everyone and collects friends, including Americans, like coins. I like him a lot.

The last player is the closest to my age. He is Japanese and is on his way to attend a university in California. He plans to graduate with a degree in business, eventually returning to his hometown of Kyoto. Really a solemn fella, he approaches the game with a seriousness, in my mind, reserved for studying and really seems a bit dull. Nothing like our gang, eh?

How different to play poker with the Americans. You know I am pretty good at watching who plays what and when, but when I look at faces so different from ours to guess their next moves, I easily get lost in what I see. I kept noticing things like their hair, which seemed to be everywhere–on their faces, arms and even in their nose, some curling in the most peculiar ways. One of the men has blue eyes, like the color of the sky. These distractions didn't help my game.

I came with coins and left with none. Everyone else, including the Americans had piles before them, a lot of which were mine. I can tell you, my cheeks burned with humiliation. Yeah, I know, you have seen me head home with empty pockets many a time, but to lose to the Americans was downright offensive. Next week, I'll pay more attention to the game, and my pockets will be full. I'll make sure of it. I can hardly wait.

Is the gang still getting together? How are you? Are your parents doing well? Do they still feed your card-playing friends? I hope so. I don't have an address yet, but will correspond again soon, assuming you'll write back. Perhaps you'd like to come see America for yourself? I could use another countryman at my side.

With best of regards,

Ricardo

### Note to Eduardo–written in Tagalog
### 10:30 a.m., July 9, 1916

Eduardo, I would like to accept your offer to visit you and your family. Could I do so tomorrow evening following supper? The company of fellow Filipinos would be a welcome change.

Kindly,

Ricardo

Yes, Ricardo, please do visit us tomorrow night. My mother in particular wants to meet the person who saved her son, and my father would like to shake your hand.

Eduardo

### JOURNAL ENTRY
10:15 p.m., July 10, 1916

I can breathe easier. All from a night where I felt accepted. Even appreciated. How I paced my room, so close to sending a note that I wouldn't be coming. The simple act of getting dressed was a chore. One shirt was too formal, another too relaxed, like I was trying to look like I belonged there, not in first-class. What shoes to wear even became an issue. Questions kept popping into my head. What if they were inviting me there simply because they thought it necessary? What would we talk about? Would I feel out of place there as well? In the end, it was the satchel of fruit I had collected that finally made me decide to go. But even at the top of the stairs, I held my breath, still unsure of what I might encounter.

To think Hubert Stein is what finally pushed me to go. Hubert— attempting to look nonchalant as he gazed out at the dark ocean. I saw his profile first, his shadow looking like what I imagine a snowman might look like. His bloated stomach, his protruding chin giving him away. From the light of the moon, his shadow enveloped me.

He followed me. How dare he! As if I was someone he couldn't trust, a criminal for standing up for a boy who was innocent. So I made him look foolish—it was his own doing, not mine. I looked down to see my fists clenched. Before I did something stupid, I flew down the stairs like a wave crashing down on the shoreline.

The stairs were well lit but narrower than I'd seen elsewhere on the ship. The handrails were made of pine, and the walls were bare. As I went further and further down, the air became moist, with a mix of smells that stung my nose. It seemed to take forever to reach the bottom, which entered into a barren hallway. A sign said, "Common Room," with an arrow pointed to the right. I turned, and there stood Eduardo, surrounded by his family.

"Ricardo, you have come!" Eduardo blurted out and stepped forward with an open hand. Every face broke into a grin. Even the little ones running around stopped and stood at attention. Eduardo's mother and father sat side by side on a bench surrounded by family.

"Ricardo, these are my parents, Pedro and Joseta Lorenzo. Mama … Papa, this is Ricardo Alvarez, the gentleman I told you about."

I suddenly felt like a full-grown man. Maybe this is what my father felt like when a family member thanked him days later for the medicine he gave them. I felt like someone had hugged me from the inside out. Then I feel a soft pat on my shoulder. *Father, is that you?*

I stepped forward and did what came naturally, knelt down and touched my lips to Mrs. Lorenzo's hand. "Ricardo," she said so softly I could barely hear her. When I presented her with a satchel of fruit, her face lit up.

"Eduardo told me you are eating for two."

She nodded and gently touched my face in appreciation. Such a simple thing, an exchange I hadn't had since I left home. Mr. Lorenzo also reached out, grabbing my hand. His shake was that of a working man—strong, almost fierce. Committed.

"Thank you, my son. We are grateful for your kindness with Eduardo."

I found it almost impossible to take my eyes off of them, even when Eduardo wanted to continue on with introductions. For the past month, I've told myself how strong I've been, how strong I am for having the courage to take this journey. To meet the Lorenzos, I see my strength is nothing in comparison.

## Letter to Nena
July 14, 1916

Dearest Sister,

Today is the first morning I woke up ready to plunge into the ship's activities rather than hide in my quarters. Many days, I have forced myself to leave my cabin to again face the challenge of conversation with other passengers. Now I fill my time in preparation by studying English with my friend Margaret, the young woman I love to dance with. I can see the results. Last night, I even dreamt in English. Life on board this ship is better.

Margaret and I continue to dance together quite often. She now floats across the dance floor. If you saw us, you would think we were quite handsome together. She no longer looks hesitant. Instead, she now stands taller and has a twinkle in her eye. Often, she will show no signs of tiring.

"Ricardo," she will say, "you can't possibly want to be done, can you?" I do believe she enjoys dancing as much as I do.

This evening, I was allowed to escort her to her quarters alone. I wanted nothing more than to take her in my arms. *"Huminahon ka aking kapatid. Ako hindi.*(Calm yourself, Sister. I didn't.) But to touch my lips on her cheek brought a surge of excitement. How long it has been since I've kissed a woman?

I, too, am friendly with her parents. We have dined together several times, and our conversation has become easier, thank goodness. Her father always shakes my hand as if I'm someone he is happy to see.

Our time together, however, will be coming to an end shortly as their destination is Honolulu. I'm not ready to say goodbye. As Margaret and I spend more time together, language barriers are less important. The other day, she gave me a look so coy I felt my face turn a shade darker and, well, I wanted to do many things not fitting to tell my sister.

The Rodriguezes remain my daily staple. Thanks to them, I sound more like an adult than a child of ten when I talk to someone for more than five minutes. The other person I have gotten to know better is

Eduardo, the young man wrongly accused of stealing whom I told you about. I visited him and his family recently. All I can say is thank the Lord I am able to travel in first-class quarters. His family was welcoming. Crowded as they were, they emanated happiness. They remind me of Juanita's family. They have little and yet are glad for what they have. Mrs. Lorenzo offered me tea she had saved for a special occasion. I drank it and thought of you, of our family.

Sister, I hope your days are filled with love and countless relatives. I miss you all.

Ricardo

### JOURNAL ENTRY
July 14, 1916

I couldn't tell Nena about Hubert Stein's continued distain. He watches my every move. First, he followed me to visit Eduardo, and then today he's in conversation with the captain. The captain looked in my direction, and I knew it was about me. When I approached him, he didn't want to admit anything. Not until it was clear I wouldn't stop asking him questions did he finally admit Mr. Stein's complaint. How could he claim I was stealing fruit to take to my friends in third-class quarters when fruit is offered throughout the day and at every meal? I've seen countless passengers take handfuls. I do an act of kindness, and the man thinks I steal.

And all the captain could say was, "Young man, you needn't worry yourself. Some men like Mr. Stein are simply prone to judge the young. Especially when they look different." I know I stood there speechless, staring at him like he was a sea monster ready to pounce until I blurted out, "Sir, we know this has little to do with my age." In my head, I was spewing what an overstuffed pompous Mr. Stein was. Finally, seconds before I walked away, he gave me what I needed—with a slight nod and sigh, he whispered, "You may be right."

His admission felt as if a lightning bolt had struck every vein in my body. I'm headed to a country that lures people from around the world with a promise of equality for all except for those who have darker skin. No, for us, we're judged inferior.

Now, even hours later, my stomach churns, and I want to spit and rid myself of the vile taste I have in my mouth. Mr. Stein takes no responsibility for wrongly accusing two innocent young men. Yet he thinks he is a better man than me? Dear Lord, I pray America isn't filled with men like Hubert.

### Note from the Captain to Mr. Rodriguez
### July 14, 1916

Mr. Rodriguez,

I write to you out of concern for a companion of yours, Mr. Alvarez. I do so in confidence. There is a fellow first-class passenger who has singled him out, casting doubts about his character. As the captain, I do not share these doubts in the least. However, I thought it important someone other than myself know of this and encourage him to be mindful, in particular in his dealings with steerage passengers.

Given Mr. Alvarez travels alone and is still quite young, your companionship is more valuable than he probably realizes. I don't believe it necessary to go into details, but if by chance you'd care to discuss this in private, I am available.

I trust you have enjoyed your time on the Tenyo Maru and will continue to do so until your departure in San Francisco.

Respectfully,
Captain Brokaw

### Invitation from Margaret's parents
### note delivered 2:00 p.m., July 15, 1916

Ricardo,

As you know, our departure destination approaches. Rather than rely on our dinners by chance, I thought we would invite you to dine with us one more time before arriving in Honolulu. Would you be able to join us tomorrow evening? If so, please meet us at the entry to the ballroom at 6 p.m.

Fondly,

Arthur Johnson

## JOURNAL ENTRY
### 9:00 p.m., July 17, 1916

I went to dinner feeling confident. Why wouldn't I? All of our conversations have gone better and better since our first dinner. I left dinner feeling naked. Like a masterful seamstress, Mr. Johnson's unending questions unraveled my carefully constructed coat of arms. It was as if one long thread was pulled, leaving all of my insecurities exposed.

I know he meant well. He has concerns about what I will do once I reach America. I tried to sound confident when I told him I had several people I knew living in San Francisco and would look them up. So many more questions: "What do your friends do?" "Do you have their addresses?" "What will you do if you can't find them?" "What about attending a university?" "You haven't applied?"

So this is how you must feel when you are accused of a crime before a judge. When in your heart you feel innocent but know, by all appearances, you look guilty. Meaningless names rambled through my head to answer his question about friends. I couldn't sit still; my right eye began to twitch, about the same time my left knee started tapping involuntarily. If I could have become invisible, I would have.

I couldn't tell them the truth, that the only two people I know in San Francisco are friends of my uncle. He had introduced me to them about five years ago when they visited him in Manila. Truth be told, no one knew if they were still in San Francisco. I hadn't cared.

I took a deep breath, and then another. All I managed to say was, "I apologize. Your questions are good, Mr. Johnson; I wish my answers were better." He's right. I should have more carefully planned what I will do once I arrive, but I was impatient to leave, to be gone. Now, all I can do is pace back and forth in my quarters, repeating his questions and having no answers. My family has never felt so far away.

## Letter to Nena
8:15 a.m., July 20, 1916

Dearest Sister,

At this moment, I truly wish you were here at my side. Instead, I write this letter to recount a dream I had last night. The dream was like one of those we both used to have about Mama, about Papa, but in this one, our little brother and sister were there as well. I could see them so clearly. You were there, too.

The dream started out well. Mama, Papa, and I were on the veranda. You were in the yard with a dog. Was it the neighbors'? None of us were talking to each other, although Mama would occasionally look up from her sewing and smile at me. She was humming a tune like she often did. I was in the middle of some kind of school project. Papa was engrossed in the weekly paper.

Then the setting changed again. I was with you, and our little Isabella and Carlos. We were playing Luksong Baka. The four of us were laughing at Isabella who struggled to jump over Carlos—the Baka. You and I encouraged her not to climb over him but to jump. Carlos tried hard to make himself as small as he could so she could succeed. You jumped in, taking Isabella by her arms, counting, "One, two, three: Jump," and then lifted her up enough that she made it. Do you remember how we all loved to play that game? My knees weaken when I think of them.

And like that, the picture changed again.

This time, I was by myself, watching Mama before she died. She didn't know I was there. I peeked in from her bedroom door that had been left ajar. She lay in bed even though it was in the middle of the day. She looked so thin, like she had vomited layers of herself away. The flesh on her arms hung like loose clothing. She was asleep, yet still held onto her stomach, moaning. I wanted to run to her, but Papa told me to not go near her, that I, too, could fall victim to cholera just by touching her. I had forgotten how he told us to stay away from Carlos and Isabella, too. Had they touched Mama?

Sister, then the picture changed again. This time, you and I sat on the steps going upstairs. The hour was late, and we were in our nightclothes. I don't think anyone knew we were there. Papa was raising his voice. "You have to take them now. I don't want my other children to see you do this." You and I looked at each other. This was the night they took Mama and our brother's and sister's bodies away to be burned. Papa didn't know we knew that is what they did. Remember, Sister, everyone was sickened and angry with the Americans for not letting anyone be blessed and buried as Christians.

We sat in silence as we watched them be taken away, each wrapped tightly in sheets. Papa touched each as they went by. I could see him fight back tears, lips quivering as he held his cross tightly to his chest.

Then suddenly I was alone in my bed. Something woke me. At first, I thought a small animal outside had been hurt, but as I listened more closely, I knew who was crying: Papa. I covered my head with my pillow. I couldn't bear to hear him. Then I woke up.

Nena, I think the night I heard Papa was when I started to truly feel all alone. After that, I sometimes would wake in the middle of the night, my pillows covered with tears, whimpering just as Papa had. After she was gone, I wanted Papa to smother me with hugs to help me forget, but Papa was a shell of himself, like a man made of straw. Do you remember? He tried hard to have our days and nights go back to normal, but how could they? The emptiness of our house reminded us daily of what we missed. You and I came together as best we could. We did for a time, didn't we? I know that for me, time seemed to stand still for weeks, maybe even months. I didn't want to forget them but needed to hurt less. I eventually let time have its way.

Oh, Nena, to think you were eleven and I only seven. What we endured. When you get this letter, I do hope you'll share your thoughts. To write to you helps. I've often wondered why I was spared. Why Carlos and

Isabella weren't. The only thing I can think of is I must have something important to do. I must.

Please take good care, Sister.

Yours affectionately,

Ricardo

### JOURNAL ENTRY
#### July 23, 1916

Sitting here coffee in hand with my journal splayed before me, I feel like my brain could explode. Too many worries, too much anger directed at whom? I'm not even sure anymore. I keep thinking of Mr. Stein and shake my head in disgust. I want to push him away, off the ship if I could. Or am I angrier with myself for my lack of preparation, for my laziness in caring about details when I would get off this ship? Maybe I didn't believe I would, maybe I couldn't image what this would be like. All of my indecisions seem to be crashing around me. And then my dream of family—how can I rid myself of memories festering within me when I thought I had buried them long ago?

I hated to ask for advice from someone but knew Mr. Rodriguez would be willing. The conversation we had, which I never want to forget, started with his simple act of extending his hand to me as he customarily did. His smile was bright and open as he sat down in the ship's empty parlor.

"I knew from your note something troubles you," he said. "How can I help?"

I had to swallow hard and take a deep breath before I could answer. I started with my conversation with Mr. and Mrs. Johnson and Margaret, then told him about not having applied for university.

"Also," I said, taking a deep breath and letting it out slowly, "I'm not sure the people who said they could help me even live in San Francisco anymore."

"Ricardo," he said. "Listen, I do not want to have you feel like I am criticizing you. I like you very much, you know this, right?" He paused to look at me and make sure he had my full attention before he continued on.

"But you might be too trusting. The city you are going to is not at all like where you come from." I tried to say something, but he stopped me.

"Locating your friends will be difficult–not impossible but problematic in part because you aren't able to communicate well enough in English yet. And the city is large."

I started to get restless, my legs suddenly unable to be still. I knew he was right. How could I think I would do well when every day I struggle to have anything beyond simple conversations? When I think of what I might do when I step off this ship alone, I freeze, my lack of nails proof of my rattled poise. Hiding my hands, I nodded.

"I haven't wanted to admit I could be better prepared," I said, "but there's more."

I took a deep breath and launched into the details of my dream. When I finished, Mr. Rodriguez reached across the table and placed his hand on my shoulder. My heartbeat slowed. I sighed, letting out some of the demons within. To experience the touch of his hand, an exchange between friends, between equals, was exactly what I needed.

"I am honored you chose me to share this with. I'm so sorry to hear of the losses that you have had. You were so very young to go through this." His tone was soft and tender. I fought back tears with all my might.

"Now, you wonder, why this dream, why now?"

I nodded.

"I think Mr. Johnson upset you enough, allowing all of these other memories to come flooding in. Sometimes dreams are the only way they can be released." He handed me his handkerchief, and I blew my nose.

I let the tears run down my face. For years and years, I haven't let myself think of Mama, Carlos, or Isabella. Instead, I push their memory away as quickly as I can. I thought I had said my goodbyes when all I did was bury them deep inside.

Carlos was my little shadow. Whatever I did, he would try to do the same, often falling to the floor in laughter. Every day, he would trot after me, ready to hear what I had to say. Eduardo gives me the same look

Carlos used to. They'd be almost the same age. Mr. Rodriquez is right. Memories, I'll now begin to set free.

### JOURNAL ENTRY
July 25, 1916

Mama used to tell me stories about her father's maid, whom he never favored when she was alive and detested once she was dead. She seemed to enjoy causing him problems. I would listen and ask Mama to tell me again and again what the maid would do. Nothing seemed beyond the maid's ghost. My Lolo was never left alone. He was pinched while eating, hit while walking down his long sweeping stairway or out his front door, his hair was pulled while he slept, and he was even tripped in front of visitors, once falling right before a dignitary. He could even hear her cackle occasionally. There were so many stories. I believed Mama. We all did.

Lately while alone in my quarters, I've felt a slight breeze, knowing full well there was no possible explanation other than a ghost. This evening, I felt a hand on my shoulder as I sat staring out at the sun setting over the horizon. I had been thinking of Mama, of Carlos and Isabella. The hand felt large emulating warmth. I knew who it was. I wasn't afraid. Oh, how I miss you, Papa.

### Note from Jaime Rodriguez
July 29, 1916

My friend,

I should have written this note sooner. We haven't spoken of this, Ricardo, and I wish we would have. Weeks ago, I received a note from the captain concerned about what he referred to as "a fellow passenger's" criticism of you. He said he could tell I cared about you and thought it good for me to know, seeing you are traveling alone. Since then, I've observed and can attest to what the captain speaks of.

Mr. Stein and increasingly his son seem to be the culprits. Whereas weeks ago I witnessed both being ill-mannered, now they seem determined to publicly display their dislike. I'm so sorry, Ricardo. When Mr. Stein made a point of calling you names as you walked past him in the parlor last evening, I fought the urge to come to your aid but realized how futile my intervention would be—we are both Filipinos, after all. I wasn't able to hear the names he called you, but I can only guess it was unkind given the hoots and hollers by his son and friends. He seems to love the attention.

I'm not sure what I might be able to do other than to let you know I'm aware and available to talk. Perhaps together we might think of a way to prevent further episodes? I would like to think we might think of something. Perhaps intervention by the captain himself.

With great sincerity,

Jaime

### JOURNAL ENTRY
July 30, 1916

When I heard the knock, I thought it was going to be Jaime. How many times I had read and reread his note. What a surprise to find Eduardo standing there with his sheepish grin. Not a word came out of his mouth. I remember thinking he looked out of place, like he knew he didn't belong. Maybe Jaime's note of warning spurred me to invite him to dinner. When I did, I felt a ping in my gut, like someone had pinched me. I ignored it. "To hell with Mr. Stein," is what I thought.

"But look at me. I am not dressed at all properly," he said.

He wasn't. He probably didn't own any proper attire. I opened up my wardrobe to show him he could use my clothes for the evening. By his reaction, you would have thought I opened a vault filled with silver. To find something to fit was a challenge, but we managed. A shirt I had forgotten I had, a vest tightened to the fullest with a pair of trousers rolled up made him presentable. Once dressed, he stood before my mirror with a mischievous grin spanning the width of his face.

"I look darn good," he chimed. He did.

When we met the Johnsons and Mr. and Mrs. Rodriguez at the entrance to the dining salon, I forgot about any concerns, excited having everyone meet. How fun to watch Eduardo experience the room's splendor. It reminded me of my first time. Jaime and I gave each other knowing nods, and like me, he was keeping a watchful eye for the Steins. I sat taller knowing Eduardo would never forget this evening, still unaware of what was coming. I let myself relax.

As everyone placed their napkins on their laps, so did he. By watching, he knew which spoon to use, same with the dinner and salad forks. Only once did he not hesitate, and that was with dessert. Once devoured, Eduardo was readying to leave, and I knew going back to steerage was for the best. But once the bare-chested men clad in loin cloths started parading through the dining hall, I could hardly ask him to leave. By the look on his face, he had never seen sumo wrestlers before.

"*Pwede ba ako?*"("Could I?" he asked)

"*Palagi.*" ("Of course.")

As we left the dining room, Jaime pulled me aside. "Be careful, Ricardo …" he began but was cut short by Margaret bounding forward asking to join us. I nodded to Jaime as we made our way to the back deck and the makeshift ring, once again ignoring the ping.

I'm not sure who was more entertaining, Margaret or the wrestlers. "Oh, my goodness," "Oh no," or "I can't watch" were among the phrases spewing out of Margaret's mouth. She alternated between quietly squealing and covering her face with her hands throughout most of the first fight. Eduardo's eyes never left the wrestlers. He looked like he wanted to be in the ring. Margaret caught me beaming at both of them. She reached out and gave me a soft kiss on my cheek. Oh, how I have longed to feel her lips on mine, just once.

"I love this," Eduardo said a bit too loudly in Tagalog. "I've never seen anything like this before!" Taking the stance of the wrestlers, he mimicked what he watched. I should have paid more attention instead of joining in with others who enjoyed watching his antics and encouraged him on. When the ship's officer asked him to stop, of course he didn't hear him as a small appreciative crowd was spurring him on. I was in my own cocoon with Margaret, finally having dared to taste those lips. We were locked together, surrounded by other passengers. Someone could have punched me. I might not have noticed.

Eduardo was in trouble, and neither of us knew. Apparently the tap on Eduardo's shoulder quickly turned into arms swinging: Eduardo's and the officer's. I finally looked up to see him being held by two officers, looking frantic. A short distance away, Stein's son stood, arms crossed before him like a commander of troops who had won a battle.

I ran to Eduardo. This time, I wasn't going to have it end as it did before with him being humiliated. We moved away from the crowd with Eduardo gripped by both officers. I stood before them and explained that Eduardo was my guest and didn't understand English. I told them in the most cordial but firm way, I would be at his side the remainder of the evening. Margaret, God love her, managed to step in and get one of Eduardo's arms free and said she'd be sure to watch out for him as well. Remarkably, they released him.

We walked away, arm in arm with Eduardo, to watch more of the match, but something inside of me shifted. I didn't walk back into the crowd—I strutted. I knew the Steins were watching. I thought, *Let them; we aren't leaving.*

Even as I write about this evening's event, I can feel the tension in my back, my neck, and my arms. I won't retreat from this father and son's trickeries. I won't walk away anymore.

# AUGUST

### *Letter to Nena*
8:30 a.m., August 2, 1916

Beloved Sister,

The port in Honolulu reminds me of home. If I close my eyes, I can imagine you portside, arms outstretched to welcome me back. But this isn't Manila, and you are many weeks away—a reality I fight to accept.

Honolulu does feel like a distant cousin we've heard about but never met. Warm, cool breezes, aromas of fish, and seagulls are all reminders of Manila, of my family.

Our usually quiet boat is bursting with voices from the dock: people calling to each other, some with urgent instructions, others friendly and cajoling. But there is one voice that stands out—our voice, Sister. The voice of Filipinos rose above the clutter. How wonderful to hear the roar of Tagalog.

Of course, many other voices are mixed in. Japanese, Chinese, dialects I have never heard before, English—they are all being spoken. Together, they sound like a disjointed chorus of non-singers. Perhaps this is what it was like when I left Manila, I don't know. I was so preoccupied with saying goodbye to you, to all of the aunts, uncles, and cousins. On board the ship, I watched, seeing you one second and losing you the next. I stood looking out until I couldn't see anything but the shoreline. I remember how naked I felt at that moment. I stayed in my room that first day, too nervous to be seen.

Although I don't know what America really looks like, the harbor tells me we are getting closer. The port shines with newness, like the buildings were built yesterday. Even the work seems more orderly. No one is yelling obscenities, nor are workers ambling about. The only thing that seems to bring work to a halt is a young lady passing by, then even the bosses have something to say.

I think this is a peek into where I am going, Nena. In four weeks, I'll arrive. Today your packet of letters will be placed on the next ship bound for the Philippines. How wonderful it will be to receive a letter from you.

With growing impatience,

Ricardo

### Letter to Nena—one I will never send
#### 5:00 p.m., August 3, 1916

Sister,

I had dreaded the moment when I had to say goodbye to Margaret. Beyond dance, we liked each other. I liked her more than I wanted to admit. I never found out how old she is—young enough to be traveling with her mother and father, young enough they keep her close most of the time.

This morning, when I approached Mr. and Mrs. Johnson as they were readying to disembark, Mr. Johnson immediately extended his hand. Then he hugged me instead. Mrs. Johnson did the same. Her whole face beamed as she said, "Ricardo, thank you for all that you have done for Margaret. You made her time at sea more enjoyable than she could have imagined. Thank you."

"This has been my pleasure," I said, a phrase they taught me how to say a short eight weeks ago.

As Margaret appeared, Mrs. Johnson stepped aside. Margaret. Dressed in traveling clothes, she looked different. Her wide-brimmed hat with matching print dress gave her the look of a woman—confident, ready for her next adventure. She was searching for someone or something in another direction. When she saw me, her face turned into sunshine. She wrapped her arms around me. I again had that urge to lift her up and carry her away. We stayed that way long enough until we both knew it was time to let go. I desperately wanted to kiss her goodbye. Instead,

I kissed her on her cheek. She turned as I did, and we briefly felt each other's lips. As she walked away, she handed me this note:

*Ricardo,*

*I want you to know how much your friendship has meant to me. I was to have been married this year, but the relationship ended quite abruptly, and so I travel with my mother and father. Yes, I was probably too young to marry, but I had thought it was what I wanted, what I needed. I hadn't laughed in a very long time, nor had I danced. You helped me do both. I wish I had more time with you. I will always remember you. Do well, Ricardo, as I know you will. The United States awaits you.*

*Your friend always,*
*Margaret*
*Miss Margaret Johnson*
*745 Magnolia Avenue*
*Richmond, Virginia*
*United States of America*

Nena, I looked up from reading, and they were gone. I wish I could tell her how much she helped me as well. She was my first American friend, a woman I would like to know more, have more time with.

She will stay with me, Nena. I'll miss her gentle nature and can't help but wonder what might have happened if we would have had more time. I try to look into my future, and no pictures enter to mind—only questions, hopes, and a dream I might find someone.

### JOURNAL ENTRY
Hours later

I stood watching Margaret walk away, down the long ramp to the port lying below. She never looked back. But when I finally decided to end my watch, who is in my pathway but Mr. Stein? He is pulling his wife along, and she appears to be struggling to keep up. Their son was nowhere to be seen. Hubert's voice told me he wasn't happy about something as usual. I stood my ground. He could go around me. He looked right at me as he strutted by to greet another couple. As he shook hands with the gentleman, Mrs. Stein and I nodded to each other. Her look seemed to say, "He doesn't know any better, I'm sorry."

I wonder, how many people she does this with, her small attempt to make up for his continual bad behavior. Does she know he and her son despise me? I think not. I would like to think there will be no others like them in America but know there will be. Hopefully I'll be ready.

**JOURNAL ENTRY**
August 4, 1916

A brief stop in Honolulu, and we're on our way, now with a whole new pool of passengers. Once again, most seem to be Americans, joined by Japanese, Hawaiians, and surprisingly even Filipinos. How refreshing to once again hear Spanish, even if it was with raised voices arguing about my country's economic status. They didn't seem to care how loud they were, which made me happy. They remind me of my cousins who were always ready to disagree. I miss their banter and their noise.

The most adamant of them is stuck in my head. He looks to be around my age, and the way he dresses and walks with long strides, head held high, tells me he is important, or so he thinks. Like me, he looks more Spanish than Filipino.

I was so transfixed by the young Filipino that I didn't notice George standing next to me. How he remains friendly, I'm not sure since I've taken bags of coins from him at the poker table. At first, I took pleasure in filling my pockets, but no longer. Now he is an appreciated fellow passenger and almost a friend. I would have never guessed.

"So, Ricardo, have you spotted another young woman to dance your way to America with?" he said, bumping me with his elbow.

I laughed and shrugged my shoulders. I hadn't even thought about dancing since Margaret walked off the ship. How fun to suggest instead of Margaret he could join me so I could teach him a few steps. "No," he declared a bit too loudly. His long arms and legs attached to his squat torso would be humorous to watch, though.

He, too, had been staring at another group of men looking like they had minutes ago stepped out of their pristine offices. All four of them were talking at once, while one held up a newspaper, pointing at a specific headline. George was like a bloodhound waiting for his master to release him. When one hollered, "Those crazy Germans!" George bolted. He had to find out if America was finally joining in on the battle.

War. Lately, I can't escape the topic. Every time I hear the discussion, images of my own war come flooding in. My grandmother's home half torn down, riddled with bullets, hollowed into nothingness. Santa Cruz chopped into small pieces—one street saved while another nothing but dirt and rubbish. Church doors once engraved with pictures of saints to greet you blown apart, stained glass destroyed, and altars stripped bare. Even today, there are signs of battles that took place before I was born. Will a war be coming to the shores of America? Will I once again need to go into hiding not knowing who is an enemy and is not?

**JOURNAL ENTRY**
August 9, 1916

The well-dressed swaggering Filipino who boarded in Honolulu is everywhere. No matter where I see him, he exudes confidence. It oozes off of him. For the past three days, we have tipped our hats to each other on the promenade, said "Good morning" at breakfast, and nodded to each other in the reading room. We even seem to be in close proximity during dinners. I steal looks. I know he does as well. I think he is as curious about me as I am about him.

*Letter to Tita Carmen*
2:20 p.m., August 13, 1916

Dearest Tita Carmen,

Here I am again, in need of sharing another experience in hopes of eventually receiving your counsel. I hate to trouble you but feel there is no one else I care to share this with.

Let me start by telling you about a new Filipino passenger, Alfonso-Rivera de Domingo. He is one of many new passengers who embarked from Honolulu. He is both delightful and offensive. He is close to my age, quite tall for a Filipino, with deep-set eyes the color of coffee that don't allow you to easily look away. I think you and Nena would find him quite handsome. He dresses immaculately with a flare that tells me he is accustomed to luxuries. In talking with him, I discovered this to be true.

I dined with him last evening, and besides discovering he was a tireless talker, I walked away feeling unprepared for America. Have you heard of the Zobel de Domingo family? Apparently, we should for all they have done. They have developed many businesses in Manila and are helping ensure schools are available to everyone. By the time Alfonzo was done, my head hurt. I asked him why he would go to America when he had so much in the Philippines?

"To attend a university, of course," he said. "To have a degree will be very beneficial in making future development decisions in my father's many enterprises." I should have been impressed. Well, I was and I wasn't. With his exorbitant display of pride, I became disgusted. You know me. This would only result in me acting bored. So, I changed the topic of conversation. I asked him if family would be waiting for him in San Francisco, thinking like me he would seek out friends of the family.

For a moment, I was hopeful. Even if he was overbearing, I thought I might have someone to be with in America. I asked him where he wanted to attend university. His look of superiority should have told me how silly I was to think he was alone. He proceeded to tell me how he was to be met at the port by friends of his family who would take him to the University of California to begin school immediately.

"They have arranged a place for me to live and promised to help me settle into San Francisco."

As he went on and on, I wanted to slide away before I had to tell him how little I have planned. For a moment, I thought I might get away. But then he asked. I tried hard to sound confident as I told him I had family friends to seek out in San Francisco and would then look for a university to attend, possibly in San Francisco.

"Wait," he said. "You need to find your friends? You have no concrete plans to attend a university? Where will you live?" This is when our conversation deteriorated as he switched to English. I started getting lost. His English is rapid and perfecto, something else I can abhor. He noticed.

"Ricardo," he said, "you are not proficient in English. That will be a problem, my friend." Much to my horror, I blurted out that I simply didn't have a strong enough desire to learn English when I was younger. That admission is probably the most honest I have been with anyone. I hated hearing myself say it. He looked aghast. All I wanted to do was to tell him what a pretentious snob he was and punch his pretty face.

Tita, I recall how you begged me to have more concrete plans. I recall your many suggestions to learn more English. I remember and now regret I didn't listen. Weeks away from arrival, and I'm as nervous as I was when I came late to Easter Mass and tried to sneak to the front of the church without being noticed. Do you remember? I fell flat on my face as I reached the pew causing the priest to lose his place in reading the benediction. There was nowhere to hide there, and neither is there here.

Prayers, Tita, I need prayers.

Ricardo

### JOURNAL ENTRY
August 15, 1916

A reprieve from my worries—that's what my visit was with Eduardo and his parents. Once again, they took me in like I was part of their family, like a distant relative that they hadn't seen for years. No judgments. No questions. My shortcomings were not important.

Like other visits, we easily laughed, and I felt accepted, even appreciated. Mrs. Lorenzo is no longer surprised by my gift of fruits but looks forward to her treasure. No baby yet.

"Very soon, Ricardo, very soon," she said as she gently rubbed her enormous belly. Did I imagine it, or did she also look worried? Underneath her tenderness, she looked pale and uncomfortable. But then how could she not be? Where once the air was only slightly disgusting, now the smells from bodily functions made me want to cover my nose. Increasing temperatures don't help. By the time I said my goodbyes, my shirt was soaked. I worry for her, for them. Two more weeks before we arrive.

### JOURNAL ENTRY
10:20 p.m., August 18, 1916

Tonight we stopped playing cards to talk. With little time remaining, interest turned to what laid ahead—our arrival in San Francisco. Howard and George have appointments set up for their businesses soon after arriving. Robert has a relative he will stay with before proceeding home to New York. Jaime is looking forward to returning to his home in Chicago, "to get back to his work," he says. Hirohito will begin his studies at the university in San Francisco.

"Well, Ricardo," Hirohito said, "What university will you attend?"

I couldn't look at Jaime, not when he knew I had so little figured out. How stupid for me to again try to bluff my way through, but I tried, even with additional ideas thrown in, like I want to attend university, but I want to travel after I spend time with friends. My explanation was weak at best.

Their questions were immediate, and, like Mr. Johnson, Jaime, and Alfonso, they started questioning what they heard. As I listened, I knew it didn't matter. I'm not able to fool myself, let alone others, any longer. Every word they said confirmed what they must think of me. I was just another boy who hasn't had to stand on his own yet. A fella who depends on his family to cover the costs while he does what he wants. A young man who has no idea what he's going to do, that's me.

I wish I could tell them how my steadfast determination was what got me here. I wish I could tell them of the heartache of breaking away from family—a clan I love. I wish I could share my reason for coming is to find my own way and not depend on my grandfather's success, on the kindness of Lola Brigida. How every year since she passed away when I was seventeen, I've felt more guilt over living in a home she paid for—thankful but guilt-ridden. She knew I was like my father. She believed my claim would be found in America, not the Philippines. Most often, I do, too, and accepted her gift to cover all of my expenses.

All of these thoughts, and I shared none of them. How could I when I feel like an overpampered dog that hasn't taken training serious enough?

### Letter to Nena early morning,
August 20, 1916

Dearest Sister,

Last night I couldn't sleep. I went to the upper deck to see the stars, to think, to be alone with all of my doubts. The moon was bright enough that I could see for miles and miles—the ocean a desert of shimmering nothingness. Currents of wind held me upright as I stared forward, my thoughts floating by me like a lost ship. Slowly the breeze washed away my concerns. Where I stood, alone on top of the ship, was exactly where I needed to be to know what to do.

I stood for a very long time embracing the quietness. I felt at peace. Then it seemed quite simple, and my decision was made. Basté, Nena, once arrived, I will turn around. I'm coming home on the next available ship. I won't come home as a failure but a wiser man.

I went back to my stateroom and slept the best I had in weeks. I'm coming home.

Ricardo

### Note from Jaime Rodriguez
10:00 a.m., August 24, 1916

I saw it in your face, Ricardo. You giving up. I won't let you. I know you have a fire in you, and I know eventually success will come your way. Your determination reminds me of myself when I was your age. So, too, does your pride. Let us help you.

I know you well enough to know you contemplate returning to the Philippines. Don't do it, Ricardo—you are stronger than what you realize. You are smarter than what you think right now. I have watched you tackle your problems. You knew you could dance and have a history of communicating through it. You helped another less able to do the same. You don't know enough English? No problem. You retreat to the Reading Room and learn more, plus you work with Esperanza like a tiger tracking his prey. Think how much you have improved in a short amount of time. When you felt uncomfortable with aristocratic snobbery, you balanced arrogance with honest down-to-earth people: the Lorenzos. You are fully capable.

You can do this, Ricardo. Esperanza and I will help. There are classes you can take in Chicago to help you perfect your English, to begin your studies. There are universities very close to our home. Come with us. We will help you find your way.

Your friend and confidant,

Jaime

### JOURNAL ENTRY
9:00 p.m., August 26, 1916

I thought my decision was final, but with Jaime's offer, I don't know. *Going home* had felt right to me. But now, faced with having a choice, I can't help but fear what people will say, what my family and friends will think if I go home. Will I go back and feel the same way when I left?

What if I did take up Jaime on his offer? I have traveled three months to get here. With their support, maybe I will be all right. But what does support even mean? Will they help me find a place to live? Will they help me settle into Chicago? And where is Chicago? How far away is this city from San Francisco? I recall Jaime saying something about a very long train ride lasting days.

But really, does it matter? They have been so very kind this entire voyage. Why would this be any different in Chicago? They have shown time and time again they care about me. Even if I find in six months that

I don't want to stay, at least I have tried.

I need to decide. Time is running out. I have moments of calm where I think I know what to do only to be followed by sheer panic over making the wrong decision. A small voice keeps telling me, "Be brave, Ricardo, be brave." Is that you, Papa? Did you, too, have doubts, fears about your own journey?

### JOURNAL ENTRY
August 28, 1916

Fourteen steps. That is how long my room is—fourteen steps. Back and forth I walk. I haven't had a conversation with anyone today. I've only conversed with myself. Back and forth I go, in between the walls of my quarters, in between staying or returning home.

### TELEGRAM TO NENA
September 1, 1916

I HAVE ARRIVED. GOING TO CHICAGO WITH JAIME AND ESPERANZA PEREZ RODRIGUEZ. TAKING TRAIN. ADDRESS IS 322 WINCHESTER AVENUE, CHICAGO, ILLINOIS, U.S.A. WILL APPLY TO A UNIVERSITY THERE. BLESSED. SHARE WITH FAMILY.

Lahat ng gubat may ahas.

**In every forest, there is a snake.**

# PART TWO

# A Strange New World

**JOURNAL ENTRY**

8:20 a.m., September 2, 1916

After months of traveling, we're finally here, only several ships' length from our destination. There is one sole ship ahead of us. Then it's our turn—my turn. I know I shouldn't be nervous. But even with the cool shore breeze, my shirt sticks to me. My forehead drips like a faucet has been left on internally. I can't turn it off.

I am dressed like I am going to a social event, even though Jaime tells me formality isn't necessary. He says as nationalists, we have nothing to worry about. My translation is we are a step below real citizenship. I can't stop pacing. To think it was only days ago I changed my mind to stay.

In the wee hours of the morning, when no one else was out and about, I watched the fog slowly lift to reveal Angel Island. I had heard so much about the immigration center. How imposing the structure was, gloomy inside and out—unfriendly is what I heard. I saw something different. From the Promenade, the building and surrounding island were basked in hues of emerald, rich yellows giving way to deep forest greens framed by a ridiculously long pier. The building itself looked neither threatening nor friendly—only large, stately, and important. This is the place where someone will determine if I can stay or if I will be sent back.

I imagine walking slowly down the pier, intent on breathing normally like I am off for my morning walk around the Promenade, enjoying the sea breeze and the fellow passengers I encounter along the way.

"Breathe in, breathe out," I tell myself. In, out, in, out. I fill my lungs and release. Finally my neck, my back, my shoulders start to feel freer, more like rubber than wood. I can even appreciate birds in their morning chorus and scents of land nearby—a sweet fragrance, alive, musty, wet with the morning's dew.

I need to be this way when I'm interviewed. I also need to trust what Jaime and others have told me. How many times has he said, for Filipinos, they simply want to make sure we are not arriving sick or with some kind of disease? He knows; he's been through this. Others have said the same, reiterating that our time in the immigration center will be several hours at most. Then we'll be bound for San Francisco on a ferry.

Although not visible this morning, I know San Francisco Port is not far away, the gateway to a new life in America. Ever since I sent the telegram to Nena, I have had endless energy. I can't seem to concentrate on one thing but jump from one task to another. The only time I can be still is when I write. Even now, I'm distracted.

With the Rodriguezes, I hope to find my way. Those two do know me; they let me be alone to make my decision. They didn't push; they offered. They let me battle my demons, my doubts, without pity. Yes, I'm afraid, afraid of so many things, but mostly of myself. I know I look like a man, but I have so much to learn. My Filipino clan is far away. Breathe, Ricardo, breathe.

✿

## Letter to Nena
September 4, 1916

Nena,

I have so much to tell you, I'm afraid I won't be able to write quick enough. First and foremost, I shudder to think of the many obstacles I would have faced if I had arrived alone. Mr. and Mrs. Rodriguez are truly a gift from God. Picture this, Sister, thousands of people in perpetual motion with horse-drawn carts mixed in with taxis of every sort, automobiles that use their horns freely and often. The noise is constant. No one seems angry or bothered by any of it, however. The buildings here are formidable. Elaborately decorated, some are more than six stories high. Block after block, they stand over you, acting as guides to the city's riches.

I am truly in a different world. But I am getting ahead of my story. Let me first tell you about Angel Island and our arrival in the Port of San Francisco. For all I had heard of Angel Island, our time there was rather uneventful. Once in the official building, we were separated into groups: Chinese in one line; Japanese in another; Filipinos, Americans, and other Europeans in still another.

From there, I was shuffled from one post to another. I waited in long lines, had a quick health inspection, and answered many questions. At the last post, a tired-looking gentleman asked us a final list of questions—name, origin's port of call, destination, and race (two choices—white or black). I was marked white, even though on the ship I certainly wasn't always treated as such. My name was added to a very long list, and minutes later, I was out the door.

We were escorted to the same pier we came in on and instructed to wait for the next ferry to take us into the Port of San Francisco. As we were leaving, the passengers from steerage were entering the building. There were hundreds and hundreds, and they kept coming. Apparently over a thousand had called steerage their home for the past three months. I'm not sure what my friend, Eduardo, and I were thinking when we said we would meet on the pier to say our goodbyes. With the Rodriquezes' address in my hand, I stopped people as they went by asking if they knew the Lorenzo family. Most simply shook their heads with their eyes on the building ahead. I was about to turn away when a young boy bolted out of line.

"I know Eduardo," he chirped. His mother was right behind him.

"Will you give him this note please?" I asked his mother. She shook her head, shooed her son back in line. And then she told me why they weren't there.

"Señor, last night, the baby, it tried to come, but there were problems. The family, all of them were taken. We haven't seen them since." My heart dropped.

"Very late, they took them to the infirmary, the two young ones with Eduardo. But if they have been taken on shore, we don't know, Señor." My mouth opened but nothing came out.

"Lo siento, Señor," she said as she hurried back in line. Behind me, our ferry had arrived. I wanted to run back into the building to find them, but what good would that do? Nena, I never saw them again. I don't even know if the baby and Mrs. Lorenzo survived. I'll never know. Now hours later, I still can't stop thinking of them. Eduardo will be in my prayers.

When we entered the port, it felt as if we were a part of a daily procession, a synchronized dance between water and land. Ferries fell in line to wait their turn; piers filled and emptied with a rhythm of civility. Somehow we found our trunks and baggage, and for a handful of coins, young men delivered them to a hotel, which I quickly learned was in the heart of the city. Here is where the newspaper and business buildings are: hotels, theaters, stores, and restaurants of every kind, even Filipino. As one passenger aboard the ship had told me, "You could live in San Francisco for a month and ask for no greater entertainment than walking through it." I had thought him foolish for saying such, but in my two days spent here, I think he was right.

In today's paper, an article appeared describing San Francisco like this:

*Life here seems to be a perpetual ferment. It is as though the city kettle had been set on the stove to boil half a century ago and had never been taken off. The steam is pouring out of the nose. The cover is dancing up and down. The very kettle is rocking and jumping. But by some miracle the explosion never happens.*

Of course, San Francisco isn't perfect. Even if the women are striking, with flowing manes of gold, bronze, and brown, they seem to have no interest in someone who looks like me. Several times, I attempted to greet women on the street by walking up to them and tipping my hat and each time was met with distain. The first was with a hand gesture, the second by a look of distaste. The third was the worst. I, like a schoolboy, had whispered, "You are beautiful." Well, this is what I thought I said. She clutched her coat and spat at me. "Get away from me, you disgusting beast." I was dumbfounded.

A young Filipino was standing nearby as she marched away, her scent of perfume lingering as she went. He couldn't stop laughing, which made me not only surprised but ready to raise a fist. He, however, quickly came to my aid, as he put it, to "set me straight about white women."

"Forget about 'em. They don't want anything to do with you."

"Where you headed?" he asked me. When I told him Chicago, he again chuckled.

"Good luck, mate. Not many Filipinos there, and I hear winters are the worst. Yup, that city is a rough place."

Sister, you can guess, this isn't what I wanted to hear at all. I'm really not sure where or what I'm headed for. And you probably know as much as I do about winter. Tomorrow morning, we leave. It can't possibly be as bad as he made it sound, can it?

You must be exhausted after this long testimony I've given you. I know my hand is tired. To think I might receive a letter from you makes me want to get up dance. Please pass on my greetings to all.

*Ang iyong kapatid na lalaki* (Your brother),

Ricardo

### JOURNAL ENTRY
September 6, 1916

I will never forget my first attempt at boarding a train in America. I had thought this would be simple, but once the whistle blew announcing the train's arrival, nothing was simple. The sound was like a dozen flock of screeching seagulls. Like the children around me, I wanted to run and hide behind someone. Instead, I froze where I stood, consumed by smoke spewing from the train. Apparently everyone else, including Jaime and Esperanza, started to move towards the train we couldn't see. Only people pushing and shoving made me start to move as well. Of course, by then, Jaime and Esperanza were nowhere to be seen. I recall repeating in my head what Jaime had told me: "We're on a train car with the sleeping compartments."

Right.

I didn't know what I was doing. I lined up behind a dozen people, pulled out my ticket, and hoped for the best. God love America, I didn't know anything. Luckily I had my ticket, but really never looked at it. I didn't know what a porter was. I'd never talked to or heard a black person speak before. I couldn't understand what he was saying and wanted to either burst into tears or laughter, I couldn't tell.

Thank the Lord he took pity on me and pointed me to the right car, four cars away. He even showed me how my ticket gave the number of the boxcar and the seat or berth I'd be staying in. "Berths are beds, where you'll be sleepin'," he confirmed. Finally, my brain clicked in, and his words took shape.

"Good luck to ye."

About then, I felt like I might require more than luck. Berths. I had thought it meant something else entirely. When I stepped into the correct boxcar, the relief I saw on Esperanza's face told me how worried she was. She had thought they had lost me. No, I'm not lost, not yet. But I do know I'm not in the Philippines anymore. If I can barely get on a train by myself, how will I manage going to a university?

## Letter to Nena
September 7, 1916

Nena,

I want to tell you about my journey by train across America. I have nothing to compare it to, seeing we have no trains in the Philippines, but I know you've seen pictures. The train car I am in has sixteen passengers who have seats that turn into sets of two beds at night, one up above and the other on the bottom. They're called berths. I share a berth with another young fellow, an American readying himself for college, off to visit family in Chicago. Initially, he wasn't happy to have me as his berth mate.

The seat I was given had my back to where we were headed, and I couldn't sit still. I craned and twisted, I stood, and I leaned over my berth mate—anything to see what was coming.

He finally exploded, yelling, "Do you mind?" I thought he was sleeping, but apparently not. Nena, I apologized, but when we were suddenly encased in blackness, I gasped and jumped up from my seat into his.

"What are you doing?" he yelled. When we reached the tunnel's end, he continued, "Look, you have your seat, and I have mine. Would you please stay in yours? And this jumping around, leaning over me—stay over there, okay? I need to sleep."

I took a deep breath and said, "This is my second day in America and my first train ride. If I could sit in your seat and see where we were going, I wouldn't bother you."

"Your second day and first time on a train?"

I nodded. Once we switched, he slept, and when he woke, we gradually discovered we could get along fine—long train rides will do that.

In two days, we've crossed through the Sierra Nevada and Rocky Mountains. I've seen fields of lush green crops, towering pine trees draped over mountains, and crossed over ravines hundreds of feet below. This morning we've passed through a wasteland of brown sand with rocks that looked like they were dipped in silver. And now we are passing by meadows that remind me of Filipino rice fields.

Someone said we are in a territory called Nebraska. Some houses stand next to each other in small neighborhoods. Others are miles apart—strangers who may want to stay that way. Many are two-storied structures made of thick slabs of wood or brownstone; others are squat, small, and made of mud. These homes aren't much different than the shacks along the Pasig River. But down the road stands a monstrosity of a house with a huge porch wrapping the home in what looks like a cloth of comfort.

And the animals! They're everywhere: horses, chickens, cats, dogs, and homely creatures called cows. They look like a cross between underdeveloped oxen and dilapidated horses. I understand they can sing. My berth companion tried to imitate the sound, "Moooooooo, mooooooooo," first in a deep voice and then with more of a groan. It didn't sound anything like singing. It sounded more like a man in mortal distress. We both laughed until our sides hurt.

Nena, it's now nine hours later, and the train has slowed down as we're passing behind people's homes, right in their backyards. I can peek into their lives as we pass by. Few have curtains or yards to speak of. Houses seem hardly furnished with plain wood tables and benches rather than chairs. Women stand on front porches, heads wrapped in scarves, hands on brooms or holding children. All of them look dust-worn and are white.

Next to the small but sturdy structures are clothes hanging on lines.

One small-framed woman was hanging out not only men's clothes the size of a sumo wrestler's but knee-high boots fit for a giant, and a monstrous night robe. The line was full with items I've never seen together before: tattered knickers that looked to have no bottoms, well-worn shawls, a dead animal with blood dripping from its body, a lone red sock, and a naked doll hanging by its arms. By the look of it, the doll had been there for some time. Sister, where have I come to?

The porter only now shouted, "Chicago, twenty minutes." More and more houses, closer together, and in the not too far distance are tall buildings. And a most disgusting smell; in fact, fellow passengers have begun to close their windows. My berth companion tells me the stench comes from the stockyards nearby we'll soon be passing. Yes, the city is near. I pray the stench isn't there as well.

Nena, I so enjoy sharing my first encounter in this place they call the United States. I look forward to eventually receiving a letter from you. I want to know about everything and everyone. I trust you are happy and well.

Ricardo

**JOURNAL ENTRY**
September 8, 1916

Not five minutes after finishing my letter to Nena, I wanted to gag. The stench had risen to a level that forced me to cover my mouth and nose. Outside our window were hundreds, maybe thousands of beasts looking more dead than alive. Most were not moving, as there wasn't room. Plumes of smoke outlined their bodies. The only sound was from hundreds of cows singing their song of despair. I wanted to cover every inch of my body to stop their misery from filling my pores. Oh, dear God, so this is where I'm going to live?

Now, hours later, sitting in Jaime's' house, there are no traces of the stockyard. Here I'm safe, but I wonder what I'm doing in such a place. I feel paralyzed, like the doll I saw hanging on the clothesline by its arms—suspended, alone, naked.

**TELEGRAM TO NENA**
September 10, 1916

IN CHICAGO. WITH RODRIGUEZES. START CLASSES AT UNIVERSITY OF CHICAGO NEXT WEEK. TAKING ENGLISH CLASS AND OTHERS. WILL WRITE SOON.

**TELEGRAM FROM NENA**
September 11, 1916

BRAVO, BROTHER. MY BLESSINGS TO THE RODRIGUEZES. RECEIVED LETTERS. WHAT A TIME YOU HAVE HAD. LETTER ON THE WAY WITH FAMILY NEWS. TELL ME OF CHICAGO. Nena

## *Letter to Nena*
8:15 a.m., October 2, 1916

Dearest Nena,

How to describe this place? Such a restless city—big, noisy, overrun with people from countries I'm unable to even name. Trains soar above streets on metal tracks. Boats vie for space on crowded rivers. Automobiles fight their way through horse-drawn carts. Horses are the losers. Today I saw one being carted away dead. Everywhere there is motion. Manila seems gentle in comparison.

Esperanza tells me Americans living in Chicago are actually outnumbered by those who hope to become one someday. "Like us," she says. Me? I'm not sure. When I walk through my neighborhood, I hear Italian and German. If I go a bit further, there is Polish and Irish. Still, no one looks like me. Unlike San Francisco, Filipinos are few in number, but it doesn't stop me from searching for some.

The city center sits on a lake. Businesses, shops, and eateries of all kinds line the street. I have been only twice, once when we first arrived, then again the other day. This is where families cheerfully saunter on Sunday afternoons to bask in the sun along the lake (a lake even bigger than Laguna de Bay), while others in their Sunday best walk hand in hand to peer into windows with lavish displays. You would enjoy looking, I know.

At Jaime and Esperanza's, I breathe easier. Today they laid out a hand-stitched table linen they were given on their recent visit home, much like the one Lola Brigida had, and the house is filled with ornaments from home—wood carvings from Paete, bamboo mats, books written in both Spanish and Tagalog, traditional Philippine art, and, most importantly, home-cooked Filipino aromas. Esperanza decided we must celebrate, as it is one month today I have been here. She is a confident cook who enjoys the kitchen. Yes, she cooks all our meals. There is no live-in housekeeper. I help clear the table and even do dishes most evenings. I imagine you being stunned, and initially so was I, but not any longer. I will need to learn to do many things others did for me at home.

The university reminds me of ours in Manila, only the students are fair-skinned, dress in a casual manner unacceptable back home, and seem to notice my more formal attire. Or perhaps they simply notice how different I look. I know I certainly stand out.

I speak English most of the time now but shudder to think of taking my first test. This language is not easy. At the university, everything is in English—rapid English. The only way I can keep up in class is to write my notes in Spanish. Then I go home to translate what I have written to English. The process is slow and tedious, but I can think of no other way.

Right now I can barely find my way to and fro. I'm still confused with the money, and I have no idea where the market is. I'm like a grown child in need of constant attention.

I do enjoy walking, though. Most people don't seem to give me any notice. Sometimes I see a person look up from their front porch, but so far, I've encountered few problems. Only in one neighborhood am I uncomfortable. There's a man who is always out in his yard, whose eyes seem to follow me. He stops his yard work and walks behind me past several more homes. I can feel his presence even after he is gone.

Enough about me. Have I told you how much I look forward to someday getting letters from you? I crave information about home, about you, family, and friends. My hand tires from all of this writing. You too must be tired of reading. I adjust, Sister, so please no worries.

Kasama mo ang aking mga dalangin. (My prayers are with you.)

Ricardo

### Letter to Tita Carmen
#### October 17, 1916

Dearest Tita Carmen,

First, on the ship there was Hubert Stein, and now this madman in Chicago. I had hoped the captain was wrong when he warned me I would encounter more like Hubert. He said this like he was telling me what the weather was going to be the next day.

This man—I heard a neighbor call him Mr. Wojcik (or something like that)—makes my blood curdle. Part of me wants to physically hurt him, the other wants to run in the opposite direction. But to get to the train, I can't avoid going by his house.

Yesterday he yelled: "You, you there. You aren't welcome here. You don't belong in this neighborhood."

Today, a woman joined him, maybe his wife. She is the foulest woman I have ever seen. With a cigarette in one hand and a broom in the other, she marched toward me like a mad dog protecting her den. She didn't scream at me, she growled, causing her already blackened eyes to narrow and her yellow teeth to look more like fangs. She reminded me of the gypsies we saw as children. You remember, Tita Carmen, the ones Nena and I hid from, sometimes behind your skirt.

"You Mexicans don't belong. You take our jobs—make our city dirty. Get, before I hurt ya," he yelled.

I started to walk as fast as I could and finally broke into a run. Both of them followed me for blocks. When I got to the train station, my shirt was soaked through, and I couldn't stop looking in every direction in fear they would appear.

My heart still pounds as I write hours later.

When I told Jaime and Esperanza what happened, their response didn't help.

"You'll have to find a different route," Jaime said.

I asked if they had ever been called a Mexican before. Neither of them had, but both admitted they had never ventured into that neighborhood. How many neighborhoods do I need to avoid?

I am tired, Tita Carmen. At the university, I watch others talk and laugh together. They don't look my way. On the tram, people are polite but most often choose to stand rather than sit by me. While walking, fair-skinned women cross the street rather than pass by me. Jaime knows I'm lonely. But what can he and Esperanza do more than they already are?

On Angel Island, they marked me down as white. But here, in the eyes of most, I'm not. I fall somewhere in between. Jaime calls us pioneers for our country. How can we be pioneers when people don't know what we are or where we come from? I feel like I'm going to explode if I don't do something.

Once again, I've shared with you my fears, questions that poke at me day and night. Do correspond when you can, Tita Carmen. I would also like to know how you and your family are.

With gratitude forever,

Ricardo

### TELEGRAM FROM TITO JUAN
October 28, 1916

RECEIVED YOUR LETTERS. YES, I KNOW AMERICA'S POEM. RECITED HERE AS WELL. OUR TIME WILL COME. HAVE FAITH IN YOUR PEOPLE. IN YOU AS WELL. ALWAYS REMEMBER. THEY ARE NOT BETTER. THEY ARE DIFFERENT. PRAYER AND PATIENCE, RICARDO.

### Note from University of Chicago English Professor
November 5, 1916

Ricardo,

I know you work hard and want to encourage you to continue to do so. Your efforts are admirable. However, we both know you struggle to keep up. You might not have a strong enough grasp of English, particularly the sentence structure required to write appropriately in a university setting.

I will continue to provide you with additional materials and personal assistance in hopes the quarter can be a success for you.

Professor Bergman

English Literature

University of Chicago

### JOURNAL ENTRY
November 5, 1916

He thinks I won't be able to pass his class. I will. I'll work even harder. I've never failed a class before, and I am not going to do it now. *Panoorin mo akong mapangahas na Amerikano.* (Watch me, you pompous American.)

### *Letter to Nena*
November 10, 1916

Nena,

Did you know trees change colors here? They do—almost all of them did about a month ago. Brilliant hues of orange and yellow, as bright as the beak of our kalaw bird, maybe even brighter. The reds are even more vibrant than the Bird of Paradise you love so much.

As the leaves have turned, so, too, has my outlook, partly because I met another Filipino: José Garcia Santos. He, too, attends the university. I know little about him other than he grew up in Manila and will finish his studies at the university here in the spring. His English is flawless. If I ever master the language as he has, I will never have another ill thought towards my English teacher again (I have had many of late). From our short conversations, I gathered José grew up humbly. He concluded I didn't.

"You were one of the rich boys we made fun of but secretly wanted to be," he said.

I do recall seeing boys like José who couldn't afford to buy new clothes or eat at nearby vendors. They were lucky to eat at all. I hadn't thought that eating was a privilege, but it was. I told him I was sorry, but he wasn't having any of it.

"For what?" he said. "Because you had much and I so little? I don't want your sympathy." He marched away.

I didn't mean to say I was sorry, but that is what came out of my mouth. I've watched for him at the place we met every day this week, but haven't seen him again. Sister, I'm excited to know there's another Filipino at the university. Now if I can only convince him to be my friend. Do send me your prayers and a letter when you can. Prayers to you as well.

Your brother,
Ricardo

❧

## Letter to Nena
November 20, 1916

Sister,

Thank the Lord. José has become my friend. Not that doing so didn't take convincing. Apparently his first impression of me was that of a privileged snob.

"I do not want to think you look down on me or worse think you're better," is what he later told me.

"I don't. I have great respect for you, in fact," I said. "You've been here for years, and you're about to graduate, something I hope to do someday." He grinned.

"Well, I speak better English than you as well, that's for sure." And he does.

José reminds me of our cousin of the same name: wide cheekbones, thick dark hair, and flighty bright eyes that match his fidgety nature. Like me, he's broader than most Filipino men, and like our cousin, the ladies like him.

Our friendship has gotten easier since we discovered we both love to dance. However, dancing here is nothing like dancing in Manila. Here, I have to pay for every dance. This wouldn't be so if my skin were fairer and my accent less. When José told me this, I didn't believe him.

"You'll see," he said and threw his head back with a laugh. Of course he was right.

We went to a place off Michigan Avenue as fancy and as big as our church in Manila. We were there only minutes before we were told, "Your kind needs to go elsewhere." This message delivered from a fair, blue-eyed young man blocking the doorway.

Instead, we went to a large, not so grand dance hall for men only. Women were there, but like I said, we pay them to dance. I'm sure you're wondering what in the world I'm talking about. They are called taxi dancers or nickel hoppers. For ten cents, they dance a song with you with half going to the musicians. As long as you are willing to pay, they dance. Men wait in line. Have you ever heard of anything so crazy?

The first time I went, I watched from the sideline. If I was going to pay, I wanted to dance with a young lady I might enjoy. One girl finally caught my attention. She didn't know all of the latest moves, but she looked like she loved to dance. I stood in line like everyone else and waited. When it was finally my turn, I felt awkward and asked if she were up for a couple more.

She looked amused and said, "Yes, I am. I appreciate you asking. My name is Sally. What's yours?"

"I am Ricardo," I said, "and I have never done this before. I mean I've never paid for a dance."

"No worries, Ricardo. Let's enjoy." She smiled convincingly, took my ticket, and slipped it into her blouse. Off we went. Our first dance turned into five, the last being the tango.

Nena, I loved being on the dance floor with her, and I could tell she enjoyed herself, too. We found our rhythm together, and if I would have had more dimes, I would have kept dancing. I have gone back several times specifically to dance with her. But then, so do many others. Sally helps me feel normal, though, like maybe I can fit in someday. I made the mistake of suggesting we might see each other outside of the dance hall, and she wouldn't look at me.

"No, Ricardo, I will dance with you. Nothing more. Please don't ask again."

I know she likes me. I watch her with other men, and they don't laugh—they fumble. She helps them not step on her feet. We fly around the dance floor with ease. She does like me. I know it. America is a peculiar place.

Sister, when will I hear from you? The mail cannot possibly be this slow. *Minamahal kong kapatid, nalimutan mo na ba ako?* (Dear sister, have you forgotten me?)

Your mournfully needy brother,
Ricardo

### JOURNAL ENTRY
November 25, 1916

What I witnessed today tells me war is close at hand. Fellow students normally who act like they don't have a care in the world act panicked. The professor could hardly stop the conversation in order to start instruction. So many different opinions. I remained silent as I watched several German students argue with others.

"The war isn't about us, but Europe," a German student said. The outrage by others, many of whom were English or Irish was palpable.

"Easy for you to say here in Chicago. I have family in England that fear for their lives," one young man said. I think his name is Robert. Another jumped in and shouted: "You think you can take over any country. How can you possibly think that is all right?"

"Wait a minute, fella, you think this is me that's doing this?" one of the German students retorted.

I was fascinated. If what I read in the paper is true, we may soon be at war—a war we don't seem to understand and one that sparks huge disagreements.

⚘

## Letter from Nena
### Received November 28, 1916

Ricardo, my dearest brother,

Has it been a year? It feels that long to me. As I write this, you have been gone for five months. I was elated to have received a second packet of letters from you, although some were difficult to read.

Your last letter was the most difficult, the one written on July 20 where you described the nightmare you had about our mother and siblings. Tears I didn't know I had flowed freely while I read. The pictures you painted were so vivid, I had to calm myself. I hadn't thought of those difficult years for such a long time, and yet I carry them with me. I, too, have buried them deep.

But my memories of the night you described are not the same. I didn't want to be on the steps to witness our family being taken away. Don't you recall? You woke me. You begged me to come sit with you. I didn't want to, but finally gave in so you wouldn't be by yourself. I didn't listen to what was going on, though. I held your hand. "Too hard," you told me. In the end, I let go and covered my ears, closed my eyes until finally I dragged you back to your room. What I recall is being angry. Not at you so much but at Father. How could he let them take our mother, our brother, our sister away without first letting us say goodbye? I don't know if I have ever forgiven him.

I pray your letter to me helped you release some of your sadness. That event is part of us, but only a small part we should remember if for no other reason than to honor them. We have endured, and look at us, Ricardo. We are alive and well. Look at you. Your bravery is something to behold. I wish I had your bold desire that burns within you.

About your travels—my prayers were answered that you would meet other Filipinos. Mr. and Mrs. Rodriguez are now both in my prayers and considered friends. You are right, Ricardo. I would truly enjoy meeting them someday. Could they possibly be saints in disguise?

Your time on the ship sounded like an odd mixture of enjoyment and torture. Your struggle with the Steins sounded the most difficult. Although here, there are more and more Americans who all seem to be in charge. We can't seem to escape them, can we? I see so many men, and now even women, every day, especially in Manila.

In the time you've been gone, life for me has changed little beyond me often thinking, "I must tell Ricardo," and then quickly scolding myself for not remembering you are far away. It is a habit I need to break. Now with your address, I will write to you instead.

I continue to work at the orphanage and marvel at the spirit of these children. We give them little, yet they are thankful. Their hopefulness is contagious. My favorite is still Rena. At three, she has bounds of energy and can't seem to grasp the meaning of rules. She makes me burst into laughter at the most inappropriate times. Usually this involves her once again not doing what she has been told to do. She wants to do it her way even if it is wrong. Hmmm, does she remind you of someone?

Ricardo, my big news is I am with child. We were quite surprised it happened so quickly. No one knows here yet, as we are only two months along. You are the first to know. If all continues to go well, we'll make an announcement next month. My hope is for a girl; no surprise, Vincente a boy.

I need to stop writing now to attend to household duties. Juanita is another who is happy to know you are well. She tells me she misses you but not the cleaning of your room. There is good news for her. She says she is in love. No one we know, but she believes this to be the one.

By the way, it was no surprise to learn it took you over a week to find my letter. Do tell me in a future letter how you fare in this regard as well.

Prayers with trust in the Lord,

Your sister, Nena

### TELEGRAM TO NENA
December 2, 1916

A BABY. WONDERFUL. YOUR SECRET IS SAFE WITH ME. EXPECTED DATE? TELL ME MORE WHEN ABLE.

### TELEGRAM FROM NENA
December 4, 1916

AN APRIL BABY. NO LONGER A SECRET. AM GROWING ROUNDER EVERY DAY. SUCH EXCITEMENT. MANY CELEBRATIONS. YOU ARE MISSED.

### JOURNAL ENTRY

She has no idea how much I miss her, our clan, the life I had. She can't. And I won't tell her. I'm going to be an uncle to a child who may have no idea who I am unless I go home. Not now. Not yet. I still don't even know who I am here.

---

### Posting of grades from University of Chicago
December 16, 1916

Mr. Alvarez,

These are your grades for the autumn quarter. They are also posted on your professors' office doors. Should you have questions, see your professor. Winter quarter begins January 8. We hope to see you then.

Cordially,

Mr. Jonathon Smith
Academic Dean
University of Chicago

### JOURNAL ENTRY
December 18, 1916

Vicente speaks of people who have nervous breakdowns over the simplest things. I wonder if receipt of my grades is the start of one for me. When I read my grades this morning, my heart pounded so hard I thought I might fall over. I was numb. This couldn't be. I worked like a madman to avoid these grades: an F, two C minuses, and one D minus. I thought I would at least get all Cs.

Nothing I do here is easy: fixing my own breakfast, washing dishes, laundering my clothes. Even going to restaurants is nerve-racking, wondering if I may be turned away. But I've always thought my mind was good. Being feeble-minded was never a question I had. I will learn English. I must.

### TELEGRAM FROM TITA CARMEN
December 20, 1916

RECEIVED LETTERS. MY DEAR RICARDO, NEVER DOUBT WHO YOU ARE. REMEMBER-BOLDNESS IS THE FRUIT OF HOPE. LETTER SENT. DAILY PRAYERS TO YOU. Tita Carmen

### *Letter to Tita Carmen*
10:00 p.m., December 24, 1916

Dearest Tita Carmen,

In a few minutes, we leave for Misa de Gaillo (Rooster's Mass). Filipinos from around Chicago will attend—not more than fifty is what Jaime says. I was relieved to hear the tradition of Mass at midnight takes place here.

Like home, we'll supper after as well. To be with fellow Filipinos will hopefully help me feel more hopeful. I didn't know Christmas without family could be absent of joy. I miss the comfort of home. Nena thinks I have faced my obstacles with little pain. I want her to think this. She already knows the demons of my mother's death haunt me. I can't let her know how much I am burdened. How I read late into the night and still can't sleep. How I sometimes imagine the ghost of my father is close by. He never frightens me. I know he wants me to be well, but I worry he is disappointed as he watches me struggle.

He must lower his head in shame over my grades as I do. I worked harder than I ever have, and still they were a step away from failing. I now bite my nails and talk in my sleep. Can I do this? I'm tired of feeling not as smart as the chap next to me. Tired of seeing my fellow students take notes in English while I take mine in Spanish, then go home and struggle to translate them into English. I'm tired. Exhausted from my effort and know I will need to do more. How many nights I lie awake praying I will be able to improve my grades, praying to accept what I can and can't do here, alone. I stare at the ceiling waiting until my eyes give in.

Jaime tells me it is time for us to go. God bless you, Tita Carmen. *Miamahal kong kapatid, nalimutan mo na ba ako* (Happy Christmas to you and your loved ones).

Your struggling nephew,
Ricardo

## Letter from Nena
Received December 30, 1916

Ricardo,

I received two more letters from you, and although I have little time to write, I want to respond. Oh my goodness, Brother, you have had a difficult time. You were ready to come home and at the last minute decided otherwise. My guess is it is the Rodriguezes who have helped you. Again, I believe them to be saints sent to you. I also know you do not give up easily.

Yes, there were those of us worried you were not fully prepared for your adventure. However, that is history. Our concern never meant we didn't support you. Trust yourself, Brother. Long ago, I knew I could. When we suddenly no longer had Papa in our lives, I saw you stand tall. Ten years old, and you were determined we would be all right. You helped me believe that we would be whole again. In your quiet way, you convinced even Lola Brigida that we didn't have to move in with her, but with Juanita's help were able to continue living at home nearby.

You will find your way. You are finding your way. Remember darkness is always followed by light. Clarity will shine through.

Your increasingly round and happy sister,

Nena

# 1917

*Letter to Nena*
January 5, 1917

My dear Sister,

I received your second letter. God bless you. You're right about me finding my way. I am. I only wish I could do so without such clumsiness. And you know, I wouldn't be me if I didn't complain and want to be better.

How I wish I could see your roundness. By now, the aunts must be busy planning the baptism and making gifts for the baby. I can imagine you happier than you have ever been. Perhaps a picture of you is what you can send next? You as a mother! I smile to think of it.

I continue my studies with some success. This semester, I aim to think, write, and speak in this godforsaken language until it becomes natural. I know people still struggle to understand what I say. I fear I might sound like I have a mouth full of food, chunks of words coming out rather than full sentences. Can you feel my determination?

Winter has arrived here. It's brutally cold, especially when you feel the blasts of wind from Lake Michigan—outbursts that cut through layers of clothing as easily as a knife slicing through a mango. The blowing seems to never stop. Last month, I purchased a coat made of wool as well as a matching hat and gloves. In Manila, I would look silly. Here I blend in— well, almost. My hat keeps the snow from covering my head, as I learned the other night when I experienced my first snowfall.

I stood outside with arms stretched out, my mouth wide open, head tilted back for the longest time. I wasn't alone. Others along our street were doing the same. First-timers is what we're called—people who have never seen snow before. Perhaps winter may not be as horrible as I originally thought. But to think this will go on for months, my Filipino blood starts to curdle.

With warmest wishes,

Ricardo

*※*

## Letter from Tito Juan
Received January 14, 1917

Ricardo,

I always believed you to be a thoughtful young man, and your letter to me concerning the independence of the Philippines confirms I was right. Our relations with the United States are perplexing, aren't they? I have always marveled at Lola Brigida for her ability to forgive the Americans for destroying the church she had devoted herself to. Then they almost did the same to her beloved home. She and I never talked about what happened; instead, she showed many of us a way to cope. Forgive, find the positive in what has taken place, and continue on.

So, here we are some twenty years later muddling along. People still can't agree about our independence. You've probably been in some of those conversations, Ricardo, where suddenly men are pounding their fists and yelling. To this day, some still cite the wrongs of 1898 when the Americans refused our independence. Perhaps with the Filipinos there, the same discussion takes place. I wouldn't be surprised.

Our relationship with the United States has been a source of confusion and contest for many years. As time goes on, it feels as if our independence is a prize we must earn—held slightly out of our country's reach. We do have more formal influence in policies but change is slow to come and we work alongside and influence as best we can.

The elders (I don't know, perhaps that is what I am now) have deep memories. Some believe our independence is long overdue. Others more familiar with world politics and our country's shortcomings embrace the Americans' desire to prepare us for independence. This is where I stand. We are not yet ready to be on our own. Being in the United States, perhaps you can see our systems are lacking, leadership wanted by many but most not yet ready to lead.

And as you say, Ricardo, this fear of war is real. With America's recent decision to join the European war, I'm not sure how that will impact you or me. What I do know is for us without the Americans, an attack on our homeland would be devastating. Given our status in America, I would hope you wouldn't be required to become a soldier. You say you won't be asked to fight. I fear this may not be true. Once under the clutches of win or lose, everyone becomes warriors.

Do continue to send me your thoughts, Ricardo. As you know, I very much enjoy sharing mine.

With respect and concern,

Tito Juan

### Note to José
### January 20, 1917

José,

I have to tell someone what happened the other day, especially someone who isn't going to suggest I take the next ship home. I trust you'll understand. I told you about my need to find a different route to the university, thanks to Mr. Wojcik, who wants only fair-skinned people to walk past his home. Even though I changed my route to avoid his neighborhood many weeks earlier, today I took a chance as I was running late to get to one of my classes. As I was walking as fast as I could, my mind was on the assignment I had completed minutes earlier.

Shouting is what finally shook me back to where I was, nearing his house. Mr. Wojcik was the one yelling, and he was yelling at me. With a bat in hand, he was coming at me with his wife right behind him. He looked possessed by demons, hordes of demons.

"We'll teach you from coming into our neighborhood," he screamed.

I wanted to run back the way I came from, but I couldn't if I wanted to get to my class on time. Instead, I ran toward them. The wife stopped to stare, tripping on the stick she carried. I ran like a deer chased by a pack of wolves, so fast I don't even think you could have caught me. Mr. Wojcik got one swing in, though, as I swerved around him. I heard the crack when he hit my back. The sound reminded me of a coconut hitting the ground after being thrown down from a tree. Didn't stop me, though. The stick the Mrs. threw didn't stop me either when it hit my left leg. A bruise the size of a washbasin and blood-stained pants were not the worse that could have happened.

Hells bells, José, I started to shake. This can't be normal, can it? What was I thinking running right past them? And what are they doing attacking me for passing by their house? I need to do something. Will you help me figure out what that might be?

Let's meet soon. I need your help to decide.

Rico

### Note from José to Jaime
### January 24, 1917

Jaime,

I'm worried about Ricardo. Have you noticed him acting any different? He told me about a run-in with a crazy Polish man and woman not far from where you live. I guess he has to pass their house to get to the tram. Maybe he told you about what happened. He didn't get hurt, badly anyway, but he sounds like he might get revenge. When I talk to him, he gets more and more steamed up about how they shouldn't be able to attack people walking in front of their house, no matter what they look like. Don't think he heard me say he needed to forget about it. I don't think he has ever had anyone do this to him before. Me? Well, growing up the way I did, I learned to fight. Sounds like you did, too. You know how fighting this man could go over here.

Maybe he'll listen to you.

José

**JOURNAL ENTRY**
February 1, 1917

Every day I think of the Wojcikes. Should I show up at their door with my own bat in hand? I know this isn't like me at all to consider such a thing. Still, I can't stop thinking of what they did. José says he won't come with me, tells me I'm a fool to even think of it. I know he's right, but what do I do with this burning rage I carry with me? For days now, every step I take causes pain, only reminding me of what happened. Only today the bruise is beginning to fade.

**JOURNAL ENTRY**
February 5, 1917

Maybe I shouldn't have talked with my professor. He tells me I'm doing better but hands me my last assignment with a great big C scribbled on it. The pages were filled with red pen marks, words crossed off, and new words placed in many of the margins. It looked like a small but deadly bomb had exploded, shedding particles of shapes and sizes all over the page.

I recall sitting in silent disbelief, loathing everything about English, loathing the effort I had put forth, loathing myself. We sat there for some time before he asked me what I hoped to do, what degree I was striving for. He might as well have asked me my grandmother's foot size. My mind was blank. To become an engineer finally came to mind, but I hesitated to say it out loud. And then he said it: "Perhaps you should think of a trade, some kind of work not requiring a high level of language proficiency."

There it was. He didn't think I could do any better. Can I?

Finally, hours later, I can think about what he asked me without my stomach going into knots. What degree do I hope to receive? I have always thought engineering, but I wonder. I think of my father's business as a pharmacist and how much he enjoyed hearing from his customers, how something he had prescribed helped cure their pains. And Mother—she, too, was always helping someone in nearby neighborhoods. Even when I met with my professor, I couldn't help but notice a slight tremor he had in his left hand and wanted to ask him about what he did for it.

Come to think of it, how many times have I found myself standing near the hospital watching sick people come and go? They often go in bent over, like every step is a chore to take. Worse yet, some are carried, sometimes dragged. When they leave, they're hardly recognizable. I'm curious.

Strange how one question can start you to think about taking a completely different pathway. Am I crazy for even thinking of medicine? No doubt my professor would think me delusional.

## Letter to Nena
### February 24, 1917

Dearest Sister,

Your letter arrived weeks ago, and the edges are already worn, I've read it so often. You told me to stand tall, and I believe I'm at least a foot taller when I see my reflection. I often repeat to myself what you wrote: "Trust yourself, Ricardo."

Every day I try. Some days, I close my book at night and know I'm meant to be here. Other days, I struggle to get out the door. Up and down I go, but mostly up. Lately, I've begun to contemplate other fields of study besides engineering. This might surprise you, considering how often you've heard me talk about my interest in engineering. But when I picture myself ten years from now, I can't imagine myself happy slogging over a desk to draw yet another design. I think I need to have more contact with people and know I've helped make their lives better, maybe in the field of medicine, like our father.

The other day, there was a family on the train that looked like they had recently arrived. They were speaking Italian. By the layers of dirt and shape of their clothes, they looked like they had been sleeping on park benches or worse. The little boy couldn't stand up and lay motionless in his mother's arms. He kept whispering, "Mama, mama. I want water, Mama." She wiped his forehead, which was covered with beads of sweat.

I couldn't bear watching. In Spanish (with a few Italian words I know tossed in), I offered the mother my bottle of water. At first, she refused but finally propped the boy up to give him a drink. He could barely hold his head up and started to cough in what sounded more like a quiet roar, spewing up the few drops he had swallowed. And blood.

We were about to reach the place that I normally get off, but I stayed on. I knew they must be headed to the hospital nearby and wondered how they were going to get there without help. No need to go into details, Nena, but I did help them by carrying the boy to the hospital, as the mother herself found walking difficult. The father wasn't much better. He carried their belongings as if he had the weight of the world on his back. Once in the hospital, I continued helping as their English was by far worse than mine. The nurse couldn't understand what they were saying, but I understood enough to translate. I stayed with them for several hours. Both the mother and son were given beds and were receiving care when I left.

Nena, I was in awe. The nurses and doctors were quick to figure out what could be done and then set out to make it happen. If I could do something like what they do, I know I could be happy. Everywhere I look now, I see people in need—men who can barely walk without the use of a cane, women with growths on their necks or hands, children with deformities.

I talked with a university administrator, and he told me a firm grasp of Latin is important for anyone considering medicine. Their university offers day and night classes. Am I ridiculous to enroll? You are probably answering, "Yes." But this is your brother—the person who obviously likes to explore, so you'll also understand if I do. Will you not? Even as I struggle to do well with my studies, the idea of medicine helps me get up each morning. For the first time in a while, I don't dread my classes. Instead, I look forward to them. Tell me what you think Nena, as you always do.

Truly yours,
Ricardo

### TELEGRAM FROM VICENTE
March 3, 1917

RICARDO, YESTERDAY WE LOST OUR BABY BOY. DON'T KNOW WHY. DOCTOR SAID WASN'T MEANT TO BE. HIS NAME IS ABELARDO. NENA RESTS, IS HEARTBROKEN. SHE IS ABLE TO HAVE ANOTHER. SHE WILL WANT TO HEAR FROM YOU. Vicente

### TELEGRAM TO NENA
March 4, 1917

SISTER, MY HEART ACHES FOR YOU. IF ONLY I COULD BE THERE. LET JUANITA DO EVERYTHING. EVEN LISTEN TO AUNTS. THEY CAN HELP. CONSTANT PRAYERS TO YOU, VICENTE, AND ABELARDO. Ricardo

### TELEGRAM TO NENA
March 7, 1917

I PRAY FOR YOU EVERY NIGHT. REST, EAT, BE WITH FAMILY AND FRIENDS. Ricardo

### TELEGRAM FROM NENA
March 9, 1917

I SENSE YOUR PRAYERS. I HEAL. VICENTE MY CONSTANT COMPANION. FAMILY SURROUNDS ME. Nena

### JOURNAL ENTRY
March 12, 1917

She was so happy to be having a child, God, why take him away? Hasn't she lost enough already? Lord, I want to be with my sister, and here I am thousands of miles away. Telegrams and letters are all I have. And prayer.

I wish I were home. If I were there, we could talk, I could distract, maybe help her to hurt less. What have I done going so far away? I can't help the one person I care about the most.

### TELEGRAM TO NENA
March 13, 1917

TODAY I WALKED IN THE PARK. I FELT YOU WITH ME. A SIGN YOU ARE BETTER? STRONGER? I PRAY AND THINK OF YOU EVERY DAY. HOPE YOU CAN FEEL MY PRAYERS. Ricardo

## TELEGRAM FROM NENA
### March 16, 1917

I HAVE FELT YOUR PRESENCE AS WELL. EVERY DAY AM STRONGER. VICENTE REMINDS ME IT ISN'T OURS TO QUESTION BUT TO ACCEPT. YOUR MESSAGES HAVE HELPED. Nena

---

### Note to José
### March 23, 1917

José,

You never would guess who I saw blocks from Jaime and Esperanza's place—that crazy man who lit after me months ago. You know, the madman I was ready to go back and battle with for what he did. Yeah, that would have been stupid, I know.

But here he was in my neighborhood. At first, I didn't think it was him. For one, he wasn't running at me, and two, he looked like a normal person. He was walking out of Mr. Van Helder's bakery, the one I had to drag you out of before you bought every loaf of bread in the place. He was by himself, taking a bite from a roll when he looked up and saw me. I was ten feet from him. We both froze.

I know I must have looked like I was about to burst; he looked like he'd seen a ghost. Our eyes were locked. He shifted his gaze right and then left, lowered his head, and came right at me. I stood, fists ready.

Mr. Van Helder opened the door and trotted out to us seconds before the man reached me. "Mr. Wojcik, you forgot your dinner rolls." He handed the man a small bag and put a hand on my shoulder. "Ricardo, are those sweet rolls calling to you? The missus just took a fresh batch out of the oven."

Mr. Wojcik grabbed the package and looking down, walked right past me. Mr. Van Helder saw the look on my face and, leading me into his shop, said, "So, you know the man, do you?" He sighed like this wasn't the first time he'd had conversations about Mr. Wojcik.

José, I didn't hold back telling him all the details as he handed me one sweet roll after another. I guess I was getting louder and louder, so eventually he suggested we step outside. His words of advice were this: "Let it be. No good will come of it if you do anything. He's angry, son, angry about all the change."

He explained. I guess ten years ago everyone around here was either Polish or German, and they gradually got along. Then the tram came and, with it, many others who didn't look or sound the same. Some like Mr. Wojcik couldn't accept what was happening and started to fight back. When I heard this, I could only shake my head. I remember hearing of Filipinos blocking off their neighborhoods from the Americans, thinking they could keep them out. Do you remember, José, men being sent to prison because they attacked Americans?

Maybe Mr. Wojcik isn't a monster—he's only a sore, fully miserable fellow ready to take his unhappiness out on a passerby he thinks too different from himself. He's angry, and so am I. But after hearing his story, I can breathe easier, maybe because I might be the change he's afraid of and maybe because I don't want to be like him. I saw fear in those crazy eyes of his, and I saw myself.

You're a friend for listening and giving me good advice.

Ricardo

### Letter from Tita Carmen
Received March 29, 1917

Ricardo, my dearest boy,

Your words cut through me like a machete. How dare these people treat you so poorly? The thought that you were first treated poorly by the gentleman on the ship and then chased out of someone's neighborhood is appalling. If this man and woman were before me, I would need to refrain myself from slapping them across their American faces. Can they not see the man you are, the man you are becoming? Can they not see you come from a respectable family with means?

When I saw you stand on top of that massive boat headed for America, I thought of your father. How proud he would be of you. You stood there looking like you belonged—unafraid and ready to tackle the world. Unbeatable.

Do not let them win, Ricardo. Your struggles will pass. Your oppressors—those who can't see beyond your speech or, God forbid, the color of your lovely skin—will find little peace. Their misguided beliefs cripple them. You need to believe this.

Don't lose your spirit, your very kind spirit. I was lucky to have been asked by your mother to help her care for you. There were days I knew she didn't require me, but I showed up regardless. How I loved to listen to your stories, your hopes and dreams. How I loved to take care of you when the slightest thing was wrong.

Write to me whenever you need. Your letters warm my heart and make me feel useful. *Oo Ricardo, ako ay palaging nandito para sa iyo.* (Yes, Ricardo, I will always be here for you.)

Your favorite aunt,

Carmen

### JOURNAL ENTRY
March 30, 1917

My dear Tita. Her words warm my heart. I want to hold on to them but know she has no idea what living here looks like. I'm sure she cannot image it, not when she lives in such comfort behind walls with housekeepers and cooks. She talks of "not letting them win" when I don't know what winning means. No, instead I bend and twist trying to find my way in a country I still don't understand. She says THEY have misguided beliefs, but don't we all? Before I met the Lorenzos, I believed I was better than those in steerage. Am I? At this moment, I only know I don't know as much as I need to know.

Masakit tanggapin ang katohanan.

**The truth hurts.**

# PART THREE

## War & Separation

I can't pull myself away from the newspaper. For the past three days, I have read any article I can find. The headlines alone have stopped me from doing anything else.

*NAVY ORDERED TO SEA — U.S. TAKES 91 INTERNED SHIPS — NAVAL, MILITIA, RESERVES ARE CALLED TO COLORS — PRESIDENT ASKS AMERICANS TO SUPPORT WAR MEASURES — THE PRESIDENT CALLS FOR VOLUNTEERS — WILL DRAFT GIANT ARMY*

The war is here. I walk out the door and know my life today is different than it was a week ago. Jaime is on edge. This morning, he raised his voice with me for the first time.

"Don't you have anything better to do than pore over the newspaper?"

I jumped from the tone he took, his mild-mannered voice replaced with almost a snarl.

"Look at the mess you make. Don't you have classes to attend to?"

"I do," I said. "I'll pick up all of these papers and be on my way." I didn't have a class to go to but knew it best to not be there.

To be on the tram was no better. One woman sat next to her son who couldn't have been more than seventeen.

"Yeah, Ma," he kept saying, "I am going to sign up as soon I can. You can't stop me." She looked ready to burst into tears. Several men argued about the decision for war. "Bloody war. What is Wilson thinking, getting us into the thing?"

"About time," a man said. "My relatives are dying over there, and here we sit, doing nothing."

I moved to the back of the tram, as I didn't need to become part of any argument about the war. I don't know what to think. José is excited. For weeks, all he's talked about is the U.S. joining the war effort. When they do, he wants to sign up. He's not a citizen, but it won't stop him. I'm not either, and some days I don't know if I want to be. Still, I want to know as much as I can about the war. I can't stop myself from reading anything

I can get my hands on. I do care about the U.S., but why would I fight for a country I'm not fully accepted in?

### TELEGRAM FROM NENA
April 15, 1917

U.S. IS GOING TO WAR? WHAT DOES THIS MEAN? YOU WON'T HAVE TO FIGHT, WILL YOU? WIRE BACK. WE ARE CONCERNED.

### TELEGRAM TO NENA
April 17, 1917

YES, USA JOINED THE WAR. MANY SIGN UP TO FIGHT. I WON'T. I AM SAFE. NO NEED TO WORRY.

### Letter from Mario
April 24, 1917

Rico,

You sent me a letter! Incredible! You said you would, and you did. Even my mother was impressed. Of course, me writing back has taken months, but as you promised, so did I. When I got your letter, our friends thought I was lying.

"Me?" I said. "When do I lie?"

They all burst out laughing. I guess I do twist the truth now and then. As you know, it is usually all in good fun. I had to show them the letter to get them to believe me, but I didn't let 'em read it. They can get their own letter is what I told them.

I bet your first days were hard, but by now you must be spouting words in English all the time, ready to talk to the president if he were to walk by. I know you, hombre. Some way or another, you would talk to him. I have seen you do it here in Manila—not with the president, but people pretty high up in our country. There you would be quietly in conversation, putting on that charm of yours. I always wished I had some more of that. I hope you are putting it to good use in America, Rico.

Nena tells me you live far from the ocean. What's that like? I know someone who has been there. Chicago, right? All I remember him saying is he'd never met so many people from countries he had never heard of before. That was years ago, but he described it as a booming but tough place. What do you say? I know you were thinking of studying engineering. Are there good opportunities there?

Glad to hear card-playing filled some of your time on the ship. This seven-card version sounds like something one of your card buddies made up. No one here has ever heard of it. Ricardo, is this your version of bluffing? Our gang still gets together to play once in a while, and yup, it's usually at my home. The first time we got together after you left, we talked more about you than we played cards. I guess we all had hoped you would change your mind at the last minute. Weren't we wrong?

Not much to say about my life. Everything is pretty much the same. Still dating Grace, still working to finish my degree in something. What do you think? Should I, too, become an engineer? Really, I have been studying accounting and like numbers. I don't know. I need to decide soon. My parents have stopped asking, which means it's time.

Rico, write to me again. Seldom do I write letters, but for you, I will. I miss that mug of yours.

Mario

## Letter to Mario
### May 1, 1917

Mario, my man,

You responded to my letter. When Jaime handed it to me, I stared at the envelope. He asked me if I was all right. "I can't believe it," was all I could think to say as I ripped open the envelope while Jaime walked away chuckling.

You're right about Chicago not being close to an ocean, in fact not close at all. At first, it bothered me, but the city sits on a lake the size of Lake Luzon, which helps. And you're right about my first days. At first, I didn't want to leave Jaime and Esperanza's home. To walk several streets nearby was nail-biting, and then to venture to the university made me as nervous as a chicken being chased for slaughter, but gradually I've become accustomed to looking amiss in masses of people.

But change is afoot. The minute war was declared, everything has changed. I don't think I exaggerate to say the city has gone mad for war. In the newspaper, it's referred to as "the war to end all wars." Young men our age and younger are signing up every day to go fight. Germans, who once paraded their heritage as a status above all others, now cower and even change their names. Because there are so few Filipinos here, I believe I will be safe from any push to join or be dishonored for not. I don't plan to sign up.

Beyond being surrounded by reminders of the war, I am well. Jaime and I talk about playing cards, but we never get around to it. His work keeps him busy, as do my studies. I miss the game. I still miss our gang as well.

I have, however, found time to dance, but it's nothing like in Manila or anywhere in the Philippines. Here, I pay a young lady to dance with me. Can you believe it? Ten cents per dance. Some dance halls, I have even been turned away from, as I am not white enough. I know, I'm one or two shades lighter than you. Here, you'd really be in trouble. *Completamente loco, no?* (Completely insane, no?)

I know you love to dance as well, so let me tell you about last night's quest to challenge this notion of keeping people like us out of white-only dance halls. My accomplice was my friend José (a fellow Filipino I met a couple of months after I arrived). He is the one who introduced me to the dance halls. He goes more often that I, but we both have gotten to know several of the dancers. My favorite partner is Sally, and his is Rose.

The girls dance for a living, and they as a rule don't go out with their regulars—the men that pay them to dance—like me. Well, I saw this announcement for the inauguration of a new outdoor garden at one of the fanciest hotels in Chicago. Dinner and dancing to an orchestra in newly opened sunken gardens. We convinced Sally and Rose to break their rules and be our dates. We offered to pay for their dinners, even though we both knew our families would disapprove of us spending their money this way. So don't go telling Nena.

What a night. The girls were dressed in stylish gowns. No one would have guessed they were taxi dancers. José and I had gone shopping, and we looked like we belonged in Chicago's finest. Dapper does not begin to describe how decked out we were. José in his newly purchased used black tailcoat, white-collar shirt, and black bow tie. Me in my black tailcoat, stripe dress pants, and a black vest and tie. I even bought black patent leather shoes. I felt like I was off for the performance of a lifetime, not a garden affair.

We arrived, gave our names, and the young man looked panicked. He excused himself. An older gentleman returned and said, "There must be some mistake as this is an event for white people only." The girls took over then, seeing as they are as pale as dried rice.

"You can see we are adequately white now, can't you? These gentlemen, the ones who paid for this evening, are our companions," Rose said.

Sally took a step closer. "So, you see, sir, unless you want to have a hullaballoo take place right now, you best seat us," she said.

Rose added, "We would like a table near the dance floor please."

What a sight to see the two of them in action. The gentleman looked around as a crowd had gathered—all white and not pleased, as they were not accustomed to waiting. He bowed and showed us to a table next to the sparkling dance floor made of marble.

We handled ourselves beautifully. Our dinner was one of the best I have had in Chicago, and the orchestra the largest I have had the pleasure of hearing. From "Me & My Gal" and "Smiles and Chuckles" to the "Tickle Toe," they played them all. No surprise, the orchestra was all white. They were excellent. So was our dancing. We waltzed, we fox-trotted, and we even did a little rumba until we could hardly stand. At one point, a couple walked up to our table and asked us if we were part of the entertainment. Sally and Rose could not contain themselves. We were in heaven—that is, until an important-looking man sat down at our table. Thank goodness the girls were in the powder room.

"Gentleman, I'm glad to see you've enjoyed yourselves, but it's time you take your leave," he said in a calm manner, confidence exuding off him. To others, he probably looked like he had simply stopped to say hello.

"I know you wouldn't want to embarrass the young women you're with. They are quite lovely, aren't they?"

José and I looked at each other, unable to speak. This, we hadn't planned for.

"Because if you don't leave this instant, I will summon officers to remove you."

"We've paid to be here, and we ..." José said.

The man didn't let José finish. "Come with me. I'll give you your money back." He said this with such civility and conviction, we stood up without out any further discussion.

As we walked with him, he greeted others and shook their hands. We did the same to the astonishment of those whose hands we shook. The girls were already at the entrance. We found out later they had been escorted there after they left the powder room. We all had wanted to dance more, but it was late, so we caught a taxi and took the girls home.

Mario, we almost succeeded in experiencing a full night reserved for whites only. And the evening didn't cost us a penny. Can you believe it? Not a typical night for me, but one I thought you'd like to hear about. José and I like to see what we can get away with. Why not, eh?

Enough about me. I am glad to hear you are making a decision about school. I could see you as an accountant. Even during our card games, I witnessed your math skills. Who adds and subtracts that quickly? I'm trying to decide what I want to do as well. You know I have always talked about engineering but now find myself wondering about other fields, medicine in particular. I am trying to trust myself. Maybe you should do the same?

Send my best wishes to your parents. I could go for some of your mother's lumpia right now. Say hello to the card gang. Tell them they can write and get their own letters.

Write again, Mario. I enjoy knowing how you are.

Ricardo

### JOURNAL ENTRY
May 2, 1917

I woke up this morning feeling like I had done something wrong. The letter I wrote to Mario played over and over in my head throughout the night. I wanted to tell Mario about dance halls but ended up bragging about our night out breaking the rules. Why did I do that? Sometimes I don't know who I'm becoming.

### TELEGRAM FROM NENA
May 9, 1917

RECEIVED YOUR LETTER TODAY. MEDICINE? DOCTOR? YES, BROTHER. LISTEN TO YOUR HEART. YOU ARE CAPABLE ONCE ENGLISH LEARNED. DO NOT DOUBT. Nena

### Posting of grades from University of Chicago
May 15, 1917

Mr. Alvarez,

These are your grades for the winter quarter. They are also posted on your professors' office doors. Should you have questions, see your professor. We will be offering classes during the summer months. Please see the written schedule and postings throughout the school.

Cordially,

Mr. Jonathon Smith
Academic Dean
University of Chicago

**JOURNAL ENTRY**
May 16, 1917

I read, write, and rewrite in English, and still my grades are not anywhere near what I expect. They don't come close to the effort I put forth. If they did, I would be first in each of my classes. But as Papa often said, "One isn't awarded medals or grades by level of exertion." At least I didn't fail a class, so there is some improvement. My grades have to improve or this idea of medical school is not an idea at all, only a fantasy.

*Letter to Nena*
May 29, 1917

Nena,

You wanted to know about the impact of the war. Where to begin? There are thousands upon thousands of Germans in Chicago, and shortly after war was declared, they were quick to remove anything German-like. German flags disappeared overnight. Names began to change. Mr. Schmidt became Mr. Smith, Mr. and Mrs. Van Helder, who make the most delicious bread I have ever tasted, are now Mr. and Mrs. Vander. Many people even fear an attack by the Germans here in Chicago. The Poles are ready to sign up as soldiers. So are many others.

For me, war has meant contributing money, listening to speeches, and attending public events. There is no need to worry about me. Outside of this household, on the matter of war, I am quiet, Sister. I am a bystander. No one recruits me when I attend events.

Few openly oppose the war. They are afraid to. Only a month after the declaration, men began giving speeches in public places around the city. They're called Four Minute Men—supposedly they are to talk no longer than four minutes. The other day, I was enjoying some quiet time in the park, and not one man but several stood in the main gazebo and promoted the war. Four minutes were more like twenty. I listened, as did everyone else. We would be noticed if we walked away.

I continue on as a dutiful student at a university, now The Lewis Institute. My grades are not the best, but I continue on. I force myself to think in English and have imaginary conversations with fellow students, the professor, and with people on the street. In conversation with myself, I'm quite witty. I still contemplate medicine. Glad to know you find the idea exciting. So do I.

You are always in my prayers.

Ricardo

### Note to José
June 7, 1917

José,

Seems like you're going to decide to go into the Army, which I fear, but down deep know it's your decision. I'm struggling with a decision, too, about this idea of becoming a doctor. I'm not sure I'm ready, but I really want to explore what it would be like. Hard to even write the word "doctor" without feeling my heart race.

Funny, I remember having this same feeling when I was only a few feet tall. I wanted to be like my papa. He often told me of his adventures coming to the Philippines. One morning, I decided to do the same by wandering in the jungle, down the road by myself. How exhilarating it was as I went further and further into what seemed like massive mountain laurels and trees twisted far above my head. I marched along in song. I made up some jingle about being captain of my own ship off to discover new lands. I was Captain Alvarez (I can hear you chuckling). On and on, I trudged until, looking around, I had no idea where I was.

Gone was my bravery like a puff of smoke. I turned in circles, and there seemed no way out. Mynah birds started their echoing taunts at me.

Spider monkeys swung wildly from branches above my head. I remember the tears streaming down my cheeks and the lump in my throat. My head swung from bush to tree, hunting for something to tell me which way to go. Finally, I looked down and saw a footprint, and then another. I placed my foot into one of them and realized they were mine. Slowly, I found my way back home.

José, right now, I feel like that little boy wanting to try something new but am afraid I might not find my way. Would I even be considered for medical school, or like the public dance halls, would they send me on my way? Do you feel the same about becoming a soldier? I bet your decision isn't easy, and mine isn't either. How about we get together and talk? No girls, no dancing, maybe a walk in the park. I'd really like to hear what you think.

Ricardo

### Letter from Nena
Received July 1, 1917

Ricardo,

How life has changed for you, Ricardo. As you describe your adventures in your letters, I picture you becoming even more sophisticated—your speech and looks more American. Would I recognize you walking down the street fully clad in Chicago wear? If I heard your voice, would I know it? Oh, but do not change too much. I very much like you the way you are.

Family have been asking about you, and I tell them you are doing stupendous, a student at university living with fellow Filipinos. No need to have anyone in this clan of ours think anything different. I know you struggle with English. We both know this, too, will change. The elders, they nod their heads in approval. As you know, an important and good thing.

I remain involved in too much. The orphanage stays full of children that I cannot stop becoming attached to. Vicente has visited several times, and the children love him. Sometimes we think we should take one home with us and start our family with a child who, for whatever reason, was cast aside. Still, we hope to have our own and pray nightly our prayers will be heard. My heart still aches from losing Alberito.

I'm not sure what time of year it will be when you read this. I would like to think it would be spring, with your first winter completed. Perhaps out enjoying the outdoors once again. You were never one to sit idly but were always off doing one thing or another-—off driving your automobile, dancing, playing tennis. I miss your whirlwind, Brother. If you were here, I might even let you photograph me. I miss you that much.

You're in my prayers always.

Nena

## Letter to Margaret
July 13, 1917

Margaret, my friend,

I do hope you remember me from our travels aboard the Tenyo Maru. I count you as my first American friend. I trust you are well and completed your extensive travel with your parents. I'm not sure exactly where Virginia is, but have been told it is not far away from our country's capital.

I am in Chicago living with Jaime and Esperanza Rodriguez, the couple from the Tenyo Maru. They've taken me into their home. Without them, I would not be here but headed back to the Philippines. I'm at a university, still struggling with English, but I improve every day. We now could have a complete conversation about many different subjects, even with your parents.

There are few Filipinos living here, as most remain in San Francisco where there are thousands. Here in Chicago, there are less than two hundred. Luckily, I've found a Filipino my age to befriend, José Lopez, but often people don't know what to make of us and are not the kindest.

I did attend the University of Chicago and now take classes from The Lewis Institute, another university close by. As you can guess, all of my classes are taught in English, and my grades show it. I pass, but barely.

Margaret, sometimes I find myself reflecting on the man who walked away from marrying you. What a fool. My bet is he regrets his decision today and may regret it his entire life. You deserve better, but then I assume you know this by now.

I hope you are well, happy, and out dancing. If this letter finds you, I would enjoy hearing back from you.

With high regards,

Ricardo

Ricardo Alvarez

322 South Winchester Avenue

Chicago, Illinois

⚘

## *Letter from Margaret*
August 17, 1917

Ricardo,

What a nice surprise to receive your letter. Of course, I remember you. How could I not? Your company made my travels more than bearable. How good to hear you are now in the throes of learning English. As you conquer English, I learn Spanish. I don't know enough to converse as you now can in English but can make myself understood. There is a Mexican family nearby, and the mother has wanted to learn English, so we help each other. Twice a week we spend several hours together. *Buenisimo para los dos.* (This is good for both of us.)

We have been home now for about five months. We were in Honolulu for most of the time, traveling to other more remote islands periodically. I never came close to learning the Hawaiian tongue. From there, we boarded another ship and headed to San Francisco. I thought of you as we disembarked at Angel Island. I know you were nervous about the process. I assume it went without any problems. I also thought of Eduardo. Did his mother have her baby beforehand, and have you heard from him? I hope so.

I plan to enroll at a university for women (they're called Normal

Schools) in the fall. Of course, studying to become a teacher is what my father believes I should do, and it's difficult to not do as he wants. I am also a volunteer for the war effort two days a week. Some women wear badges to show they are important as they do their part for our boys fighting. I don't bother. We do such menial tasks: rip material into strips for treating wounds, collect paper and pencils, and sort through clothes donations. I do what I can.

I am much better now, Ricardo. I actually giggled when I read your kind words about my past betrothed being an idiot. I agree. As time has passed, I recall many other things about that relationship. I had thought it was perfect. It was far from it. He was often short-tempered and critical of me, demanding at times that I do things only his way. Even what I chose to wear was a point of stress for me. And, Ricardo, he wasn't much of a dancer either. You would dance circles around the poor man.

I haven't danced in such a long time. On our return trip home, however, I did and had the confidence to say "yes" to many young men thanks to my previous experience with you. None danced as we did, however. How I enjoyed being swept across the dance floor with you. I use to imagine I was an exotic bird that floated through the air in your arms. I do hope you have found places in Chicago to keep you on the dance floor.

My only sad news is the loss of a close friend. When we left on our journey, she had been ill with consumption. Only weeks after my return, she passed. She was a person I shared everything with and one I will, I fear, always miss. She was my age, only twenty, and much too young to die. Please do stay in touch, Ricardo. I would like to continue to hear of your many escapades.

Fondly,

Margaret

**JOURNAL ENTRY**
September 7, 1917

José, you're gone. Nothing I said mattered. How many times I asked "why?"

"Because this is my home, my country now," you said. "I will defend it."

Even when I reminded him he isn't a citizen, his answer was the same.

"This is my decision, Ricardo. Me going doesn't mean you have to."

Me, be a solider? I could no more imagine walking down the street naked than having a gun in hand. I'd sooner take a bullet than shoot one. But I'd probably take one for you, José. When we said goodbye, I felt as if a body part was being ripped away.

You're my friend, my comrade—the fella I share all of my mistakes with, and you've left. So many escapades we dared each other through, unaware we were crossing lines.

The night we decided we had to go to a jazz place on State Street in the middle of Black Chicago was probably the worst. We should have turned around, but of course we didn't. Not us. We made our way into that crowded saloon and were quickly surrounded by big men, big black men—blacker than coal with arms twice the size of my own. I remember their faces. None of them looked pleased. How we politely tried to wiggle our way back to the bellowing tunes blazing from the back room, trying hard to act like we belonged, knowing full well we didn't. We only made it ten feet into the saloon, still nowhere near the music we came to hear, when that oversized black woman strutted over and put a halt to us taking another step. Her meaty arms were enough to stop us in our tracks.

"Boys, now you all know better than comin' on in here. I just walk you back on out so's you don't go getting hurt," she said. We tried using our charm but suggesting she instead escort us to the back room.

I jumped in: "Really, Miss, we won't be a bother …" I didn't get to finish.

"Ha, you worrying about being a bother is cute. Look around you, fellas. Do you think you belong here?"

She said this as she nodded to two men nearby, and seconds later, they were at our sides. To them, she said, "Get 'em outta here—and, Jimmy, try not to be too rough."

They came at us like two bulls, making us walk backwards. We ran into men who shoved, kicked, and yelled at us. At the door, Jimmy and his friend pushed while someone behind us stuck out their feet. We landed hard on the wood platform to the hoots and hollers of everyone nearby. Jimmy wasn't done, but before he got his hands on us, we jumped up and ran. Took us a while to laugh about that one.

And now, José, you're gone. I can't believe you're off to be trained to kill.

### JOURNAL ENTRY
September 13, 1917

Why must there be reminders everywhere? Bad enough there are signs and banners. Now there are songs about the war. "Over There, Over There," is the latest. The words feel like oil thrown on an open wound.

*Johnny, get your gun, get your gun, get your gun.*

*Take it on the run, on the run, on the run.*

*Hear them calling you and me?*

*Everyone for liberty.*

*Hurry right away, go today, no delay.*

Yes, hurry like José did, so you can get over there sooner. Doesn't matter who you are or what color your skin is. They'll take anyone willing—even my friend.

Yes, the Yanks are coming. The Yanks are coming. Some are not citizens yet. I wonder. Will the others call José a Yank? If I put on a soldier's uniform, would they call me one?

### Letter from Mario
September 16, 1917

Rico,

I've been thinking about you a lot. Ever since I heard America joined the war. Well, that and your crazy story about you and your Filipino friend going to an affair that hotel didn't want you at. I try to picture the whole thing. No, I try to picture a place, a country where you can't go where you please if you don't have the right color of skin. Heck, we let Americans with money go anywhere here, and you have the money. Why wouldn't it be the same there?

Then you tell me about your night out. Man, you must have been sweating bullets 'cause you're brave and all, but what you described is not something I would think you'd do. Yeah, we used to sneak around a little, push the rules at school sometimes. We even snuck out late at night once. Remember how brave we thought we were? But Rico, what were you thinking doing what you did? Be careful, all right? I hope you're not about to sign up to fight the war. Now that would be downright stupid. All I can say is let the Americans, those people who have lived there for a lot longer than you, go fight.

I have news. I'm about to finish my studies to become an accountant. Can you believe it? My parents want to throw me a party, they're so happy. Yeah, and Clarita and I are pretty serious, not getting-married serious, but maybe. Who knows? We're still young, and I need to get a job before I do anything.

The card gang still gets together once in a while. It's not the same, though, as everyone is busy. Domingo and Carlo talk about moving to other parts of the Philippines. Wally may even go to Japan. I haven't seen anyone from your clan for some time. Not even Nena. So the next time you write, you'll have to give me news about them if you have any.

Take care, Rico. Be safe. Any chance you'll come home?

Mario

## Letter to Margaret
September 20, 1917

Margaret,

I was so happy to receive your letter and to hear you're doing well. I'm sure you'll be a perfect student at Normal School. I am forever grateful you helped me tackle words like they were something sweet I wouldn't want to miss. And then you're learning Spanish as well. *Que bueño para ti.*

If you recall, I talked about becoming an engineer but am no longer sure. Medicine has become my fascination. I'm drawn to it like I am to a dance floor. I guess it's the difference between being on the dance floor versus designing one.

As you guessed, Angel Island was no problem. We were in and out in less than two hours. I did not get to say goodbye to Eduardo, though. I wish there was some way to find him. I hope he, too, is learning some English, but I fear work to feed his family will be his primary focus.

Margaret, I'm sorry to hear of the death of your friend. She sounds like she was very important to you. I know firsthand how difficult death can be to accept. It has taken me years to accept my parents' deaths. I don't think I ever talked to you about this—really, I have hardly talked to anyone about them. I was so young when both died. Only now am I starting to better understand the impact their loss has had on me.

My hope is that you don't do as I have: carry a burden of loss for too long over your friend. You're much too lovely and kind to be sad. You deserve great happiness Margaret.

Your Spanish-Filipino friend,

Ricardo

*※*

### Letter from Margaret
September 30, 1917

Ricardo,

Oh, my goodness, I knew your father and mother were no longer in your life and had guessed they had both passed, God rest their souls. I didn't know you were only a child when it happened. If you recall, I asked you about them, and you only gave me a short answer and changed the subject. I sensed your privacy on this matter to be important to you, so I didn't persist. I'm sorry I didn't.

But now, please, Ricardo, tell me as much as you like. Perhaps it will be easier in a letter and help rid you of your sadness. I would see this as a gift of friendship that I hold dearly.

Affectionately,

Margaret

## Letter to Margaret
October 11, 1917

Margaret,

Thank you for your kind words. I do remember you asking about my mother and father. I wasn't ready to talk about their deaths then. But I am now, although my hand shakes as I begin.

When I was seven, my mother and two siblings died from cholera. First our housekeeper fell ill, and then my family. It spread so easily. My older sister and I were not even able to hug my mother goodbye or our baby brother or sister. We helped each other first survive and then learn to live on without them. My father suffered the most—at least this is what I discovered years later.

Margaret, as I write this, I realize my story may be too painful to read. If so, please set my letter aside. I will understand. I'm afraid the worst is yet to come. The unthinkable happened. Several years later, my sister and I came home from school, and we found him. The house became flooded with our blood-curdling screams. In our parlor, he lie in a pool of blood, the pistol still in his hand. I kept yelling, "No, no, Papa, no!" My sister had to drag me away, both of us lost in the horror of the scene, the silence, the finality of what he chose to do.

Misery became my daily companion. I wore it like an overcoat made of coarse straw; it poked, prodded, and pricked me as I tried to move throughout the days that followed. My mouth no longer functioned. Words were forgotten before they were released. My aunts tell me I was not really there. They helped my sister and me shuffle through the days, through the nights, and tucked us in at night afraid to leave us alone.

Perhaps I have told you too much, but once started, I couldn't stop (believe me, I have almost thrown this letter away several times). My father's death in particular has been such a dark secret, a burden I've carried for far too long. Thank you for helping me finally release memories I've hidden from, thinking they would go away. I imagine you reading this and gasping in horror. If you are, that was not my intention.

I, too, treasure our friendship, Margaret. Hopefully I will receive correspondence from you shortly. I wonder, do you have a beau at your side now? If you do, I hope he is everything you deserve.

Ricardo

### Letter to Tito Juan
October 12, 1917

Tito Juan,

I pray you can help me. My father's death has come to haunt me. For the first time, I told a friend the story of how he died, and ever since, I'm flooded with memories—like the walls of a dam have been broken wide open. Images I thought forgotten come into focus at the oddest times—getting on the tram or in the middle of a conversation. When I see someone who remotely looks like my father, moments of curdling pain rush out.

The day we found him, I tried to make him wake up, but now I remember his face was half-gone. Nena tried to pull me away but couldn't. I was covered with his blood. I recall thinking that somehow I had done something wrong, or didn't do something he wanted. Were we not enough for him?

Now, ten years later, I need to have a better understanding, a clearer picture to answer my ultimate question: Why did he pull the trigger? Was he not over the deaths of my mother, brother, and sister? I thought he was. I thought we were all finding our way together. He was more himself, although I remember often waking late at night to see him poring over papers at his desk.

Can you help me, Tito Juan? What would lead him to leave his two children whom I know he loved? Sometimes he would hold our hands while we said our prayers at supper and not want to let go. "You are my blessings," he would say. "I pray every night in thanks. I hope you know how much I love you both."

You knew my father well. I believe you hold some answers. If not, you know others who may. Please share with me as much as you can.

Always with high regard,

Ricardo

## Letter from José
### October 15, 1917

Hey, Ricardo,

Finally have some time to write ya. They keep us darn busy. I'm good, though, and look even better. In another month, you won't recognize me with all this muscle. Hard not to get stronger with the routine we keep. My body screams at me every night from the running, jumping over fences, and exercises they have us do. Yesterday, we had to run an obstacle course with an eighty-pound pack on our back and then climb under imaginary enemy lines. My boots were filled with mud, and my helmet was crusted with items I couldn't identify. The smell was enough to make me want to keel over.

Every day, we march until they tell us to stop. My legs sometimes go numb. They ache so bad I have to tell myself to keep moving, one foot in front of the other. Doesn't help when some of the officers yell commands all the time. They say the commands toughen us up for the reality of war. I don't think tough describes the aches and pain I feel. And their yelling? Don't even hear them anymore.

I know this camp is a place to train us to fight and, yeah, eventually to kill, but this place is good for me. It's not like Chicago, where what you look like and where you come from matters. My bunkmates are Italian, Polish, Jewish, Irish, and even German. Germans and Polish outnumber everyone. What's incredible is I know I can trust every one of them. In Chicago, we would never have met or looked at each other. Here, we are brothers, and most of us are hungry to join the war, although we aren't anywhere near ready. Every day, we train from dawn to dusk, except on

Sunday when most of us attend a church service and relax. Yeah, I'm goin' to church, Rico. I like it.

It turns out my ability to figure out how to fix things is needed here, so I'm asked to fix one thing or another all the time: motorcars, horse-drawn carts, plumbing gone bad. Buildings are still being built as more and more men arrive each week. There are several thousand of us here now, and that will double soon. Only a handful of Filipinos are in the camp, and we make sure to watch out for each other, although there isn't really a need. The general has made it darn clear that at this camp we are all family.

No news about when we will be sent overseas. For now, we work hard to learn what they call "the art of warfare." There's nothing glorious about what we do. The thought of using a weapon to kill someone still makes me a little sick to my stomach.

Will write you again, Ricardo. I hope all is fine for you. How is The Lewis Institute? Do you make your way to the dance hall? Do you see Sally or Rose? I miss the music and dance—not much more. Write when you can.

Your friend (the brave Filipino),

José

José Mendez

Camp Grant

Rockford, Illinois

### Letter to José
October 25, 1917

José,

You are right, I will not recognize you with muscles. Especially covered in mud! Are they making you taller as well? That might not be a bad thing. Some of those dance girls would like you even better slightly taller, and then with muscles!

I am glad to hear the camp is good for you. So tell me, whom have you most enjoyed getting to know—the Poles or the Germans? Having had such little contact with them really, I am curious. My guess is the Poles. They seem to have more fun and are less worried about what that looks like. Well, except for the Pole who attacked me for being in his neighborhood. He was a real pea-head. Do tell me, will you?

The Lewis Institute is much more to my liking. I'm even enjoying my Latin class. It makes more sense to me than English. I can now understand the basis of English better. I'm not sure how much longer I want to be studying at any university, though. I know you said you could see me as a doc, but how do I find out if that's what I really want to do? Not sure studying at a university will give me the answer.

José, I do make it to the dance hall occasionally, and yes, Sally and Rose are still there. With the war, the dance lines are a lot shorter. Sally is still willing to dance with me—nothing more, though. I've asked her to do something with me outside the dance hall, and she always answers the same. "Ricardo, you know how much I like you, but I can't. People will talk."

You can picture her saying this to me, can't you? She's sweet even as she rejects me, her hands held up as she looks into my face with those green eyes of hers. I pay her my coins, still glad we have the dance floor. She, too, wonders what to do next. Chicago continues to be absorbed by war. Speeches now take place everywhere to encourage support in any way possible. The newspaper says few Americans have left our shores, and the English and French are anxious for more to arrive. I can't imagine what you will find once you go.

Thanks for your letter, José. I have wondered how you are doing and glad you won't be overseas for some time. Would you like me to send you anything? I can't send you a dancing girl (Rose most likely your preference), but could send a missing item.

Let me know, my friend.

Ricardo

## Letter from Margaret
November 2, 1917

Ricardo,

To read your letter made me wish we were still on the Tenyo Maru. I could hold your hand, look into your face, and tell you how sorry I am. You were so young to experience such great losses and to see what you saw—all without a mother. I'm glad sharing your secret with me helped lighten your burden, and I am touched you chose to share this with me.

The loss of a friend, although dear to me, is nothing like what you've been through. I'm thankful you and your sister have each other. I imagine she feels very much the same way. You'll always have that and, if I recall correctly, too many cousins, aunts, and uncles to keep track of. They, too, are your family.

About me being in another relationship, the answer is no. I do believe that someday I will, though. My parents worry much less about me. They support me in becoming a teacher. Both of them are happy to hear we are in contact. They admire your bravery, Ricardo, and are glad to know you are doing what you want. We would be happy to have you as a guest if you are ever able to break away. I would especially like that.

The war is having an impact on all of us. Many men have left to be trained to fight. I collect items to send to the soldiers regularly and see firsthand the fear of mothers who have allowed their sons to go. I can't imagine it.

I wonder what Chicago is like. I have never been but hear stories of its chaos. Friends who have visited describe it as a large city that demands constant attention. Is that true?

Do continue to write, Ricardo. I take great pleasure from our correspondence. I am glad I am your first American friend. I hold that dearly.

Be well, Ricardo.

Margaret

**JOURNAL ENTRY**
November 11, 1917

Could there ever be something more than friendship between Margaret and me? To write the question makes my heart tighten. I immediately think how ridiculous I am to even think it. She's white, and I'm not. It's taken me over a year to fully grasp what that even means. Look around, Ricardo. Have you seen young white women on the arms of brown-skinned men on the streets, in the movie theaters, or in church?

I have seen one couple. I couldn't take my eyes off of them—a woman who looked Mexican with a light-haired chap with an accent that sounded like Mr. Van Helder. They were in church together sitting hand in hand. From the way they looked at each other during the service, I could tell they were in love. Maybe there is hope. Not necessarily for Margaret. She lives far away, and here I am still living on the kindness of Jaime and Esperanza and on my grandmother's money. But maybe someday, somehow, I could, we could …

# 1918

### Letter to Tita Carmen
January 5, 1918

Dearest Tita Carmen,

The ink in my pen has been dry for weeks. I haven't pestered you, which is a good sign. Perhaps this means I am doing better, which I am, except for my studies. I received third-quarter grades today. Monkeys may well be capable of doing better than I did. Tonight I've paced back and forth in my room muttering loud enough to cause Jaime to come find out what was the matter. I had thought I was arguing with myself in my head. Turns out, I wasn't completely silent.

I must have looked like a cross between a mad man and a worn-out schoolboy. I blurted out, "Studying, classes, grades—I am done with it all. I've wasted my time and Lola Brigida's money. Look, I got another 'F.'"

Jaime took the sheet from me and shook his head, "I'm sorry, Ricardo. I know you were working hard."

Was I? I don't know anymore. Lately, I sit in class and sometimes find I'm not listening. One time, the children outside caught my attention, and another time, it was a group of old men. Other days, it might be a fly on the chalkboard or the worn shoes of the student next to me. My legs no long sit quietly but jitter like they need to get up and move. Sometimes I doodle rather than take notes. Something is missing for me.

Tita Carmen, I'm not sure what I'm working towards anymore. When I asked you if you thought medicine was for me, you said yes. So did Nena, but I need more convincing. The only thing I know is I can't stop thinking about the many aliments I see people have.

What makes the woman I see every day have such a pronounced limp? Why does Joe, our neighbor, have disfigured hands and growths on his arms? Why are some elderly women bent over, their backs forming an arch rather than a straight line? There has to be a way to chase that curiosity outside of sitting in a class, hasn't there? I explained this to Jaime, and he had an intriguing idea.

"Offer to help at a hospital," he said. "They may need you."

Even though I'm afraid they won't want my help or, worse yet, find my offer humorous, I am going to go tomorrow and see if they need my help. Maybe then I can either stop my persistent enchantment with medicine or do something more real than sitting in a classroom where success eludes me.

My blessings to you and your family,
Ricardo

### TELEGRAM TO NENA
January 10, 1918

DECIDED TO TAKE A BREAK FROM UNIVERSITY. WILL REMAIN IN CHICAGO WITH THE RODRIGUEZES. I AM FINE. BEST TO YOU AND VICENTE Ricardo

### TELEGRAM FROM NENA
January 15, 1918

BROTHER, DO BE SENSIBLE. TRUST YOURSELF AND WHAT YOU NEED TO DO. I AM PREGNANT. JUANITA DOESN'T EVEN KNOW. OUR SECRET. Nena

### TELEGRAM TO NENA
January 16, 1918

MAGNIFICO! PRAYERS DO GET ANSWERED. NOT A WORD TO ANYONE. Ricardo

### *Letter to Margaret*
January 28, 1918

Margaret,

Thank you for your letter. Your words were a comfort to me. As I had hoped, after writing to you about my parents' death, I am now able to remember without suddenly feeling choked, unable to take a breath for fear it might cause me to break down.

So much has happened since our last correspondence. I'm not sure where to start. I'm no longer a student but now volunteer at a nearby hospital to help me decide if medicine is something I want to explore or not. For the past month, I've been at the hospital every day. I do pretty much everything. My favorite is helping translate anything remotely Spanish and sitting with people to help calm them down. I think this is where I belong because every morning I wake up ready to go again. An added benefit is my English improves every day.

Yes, I would very much like to visit you and your parents. Or when the war ends, maybe you could venture to Chicago for a visit? Perhaps with your parents, I could show you the city or maybe we could even find a place to dance.

Fondly,

Ricardo

## Letter from José at Camp Grant
February 3, 1918

Ricardo,

About time I get a letter from you. Whenever anyone who isn't married receives a letter here, bunkmates assume it's your girl and hoot and holler, hoping you'll share details. Yours arrived, and they stared at me. "Ricardo?" they said. "That's no woman. Don't need to share any of that." Sure wish I had gotten me one—a woman, that is—before I got here, though.

Not many of the fellas get mail. I actually got a letter from my parents this last month and couldn't believe it. They're so proud that I am training to become a soldier. I guess my father fought in the war against Spain. I had no idea. He never talked about it.

No need to send me anything as I got word that some of us are going to be sent over to France soon. We thought this was a little strange because we were told we would all be going as a unit. Instead, a handful of my unit are being sent. I'm going because of my ability to fix things. I am excited and scared to even think about getting on a boat to go over there. We first get sent to another camp somewhere out East, and then the plan is to send thousands of us overseas.

Some of my buddies are really upset they weren't chosen to go. We've been here now for five months, and they thought they'd be in battle by now. Me? I can wait, although I do know how to fight a lot better, so I may have a better chance of staying alive. Bigger muscles, Ricardo, but same height. Those taller girls, they like us smaller men anyway.

These fellas here sometimes say things or use words that make no sense to me. They love it when I say, "Huh? What does that mean?" The other day, one of them said, "Yeah, my buddy and me we were on the make." Now would you guess it means they were both flirting with girls? I didn't. Like an idiot, I asked what they were making. Boy, did they laugh. Then there are the words they use. A "simp" is someone who is stupid, a "goldbrick" a lazy person, a "dingbat" … well, maybe you can guess that one. The guys who have been in the U.S. for a while have plenty of surprise phrases they like to teach me. Also, you're right. I like the Poles the best.

Not sure when we will be leaving. If I can, I'll write you from the next camp. Send me those prayers, Ricardo, I may need them in the months ahead.

José

Black Hawk Division—86th

P.S. If something happens to me, will you let my family know? I worry they wouldn't find out. I have listed your address in my records along with theirs. With the mail the way it is, I don't trust it.

Purok 5

Salvacion, Panabo City

8105 Davao del Norte PI

### TELEGRAM TO JOSÉ
February 5, 1918

YOU JOKE. YOU TAUGHT ME HOW TO BE ON THE MAKE. BE CAREFUL. PRAYERS FOR YOU. Ricardo

## Letter to Nena
February 19, 1918

Sister,

How are you? You didn't say how far along you were in your telegram, but by now, you must have begun to show. Our cousins probably guessed before your stomach began to become round. Those women, they do pay attention.

In one of your last letters, you worried that I might have changed so much that you wouldn't recognize me. I don't think so on the outside— only a bit older, which is probably good. Haven't gotten one bit taller. I don't know, maybe I've lost some of my charm, though; haven't had hardly any luck with the girls.

But on the inside, I have changed. In this city, how could I not? I'm living in a place that prides itself on being a mecca for the adventurous, a city that redefines itself every day, a place that dares you to dream big but won't catch you when you fall.

Believe me, I've fallen. They weren't huge falls—failing classes is not like losing an arm from a passing train. (I have seen that, and it was terrible to witness. Far worse was how few people came to the man's aid. When I tried to run to the injured man, I was pushed back and told to stay away.)

Taking a break from attending university has been good for me. I find myself humming tunes more often, eating less (I really was becoming a bit portly, which was not a pretty sight), and choosing to stroll rather than rush. Most of my time, I spend at a local hospital helping doctors and nurses take care of patients. Many doctors have left to join the war effort. As the hospital administrator put it, "We need hands, bodies, anyone who can help us take care of all the sick people."

I like being needed. I help wash patients, clean up after procedures, wrap bandages, and, when needed, translate for those who speak little English. But Nena, I've never done such physical work, nor have I ever taken orders from not one but many. Still, what I do helps both the hospital and me. This morning I was humming away to myself.

Jaime laughed, saying, "It's been a while since I've seen you this relaxed."

I am calmer. Now, I spend more time with Jaime and Esperanza in the evenings rather than hide away in my room poring over a day's lecture. Don't worry about me, Nena. As I work alongside doctors and nurses, I become more convinced the field of medicine is something I need to pursue.

I appreciate your trust, Sister. Do take the greatest care.

Ricardo

### Letter from Tito Juan
Received March 21, 1918

Ricardo,

I wrote days after receiving your letter, but I know months will have passed before you read this. I knew someday you would want to know more about your father's death and am glad you asked. To give you the best answers, I spoke with several other elders who also knew your father well.

I loved your father. Although quite different than me, he reminded me of myself when I was younger. It was your father's mischievous nature that I loved. He was a somber and quiet man but still enjoyed himself. He didn't, however, do anything without serious thought for consequences. He wanted always to do what he thought was best for everyone concerned. Always.

How he loved your mother! And you children! You are correct that his world fell apart after her death. As his son, you more than anyone felt this. How he doted on you all. His smile often filled the room when he was with his family. Never doubt his love for you, Ricardo.

You are also right to think there was something more. His status as a highly regarded Spaniard was severely shaken when Spain was defeated by America in 1898. You were but three years old, I'm sure you recall little. During that war, his business remained solvent. Filipinos continued to accept him as their pharmacist. After all, your mother was from a prominent mestizo family. You know how respected Lola Brigida was by all.

When your mother died and the war between America and the Philippines droned on, his business began to fail. Lines were drawn even further, causing Filipinos to choose Filipino businesses over others. You say you recall waking to your father poring over his books. He was. With fewer and fewer customers, he didn't know how he was going to cover the expenses. He didn't know how he, looking like such a Spaniard, would ever be fully accepted again.

I believe, as do others, Ricardo, that he saw no other way out that would leave you and Nena in a good place. He knew Lola Brigida would step in to make sure his children, her beloved grandchildren, were well cared for. He was a bright man, a realistic man with little money left who again only wanted what was best for his children.

But without your mother he was lost. You may have faint memories of a distant Aunt often being at your home after your mother passed. She knew your father was struggling, and quickly became a close companion. In fact he had hoped they might marry and have a complete family again. But the elders at the time said, "No." His business was failing, and it was questionable whether or not he could support her in the way she was accustomed. Perhaps this too played a role in his decision to end his life. It was never from anything you or Nena did or didn't do. This I know in my heart. Ricardo. If you believe anything, believe this.

Hopefully my letter helps you let go of any burden you carry. The heart has great capacity, Ricardo. My hope is you are able to forgive. Your father once told me his life was blessed to have met your mother and have children of such high character. Hold this dearly. Many never know those words were uttered from their father's lips.

I trust you are doing well, Ricardo. We are all cheering for you. So is your father from up above.

Tito Juan

### TELEGRAM TO TITO JUAN
April 1, 1918

YES. HE DID LOVE US. HE TOLD US OFTEN. MY POOR FATHER. FAILING BUSINESS. IMPOSSIBLE LOVE. NO WONDER LOLA BRIGADA VISITED OFTEN. LESS BURDENED KNOWING MORE. GOD BLESS. Ricardo

### JOURNAL ENTRY
April 1, 1918

Papa, I didn't know. I was too young to understand. I do now, or I'm starting to …

### TELEGRAM FROM JOSÉ–FROM ENGLAND
April 12, 1918

TODAY WE GO TO THE FRONT. I PRAY I AM READY. SEND ME YOUR PRAYERS, MY FRIEND. José

### JOURNAL ENTRY
8:30 a.m., April 23, 1918

I should find another place to live but haven't wanted to admit it. Where would I go? I never intended to stay this long. Oh, Lord, I have overstayed their welcome. Of course I have. I have been their guest for almost two years. Last week, I came home early, and they were having a serious conversation until I walked in the room and they abruptly stopped. Yesterday I overheard them talking softly about the need to make changes to their home. Life before Ricardo, I am sure was quite different.

But leaving is hard to think about. I'm comfortable here. I come and go as I please. I do the dishes, and I do pay rent. Maybe I need to do more. When was the last time I went to market, washed my bed linen, or helped clean? Lord in heaven, I can't remember the last time I did something nice for them or even said thank you. Of course they want me gone.

**JOURNAL ENTRY**
April 27, 1918

In Santa Cruz and Manila, I saw pain from a distance. Here at the hospital, I can taste it—a bitterness that makes it difficult to swallow, like salty sweat that runs down your brow into the corners of your mouth. I even hear the patients' whispers of desperation in my sleep. Their sickness doesn't frighten or disgust me. I simply want to help them in any way I can.

When I ask them where they live, they have despairing answers: "Wherever I can find a place." "Sometimes we are able to stay with family." "We are looking for somewhere to live." Many of the patients tell me they don't have a place they call home. When they do, I know they are crowded into spaces fit for two not ten.

Ever more people come to the hospital for la grippe or influenza. One patient said one minute he was fine, and the next he could barely stand. "The cough," he said, "I never knew I could cough this hard. I pray it will end soon." It did end for him; he died the next day.

Doctors and nurses are starting to wear masks. They suggest I do the same. I heard one nurse say to another, "I can't understand why so many young, healthy men are coming down with the flu. It doesn't make sense." The other whispered, "I know. Dr. Webster wonders if this is a new disease or something. He says he has never seen anything like it. I'm scared." They scurried away as if they wanted to break into a run.

If they are frightened, I can only guess what the patients who struggle to get their next breath feel. What is this? Is it a new disease? Will I get it?

## *Letter to Nena*
April 29, 1918

Dearest Sister,

I am applying to medical school. I know there is a strong possibility I won't be accepted, but I hear there aren't enough doctors because of the war. This conversation between two doctors convinced me:

"For crying out loud, don't tell me we lost another one," Dr. Webster said. "Pretty soon nurses will be doing our jobs."

"Oh, it's not that bad," the other doctor said. "We've seen the worst of it. All the docs who want to go fight the bloody war are there already."

"I think more men will go." Dr. Webster looked up and saw me. "Ricardo, be careful. You may be doing bandages now, but the way things are going, we may need to pull you into surgeries." We all chuckled, although I thought: This could be the moment I've been waiting for to ask him what he thinks about me someday becoming a doctor.

Sister, the other doctor left, and I summoned up the courage to ask.

"Dr. Webster, what would you think about me applying to medical school?"

"Well, Ricardo," he said. "I know you've attended university. How have your grades been?"

"Not the best. English is still a challenge."

"No matter. You'll learn English. As you know, we are in desperate need of more doctors. I've watched you with patients. You're sympathetic, kind, and you're not afraid. Why not apply and see what happens?"

Nena, my heart pounds as I write. He didn't think I am a fool to want to apply to medical school. So I am. If you were here, I would twirl you around in circles. I'd make you dance with me, carefully given your current condition. I do hope you feel well and are growing round as a ball. I can't write anymore, I need to think about what I might say in my application.

Ricardo

## JOURNAL ENTRY
May 1, 1918

No letter from José. Every night, I pray he is alive and coping as best he can. Men, too many men, are dying every day. In the daily newspaper's list of the dead, his name is absent, and every day my heart pounds until I've reached the bottom of the list that gets longer and longer. I'm so alone, more an orphan than ever before. But my struggle is nothing in comparison to what José is facing. I won't die from loneliness or from confusion about my future. On the battlefield, José could.

## TELEGRAM TO NENA
May 14, 1918

INTERVIEW FOR MEDICAL SCHOOL IN DAYS. NERVOUS. NOT SURE THEY WILL WANT ME. WILL DO BEST TO CONVINCE THEM. SEND ME PRAYERS. OUR SECRET.

## TELEGRAM FROM NENA
May 15, 1918

MY PRAYERS FOR YOU DAILY. I WILL ADD TO THEM. YOU NEED BE ONLY YOURSELF, BROTHER. Nena

## TELEGRAM TO NENA
May 16, 1918

MEETING WENT WELL. LIKED MY FREE WORK AT HOSPITAL. MY ENGLISH COULD BE BETTER. TOLD HIM I PRACTICE EVERY DAY. NOW I WAIT. WEEKS OR MORE. Ricardo

## *Letter from José*
June 9, 1918

Rico, my friend,

I have been injured. I'm in a hospital somewhere in England. I don't know how I got here. I lost about a week I can't remember. They tell me I was found among dead men in a trench half-filled with blood and water. Most of the men I came over with are dead. They were men that I knew and trusted. Now they're gone. One minute, we were taking turns watching for … what we were watching for? The enemy? I keep asking: Why not me? Why them?

They tell me I am lucky to be alive, but life will never be the same. I'm not glad I didn't die. I'm not sad either. I'm not anything. I feel broken. I lost one of my arms, Ricardo. My left arm, thank God, or I wouldn't be able to write. I am trying to not feel like my life is over. I also took a bullet in my chest. Missed my heart by inches, but that will heal. I look around here and see I could be worse off, a lot worse off. The fella to the right of me will never see again, the one on the left has no legs, and another lies in bed motionless. So many others are no longer with us. War is not what I expected, not any of us.

I hate this war. I hate what it has taken, is taking every day. With or without an arm, I would like to go back and help us win, but it means killing. I have had enough.

I'm glad you're my friend, Ricardo. I am glad I have good memories of our times together. I don't know when I will come back to Chicago or if I will. I have no family there but have no idea where else to go. I won't go back to Manila this broken.

Send me a letter when you can.

José

## Letter to José
### June 15, 1918

José, you are alive. Thank God. I have prayed for your safety every day. I seldom feel prayers are answered, but this one was. Every day, I've checked the paper for posted lists of soldiers perished. Every day, I've sighed with relief when your name wasn't there. By the size of the lists, my guess is you have endured seeing enough death to last a lifetime.

Come home to Chicago, José. I am here, and I know you have many other friends, people who care about you. Come home. With time, you will figure out what to do. You know you'd be welcomed back by the family you lived with. If you are worried about work, you will be able to find work here. Many companies struggle to find workers. Women fill in to keep businesses going. As a soldier who fought for this country, you will be welcomed back with or without an arm.

Let's not rely on memories, José. Let's make some more. You can still dance, my friend, and I know you like that. Rose asks about you often, saying she wishes you had written like you said you would.

Put that stubbornness of yours to use, my friend. When we win this war, you are going to be a hero. Pen me back to tell me when I will see you.

Ricardo

## Letter to Tito Juan
### July 4, 1918

Today is Independence Day. As you know, the day Americans declared their independence from the English back in 1776 (if you recall, I sent you their poem—now national anthem—when I was on the ship). They remember the date every year by having picnics and parades. Some don't have to work. With the war this year, the celebration is even bigger. They now call it the War for Peace or President Wilson's War for Democracy.

While men fight and die on the battlefield, here it seems to be a daily fight for the minds of men, women, and children. I saw a headline the other day in the newspaper that read "Are you 100% American?" Who would dare say they aren't? Slackers are what they're called, and no one wants to be seen as one. American bonds are the way to show you're a supporter—basically a piece of paper you receive after you give money. I understand some have the papers framed and hung in their homes. Others compete to give more than their neighbors. I have bought several. I also have volunteered here and there. I don't want to be seen as a slacker.

Can you imagine, Tito Juan, over a million men have been trained and now fight alongside the French and English? Many have already died. Families who have lost a son or uncle now wear armbands with a star telling how many men their family has lost. The most I have seen are three stars, and the man that wore them walked like a man completely worn out, consumed by loss, forever marred. My guess is that there are families all over who are in mourning, praying for no more stars.

It makes me wonder what war is like when you are in it, when it surrounds you, binds you to a hideousness you can't escape. My Filipino friend José was actually one of the first to be shipped over. He was struck down but survived. He lost an arm and is recovering in a hospital in England. He wrote me about all the friends he has lost over there and his fear about coming home "ruined," as he puts it.

Tito Juan, what was it like for you during the Philippine-American War? I was only four. I have little memory of it, other than clinging to my father's hand as we left our home. I can't remember where we went to hide. I heard stories of hiding in the mountainside but little of the actual hardship. Could you tell me? Your recollections might help me have better insights about what our family and my parents endured. They might even help me make sense of this war as well.

My best to you and family,

Ricardo

## *Letter from Thomas Clarke*
July 24, 1918
Official Correspondence from University of Illinois

Dear Mr. Alvarez,

Congratulations on your acceptance to the University of Illinois–Champaign, School of Medicine. Your acceptance recognizes all the hard work and achievements in your academic and personal past. We are honored to have you join our elite group of individuals. From the first days of your medical school career, you are entering a different level of demand and professional obligation as a physician in training. Every step of the process is a building block toward the next, and has important elements of training and a depth of knowledge expected by patients in their physician. We encourage you to continue to enhance the level of attention and academic achievement that got you here so your training might be distinguished not only by its length but also by its depth. To accept our offer, we need to hear back from you in the next several weeks. We warmly welcome you to the School of Medicine community and look forward to helping you pursue your best future at University of Illinois–Champaign School of Medicine.

Sincerely,

Thomas Clarke

Dean of Students

University of Illinois–Champaign

College of Medicine

### JOURNAL ENTRY
July 26, 1918

Can this possibly be? I'm accepted. I am going to medical school and start in September. Even with my grades, they want me. Only seven weeks away. I don't know what to think. I thrust my letter of acceptance into the hands of Dr. Webster who simply nodded and said, "So now your work begins." Yes, work and long hours of study.

I don't know anything about Champaign, except from what Mr. Clarke told me in my interview. Two hours by train, I can easily come back to visit. I am ready for something different. Jaime and Esperanza will be excited. I need to say goodbye to Sally. I hardly see her anymore. There are few others. It's time.

### TELEGRAM TO NENA
August. 1, 1918

ACCEPTED TO MEDICAL SCHOOL. UNIVERSITY OF ILLINOIS-CHAMPAIGN. MOVING SOON, NOT FAR FROM CHICAGO. SPREAD THE NEWS. Ricardo

### TELEGRAM FROM NENA
August 4, 1918

EXCITED FOR YOU. FAMILY VERY PROUD. Nena

### TELEGRAM FROM NENA
August 15, 1918

PINA HAS ARRIVED. HER CRY HEARD THROUGHOUT SANTA CRUZ. MINE AS WELL. YOU ARE AN UNCLE. Nena

### TELEGRAM TO NENA
August 16, 1918

PINA. LOVELY NAME. OVERJOYED FOR YOU AND VICENTE. I AM HER PROUD UNCLE. BLESSINGS SISTER. Ricardo

### Note from Jaime and Esperanza
### discovered August 30, 1918

Ricardo,

You leave today and some things are best put down to paper. We recalled your tale of finding a letter from your sister on board the ship and thought it a perfect way to send you on your way. We hope you find our letter within days. We didn't hide it well purposely.

We're writing to make sure you know certain things, like how thankful we are for the time you have spent with us. We will always be your friends, but having been with you now for close to two years, you're like family. We know you better than most of our cousins, better than several of my brothers. Better yet, we still like you.

You have never been a burden. Sometimes you were so quiet poring over books in your room or living at the university, and most recently the hospital, we didn't know you were here. We will miss you, Ricardo. How we enjoyed hearing of your quests. Our lives seemed boring in comparison. I know you felt your stay was too long, but we would not have had it any other way.

The two years brought us great satisfaction. We have watched you become the man you had hoped to be, comfortable in your own skin, dark as it is. Here in Chicago, that is no small feat. It speaks to your full-strength determination. A parent might call it stubbornness bordering on pigheadedness, but it has helped you and will continue to do so.

Esperanza will also miss your continual help in cleaning up after dinners, which means I'll be there instead. I liked the two years off. You've also been more than kind in providing us with finances to cover added "living expenses," as you put it. We won't miss the sometimes cyclone that takes place in your room, but that was easily dealt with. We do have doors for a reason.

We also want you to know in six months or so we will have another family member join us. Esperanza is expecting. We are thrilled, surprised, and honestly shocked. We had thought our time had passed, but here we are. I'll be an old man just when he is about to become one. Imagine that. Esperanza is feeling well. If you look closely, you can see her thin frame is becoming a bit rounder. Your room will be put to good use, and you, my friend, will be an uncle.

We hope you choose to visit us. You are only hours away by train, and we will want to know how you are faring, what medical school is like, and hear stories of your life in a new place.

Take good care, Ricardo. We are here when you need us.

Jaime and Esperanza

**TELEGRAM TO JAIME AND ESPERANZA**
September 1, 1918

I FOUND YOUR LETTER. TOOK LESS THAN A WEEK. THRILLED FOR YOU TWO. YOU WILL BE THE BEST PARENTS IN AMERICA. I WILL VISIT. ADDRESS HERE: 112 BIRCH STREET, CHAMPAIGN, ILLINOIS. STUDENT BOARDINGHOUSE. Ricardo

## Letter to Nena
September 3, 1918

My dear Nena,

I must tell you of my new home. Two weeks living in Champaign, Illinois, isn't anything like living in Chicago. I could walk through this whole city if I wanted to. Everyone looks the same—light hair, light skin, friendly but untrusting eyes. When I walk down the street, I don't see anyone else close to resembling me. Some greet me; some do so but give me a look. Not sure if they don't know what to say or wonder who the tarnation I am. Today, one family crossed the street when nearing me. Another family stayed their course, but the father moved to the inside so he would be nearest me. They like to talk, only not to me. Tipping of the hat here is mandatory, though, even when you see a Filipino for the first time. I may well be the first Spanish Filipino they've ever seen.

Like Santa Cruz, Sister, there is a local rhythm to the place. I like that. The church bell rings at noon, the whistle at the local factory blows every day at five o'clock (except Sunday). Friday is the day for cake-making by the local baker (emitting plumes of tempting sweetness I have to stop giving into), and laundry is only received on Mondays. Only taverns betray the tempo, being open whenever you walk through the door.

So here I sit, in my small room at a boardinghouse. All the furniture looks like it came from a country I've never been to. My headboard is the size of a ceiling beam, with posts to match. My dresser has carvings of ships around the mirror that look like they are battling to stay afloat. Wherever the furniture came from, the people must be big. I've never felt this small.

I'm ready. I have my books, know my class schedule, and know where my classes are. I've read five books in the last four weeks, all in English, and now feel I could write a book—well, maybe a short one for children.

So far most students leave me alone. A few greet me, and one, Frank Olsen, offered to show me around. It turns out he is a classmate. He doesn't live far away—a "farm boy" he tells me—has five sisters and brothers, and cows, pigs, and oh, yes, lots of cornfields. He has no idea where the Philippine Islands are. Even when I mentioned Hawaii or Japan, he looked at me blank-faced.

"Now what languages do you speak?" he keeps asking me. He has a difficult time understanding what I say as well. "What was that?" he'll say. "I can't understand." But it is nice to have Frank as a friendly face.

I still need to work on my pronunciation.

Honestly, Nena, I can't believe I'm here. I'm going to become a doctor. And you are a mother. Perhaps we are doing what Mama and Papa had envisioned. For both of us, the road has not been easy. I know mine may become harder than I can imagine. I think I'm ready.

Blessing to you, Pina, and Vicente,

Ricardo

## Letter from Tito Juan
October 19, 1918 (sent on by Jaime)

Ricardo,

In your last letter, you asked me about our war with the United States. I'm not surprised you don't remember much. You were only a little boy. My memory of it is difficult to share, but I will because, you're right, perhaps you'll understand your country and war in general better.

Like you, we lived in Santa Cruz. I was a young man and conflicted about what I saw. I wanted to fight to join my countrymen, the revolutionaries against the Americans. My father refused to let me go, telling me wisely the battle could only end in one way, with the Americans winning. He was right, of course.

Right here in Santa Cruz, men were lined up and shot to death as traitors—not by Americans but by fellow Filipino soldiers when all they were doing was trying to protect their families. Women refused to leave their husbands' bodies that lay rotting in the merciless Filipino sun. Children called for their mothers and fathers lost in the confusion of hiding from the enemy, when really we often couldn't tell who to be most afraid of—the Americans or the revolutionists. The images haunt me to this day.

Like your grandmother, we hid in the dense mountains above Santa Cruz. For months, we lived in the shadows of steep cliffs, palm trees, and caves and listened in fear of being found. Given my youth, I was a member of a small group of men who would travel by night to the city's edge to gather additional provisions and hopefully information. Usually we returned without a problem with both. One night, we weren't so lucky. That night, we came home with one fewer man and no provisions.

I remember that night like it was yesterday, Ricardo—it was eerily still. Practiced as we were to be quiet, that night we sounded like giants crushing through a lifeless jungle. The moon and wind were absent, and mosquitos fierce. We trudged on, knowing supplies were needed. Finally we reached the city and spread out as we always did. All was well until a piercing cry from a familiar voice stopped each of us in our tracks. We knew instantly our friend had been found. Worse yet, he was potentially dying. I don't recall how the rest of us made it back. We only knew we had failed and shuddered to think of our friend's fate.

Today, when I reflect on war in general, it seems a cesspool of injustices. Men dying for their beliefs but in the process, losing their souls—families left to deal with the destruction for years to follow.

Be glad you are not in the war, Ricardo, only a witness to it. The inside view is a hideous current of disillusion. Chicago, like many other cities in America, is impacted by the war but will not be forever damaged, only changed. Those of you not fighting the war but supporting it will carry that change but with much less pain than those who fight.

As to your friend, I send prayers of hope for the war to end soon and for his safe return.

Your uncle,

Tito Juan

### TELEGRAM TO TITO JUAN
October 21, 1918

TO HEAR YOUR STORY MAKES MY HEART ACHE. TO SEE PEOPLE DIE. TO HIDE AFRAID. I WATCH AND LEARN. WORLD GONE CRAZY? Ricardo

### TELEGRAM FROM TITO JUAN
October 23. 1918

FEW WIN IN WAR. MANY LOSE. YES, CRAZY WORLD. YOU STUDY MEDICINE NOW. EXCELLENT. WILL CELEBRATE YOUR SUCCESS. WILL REGALE YOUR INTELLIGENCE TO FAMILY. HOW FUN. Your favorite Tito

**JOURNAL ENTRY**
October 23, 1918

I pray I don't disappoint him. I can't. I won't.

**JOURNAL ENTRY**
October 26, 1918

This flu is the same I saw in Chicago before I left. I'm sure of it. That horrible flu came back. The papers say not to worry, but I remember the fear I saw in the faces of doctors and patients. At the university, no one notices. Classes go on as normal—so easy to ignore if it doesn't affect you. This, whatever it is, is why I want to become a doctor. I need to help with what might be coming, what might be already here.

My studies overwhelm me, though. I study late into the night only to wake up finding myself trying to solve a problem or remember a definition. I can't fall behind. I know what could happen.

*Letter from José*
Written September 21, delivered to Chicago;
received in Champaign October 29, 1918

Ricardo,

If I have it right, I asked you to send me a letter, probably begged, and then you heard nothing from me. I know I sounded miserable. I was. I got your letter but don't remember much else. When was that, six months ago? All I could do was feel sorry for myself. For months, all I thought about was what had happened, what I lost. Nothing else mattered.

I'm still here at the now overloaded hospital outside Sussex in England. Rico, the telegram you sent helped me break out of my misery. At first, I threw the message aside, but every morning I'd find the thing on my bedside. Turns out a nurse here kept putting it out for me to see. I guess she didn't want me to give up. I am more myself now, clear enough to see things as they are. I didn't die, and my life isn't over. It will never be the same, though. I look around and know we are all damaged in one way or another. Ruined but (hopefully) not destroyed.

These men, like me, stepped forward to fight for our country, and now here we are on a battlefield with ourselves. I know, Rico, you didn't think I should go, but I had to. Sometimes you can't stop yourself from doing what you think is right, even when you know others don't agree. You know what I'm talking about or you wouldn't be sitting in America right now.

I've decided to stay and help out here. If I can break out of my depression, so can some of these other men. I am one of them. I think they'll let me help them. That's why I'm still here—that and a sickness that kills dozens of men every day. Has this hit Chicago as well? They say it is a flu gone wild. Soldiers come in with signs of flu—bad headaches, raw throats, and feeling weak. Two hours later, they're turning blue, gasping for air, and coughing up blood. Some vomit, others bleed from their eyes and ears. Then they're gone. The doctors work around the clock and can't keep up. Those of us healthy enough help bring patients in but too soon help take them out. I wouldn't believe it if I didn't see this with my own eyes.

I'll stay here until they don't need me, but that doesn't look like it will be very soon. I'm learning to use the stub of an arm I still have, and Ricardo, the other night I even dreamt of dancing. I am doing what I need to do.

You're in medical school. All of that studying paid off. I bet you'll make a damn good doc someday. We could use you here. Pen me back. I'll look forward to your letter.

José

## *Letter to José*
### October 30, 1918

José,

I ripped open your letter. The envelope had the hospital listed, and since I hadn't heard from you for so long, I thought the worst. To see your handwriting … well, you can bet I took a deep breath and sat down heavily with relief.

I would like to be able to say I understand your circumstances, but we both know that's not true. Frankly, I can't imagine what you have been through, what you're still going through. Your letter gives me a glimpse into a world I hope to never experience firsthand.

Believe me, you wouldn't want me as a doctor over there. I have barely started my training and would only get in the way. I am in Champaign, Illinois, now in my first quarter of medical school. You thought I spent hours with my nose stuck in books in Chicago? That was nothing. Here, I barely look up from the too many pages of material I'm supposed to know. I'm learning about becoming a doctor and am not anywhere close to being the real thing. What you are doing sounds much more impactful and real. You're helping save people, José.

You asked if we are also experiencing influenza. We are, but not anywhere near the extent that you describe. Here, the newspapers downplay the flu as nothing exceptional or no more deadly than influenza that has gone on for centuries. In the newspaper, the surgeon general recently stated, "There is no cause for alarm if precautions are observed." His advice is to make yourself cough every morning and to stay away from anyone who is coughing in public. He also issued a rule saying people can't spit outside their homes anymore. Really? Like those steps will prevent people from getting sick. On the other hand, theaters and dance halls have been closed indefinitely, which does make more sense. I'm not sure what that means for Sally and Rose.

Here in Champaign, the university has remained open, but other universities have closed their doors until whatever this is passes. Already three students here have died. A couple of students in my classes no longer come. This is nothing like what you describe, but I am sure Chicago is much worse than here.

Stay in touch, my friend. You and I will both return to the dance floor. The last time I did was in Chicago, and I found more fellow Filipinos showing off their dance skills. Sally called them my competition, and Rose wanted to know if I had heard from you. As you know, she liked you beyond the dance floor. She still does.

Proud of what you're doing, José. Proud to call you my friend.

Ricardo

### TELEGRAM FROM JAIME
November 1, 1918

TRUST YOU ARE WELL. WE'RE HEALTHY BUT VERY CAREFUL. DEADLY INFLUENZA. SEVERAL IN NEIGHBORHOOD HAVE DIED. DO NOT COME TO CHICAGO NOW. WRITE INSTEAD. BE SAFE. ESPERANZA GROWS. Jaime

### TELEGRAM TO JAIME
November 2, 1918

GLAD ESPERANZA IS WELL. SEVERAL STUDENTS HERE DIED. YET CLASSES CONTINUE? SOME PROFESSORS DONT SHOW UP. AM NERVOUS. JOSÉ STILL IN ENGLAND HELPING OTHER SOLDIERS. Ricardo

### Letter to Tita Carmen
November 7, 1918

Tita Carmen,

I was sitting in a small café near the university this morning, trying to remember chemistry formulas for a test hours away. My brain had decided to ignore my plea to function, and formulas bounced around my head like a tennis ball slammed too hard against a wall. Overwhelmed is what I was, trying hard to focus and not succeeding. No, something else caught my attention that I have to tell you about.

Near me, two doctors were having breakfast. One was from the medical school, Dr. Wilson. The other doctor I didn't know. He looked out of place. He was a small silhouette of a man, haggard, with a full beard that badly needed a trim. His eyes sunk in like he hadn't slept in days. When he spoke, there was a tinge of desperation. I was managing to not listen to their conversation until they started talking about the flu outbreak. Then I couldn't stop. I wanted to pull my chair closer.

"It's horrible, I tell you. The men, the bodies, there was a steady, bloody stream of 'em," the haggard doctor said. "We were averaging about 100 deaths per day, and we couldn't keep up. One day these young men, healthy soldiers, were walking around feelin' good, and the next day they were be dying. I've never seen nothing like it."

Dr. Wilson spoke quietly. "You say they are calling it the Spanish flu? Can it really be a flu that kills so rapidly? We had thought it must be a disease."

"Yes, that's one of the many names I've heard it called. They liken it to the Black Plague that spread through Europe some three hundred years ago. This plague has struck down military men all over Europe."

I looked over to see Dr. Wilson's reaction. He was staring at the other man like he couldn't believe what he was hearing.

"Imagine, they survive a stinking, bloody war and get struck down by this evil virus. No disease—a virus for God's sake." The other doctor stopped to take a long gulp of coffee, wiping his mouth off with his sleeve before continuing on. "There were several days where no coffins could be found, and the bodies piled up something fierce. Glad I didn't have to see that firsthand."

"Wait, you're saying there were so many dying that they ran out of coffins? Dear God!"

"I couldn't handle it, not after seeing men in their prime die right before me, and I couldn't do a damn thing for 'em. Told my superiors I needed to go home, that I wasn't fit to do anything else."

"Fred, my friend," Dr. Wilson said, "you did the best you could, and I'm thankful you were spared."

"Spared? Sometimes I'm not so sure." Neither of them spoke for a few minutes. I snuck a look. They both seemed deep in thought, eyes blank, locked on nothing.

"Well, it's here," Dr. Wilson finally said. "Community folk, students, and teachers have come down with it. Our hospital is usually a thirty-bed facility. We have expanded it to 300, which is barely enough."

Fred gripped his coffee cup with both his hands. I looked away, afraid the cup might burst.

"It isn't as deadly, though, thank God. Many get very ill but survive. Ten have died so far. Can you come in and help us, advise us if nothing else?"

As the men talked, my chemistry test suddenly didn't seem important. I wanted to turn to both of them and shout, "Is there nothing we can do to protect more from getting it? Why do the newspapers say we have nothing to worry about? Shouldn't we all lock ourselves in our homes until this passes?" But I didn't. Instead, I packed up and left. Somehow I had to block this from my mind and get ready for the test, now only two hours away. I knew I wasn't ready. There were still gaping holes. Only two hours to fill them.

But, Tita Carmen, this flu—can it be similar to what took my mother and siblings? No, no, that was cholera, but how many thousands died from that as well? I pray this isn't as deadly. No such illness is taking place there, is it? I fear for Nena's little girl not even two months old. Do let me know how you are.

Your trusted nephew,

Ricardo

### TELEGRAM FROM NENA
November 19, 1918

YOUR WAR ENDS. YOU MUST BE CELEBRATING. WE CELEBRATE IN YOUR HONOR. HAVE HEARD OF THE FLU. AT YOUR UNIVERSITY? ARE YOU WELL? LET US KNOW. Nena

### TELEGRAM TO NENA
November 22, 1918

FEW CELEBRATE THE END OF WAR NOW. WIDESPREAD INFLUENZA. BY GOD'S GRACE, AM WELL. FEWER DYING. FEAR REMAINS. I AM CAREFUL. NO FLU THERE, RIGHT? WILL WRITE SOON. Ricardo

### TELEGRAM FROM NENA
November 24, 1918

SOME FLU. MAINLY SOLDIERS. WE ARE WELL. THANK GOD YOU ARE TOO. PRAYERS Nena

### Letter from Margaret
December 6, 1918

Ricardo,

I have thought of you often in the past several months, but with the war and this raging influenza that has killed so many, I haven't had the capacity to write. My parents and I are well. So far, we've escaped the illness that seems to target the healthiest young men and women in our community. They say it is a virus, but how can a virus be so deadly and unmerciful? At the College of Medicine, are they teaching you about it? I hope they are.

Everyone is frightened. We have neighbors who refuse to answer their door. We haven't seen them in weeks, but they wave to us from an upstairs window or post messages on their front door. My father will hardly let me out of the house without knowing exactly where I go. When I do go out, I do so only briefly. To pass the time, we spend a great deal of it reading to each other.

Your university remained open? I understand many have. I had started to take several classes this last semester at a nearby Normal School, but they closed their doors, saying they will reopen once the flu has passed.

How is medical school, Ricardo? Is it what you hoped it would be? I imagine you with your head stuck in books piled high around you. I have heard from others the classes are quite difficult. Don't get disheartened. A friend once told me "a poco, a poco" about trying to learn something new. I have no doubt it will come.

Please let me know how you fare. If I don't hear from you, I trust you know I will worry. My parents send their greetings.

Margaret

**TELEGRAM TO MARGARET**
December 9, 1918

GLAD TO KNOW YOU ARE WELL. MEDICAL SCHOOL IS DEMANDING. BOOKS HAVE BECOME MY PILLOWS. NO NEED FOR WORRIES FOR MY HEALTH. I AM CAREFUL. Ricardo

*Letter to Nena*
December 14, 1918

Nena,

I have thought of writing, but my days are consumed with studies. I often fall into bed at the end of the day. The other night in my dream, I was giving a speech to a large crowd, all in English! Ha, only in my dreams could this be possible.

Medical school is difficult, like I'm mentally rowing a boat across Laguna Bay every day against a strong wind. My brain aches, especially in chemistry with its sphere of chemical compounds, elements, and substances. General medicine is filled with words I can barely pronounce, and sometimes my mouth refuses to participate. I wish I wasn't the only student in my class who didn't grow up speaking English. When I speak in class, some classmates snicker, amused by my garbling of medical terminology.

Nena, at times, I think I am not yet ready for this challenge. You were right, you know. I wasn't prepared to go to the United States. Can you believe I left over two years ago? So much has changed for me. Medicine is what I choose. I often feel like an outcast, a stray dog who has wandered in uninvited. English is still a challenge, let alone scientific names thrown out like daily greetings. One student, Frank Olsen, has offered help. I'm not sure what he might be able to do, but I may need to accept his offer.

I will come home someday to visit, to meet your daughter. By then, you may have more than one? When I come, I will be there long enough for her to know she has an uncle who will make her giggle and help her embrace life as fully as she can.

Love and prayers,

Ricardo

**JOURNAL ENTRY**
December 17, 1918

I can't think clearly. I review my formulas and go, "Yes, yes, this makes sense." Then there's a point where none of it makes any sense at all. I try hard to calm myself down. I tell myself, *"Ricardo, you are good at math, and chemistry is simply using those skills in another way."* But it doesn't work. I know I have missing pieces. I go back to my notes, to the book that looks like I have thrown it against the wall and chewed on its edges, but I can't seem to figure out where the errors are.

I've tried to talk to Professor Jorgensen, but each time, I walk away more confused. How many times has he said, "Ricardo, you must learn to pronounce your words more clearly. I can't understand what you say. Now tell me again what the problem is. What's your question?"

I'm not sure what else to do. I speak slowly, I point to words, the formulas. I pull out my notes, which he says he can't read as the print is too small. Still, he complains of my accent. I say "in your lecture," and he tells me he can't understand.

"You sound like you are saying 'letter,' not 'lecture.' Say it again."

I take a deep breath and say as clearly as I can what my question is. When he finally understands, he quickly rattles off his answer. An answer I don't comprehend because he speaks too quickly.

I hate feeling stupid and even worse when he looks at me like I am. I've gone to him a half a dozen times. Each time, I have walked away embarrassed for both of us. I despise his lack of patience and his superior attitude. I've seen him with other students, and the man is friendly and helpful. He looks like a different person.

My final test is in several weeks, and if I don't do well, I won't pass the class. Yesterday Frank asked me again how I was doing. I don't want to, but I need to ask him for help.

# 1919

### JOURNAL ENTRY
January 16, 1919

I've been an idiot, careless, a complete dupe. What was I thinking? Frank told me I had nothing to worry about. "No one will know," he said. "Don't let your struggles with English get in the way. This will work this one time."

I believed him. But look at where I am now: I can't even step foot on campus. I can't register for classes next semester. They may very well tell me I can't return, ever.

When Professor Jorgensen called me to his office, he could hardly look at me. Usually a small-looking man, he seemed to tower over me—his anger and disgust permeated off his now expanded frame. I stood at the doorway, afraid to go any further. Seeing me, he slipped by to close the door and turned to face me. His words will be ingrained forever in my brain.

"Did you think you could get away with this?" he hissed. "Buying answers to give you a near perfect score on your exam?"

I was speechless. I stared at him, inside registering what was about to take place. My heart pounded. I felt I might pass out. I looked down, to hide my sense of terror. I had been caught.

"How could you do this? You struggle, and your answer is to cheat? How dare you?" And still I couldn't find words. His final question was like a jolt of lightening.

"You think this is acceptable for someone who hopes to become a doctor?"

My response was feeble. "I was desperate. I didn't want to fail. I've never done something like this before."

"Mr. Alvarez, I thought you a better man than this."

All I could think at that moment was: Then why didn't he treat me with the respect he gave others? Why was he irritated and continually critical of my speech? Why did he act unhappy to help me? I finally asked if there was anything, anything I could do.

"No," he said. "What's done is done."

I couldn't look at him, much less think of anything to say.

When he spoke again, his voice was quieter, and he stared at his desk. "I have to report this. You'll be suspended from the university. Barred from taking classes. Barred from stepping foot on campus." He raised his eyes. "We're done here. Get out."

*Out.* The word is so final. This is what I am—out of medical school. Out. Was I ever really in? I've done what my father would consider to be a mortal sin. He would be ashamed. He wouldn't want anyone to know what his son had done. I don't either. Dear God, I don't either.

### Note to Mr. Thomas Clarke, Dean of Students
### January 18, 1919
### University of Illinois–Champaign

Mr. Clarke,

I know you are fully aware of the situation regarding a student within the medical school and his decision to purchase the answers for a final examination. Ricardo Alvarez is of whom I speak. Per university requirements, I have submitted all of the necessary papers and believe the student is no longer allowed on campus. I wholeheartedly support the university's policy as it pertains to cheating.

Today, I write separately to express my concern over the decision to admit students of this caliber in the first place. Mr. Alvarez is a prime example of someone who was ill-prepared to excel at the rigor required to become a physician. He lacked proficiency in English. I can attest to this firsthand. On many occasions, he came to my office, and I could barely understand him. To think he would have eventually been working with patients in the hospital is appalling. Looking as he does, I doubt patients would even want to be treated by him.

I would encourage you and the larger administration to think hard before taking on students who are so utterly different from those who reside in our community. I believe we only hurt our community and other students by doing so.

Respectfully,

Professor Jorgenson

### Note from Mr. Thomas Clarke to Professor Jorgenson
### January 25, 1919

Professor Jorgenson,

I appreciate you taking the time to express your support of the university policy regarding illicit behaviors of students. For the said student, we have taken the appropriate measures as outlined by this policy. However, regarding your suggested stance taken on future admissions of students who are utterly *different* as you stated, I am frankly dismayed. Were you not once a person from another country struggling to become what you are today? Did you not sound and look different from others?

For those of us who have been here for a generation or more, we can easily think negatively toward those who venture to become Americans now. As a university, especially during this time of war and this impudent influenza, we need to be open to those who have the abilities to succeed. Having met Mr. Alvarez, I know he does. His decision to purchase answers for a final exam is unfortunate and quite surprising. I'm sure he regrets his act more than you or I can imagine. He was a brave young man for coming to the university. Look around, Professor Jorgenson. He was one of a handful of different students—none of whom were in the medical school.

We will continue to be open to others, and in terms of hurting other students, I can tell you that I have heard from several of your students who have argued for leniency for Mr. Alvarez.

Respectfully,

Mr. Clarke

### Letter from University of Illinois-College of Medicine
February 5, 1919

My dear Mr. Alvarez:

I am sorry to inform you that at a meeting of the Council of Administration on February 4, it was voted that you be dismissed from the College of Medicine for buying and using examination questions in Chemistry in the first quarter of the year. This is pursuant to university policies.

Very truly yours,

Thomas Arkle Clark

# A Dubious Midpoint

**1919: Champaign, Illinois**

What have I done? I don't eat. I shove food in without recalling what I ate. My room reeks of pork, cheese, and stale bread—well, and other things I'm not able to identify anymore. I can't recall the last time I went downstairs to breakfast or dinner. I'm not ready to be seen yet—the reprehensible medical student who tried to cheat on a final exam and got caught. I've become a caveman, hiding from any and everyone. If I could, I'd run away from myself.

My conversation with Professor Jorgensen runs endlessly through my brain. His words—*Ricardo, I thought you a better man than this*—have become my involuntary hymn. I thought so, too, Professor, I thought so, too. I have repeated his words enough to conclude he's right. Me, a Catholic raised to atone for anything I've ever done wrong. How do I atone for this? I try to pray. Nothing happens, only the hymn.

This morning, I was in the middle of this daily ritual when someone pounded on my bedroom door so hard I thought it might break apart. It was the landlady, and although I had paid no heed to her for days, maybe longer, today she was determined.

"Richard, I know you're in there. I'm staying put right here for as long as it takes for you to open this door," she bellowed.

I heard her breath through the door and felt her presence. If she could, I know she would slither under the door and stand before me.

"You open the door, or I will." I was half-dressed, and my room looked like a monsoon had hit. I thought it best to respond.

"Please give me a minute, Mrs. Cranston. I need to get a shirt on." Patient she is not, and in minutes, I heard the key slide into the door just as I was throwing clothes strewn throughout the room into a pile on my bed. She literally shrieked when she entered my room.

"Lordy, you must be plumb out of your mind. Look at this place. What's that smell? I've been in barns that smelled better." She walked across the room and threw open the window. When she turned to look at me, she placed her hands on her hips.

"Look at you. You're a mess. Now what in tarnation is going on, Richard?"

"I don't mean to be a bother," I said.

"A bother? I think you best be saying more than that if you want to stay on here." Her eyes softened, and she let out a long sigh. "I've heard talk about you not being at the university anymore. Is that what all this is about?"

"Yes, ma'am. These past few days, I've been trying to work out what I'm going to do."

"Harrumph. Feeling sorry for yourself is more like it, and from the looks of this room and you, I'd say you haven't worked out much of anything. And, young man, it hasn't been a few days. It's been over a week. Furthermore, this," she said as she picked up a plate with a moldy piece of bread on it, "isn't acceptable. Not for either one of us."

"I didn't think anyone would see my room before I cleaned it, especially you."

"This isn't only about your room. I expect my boarders to be at meals, and I expect them to have activities during the day. That's why I like students. They're gone most of the day. I want my rooms clean and my boarders sober."

I opened my mouth, but she silenced me with a wave of her hand. "Don't bother. I can smell it. I won't say more, but it's not all right with me. Do you understand?"

I nodded. "Is there any way you would bring food up for just a couple more days? I'm not ready to deal with the others."

"I'll bring up food tonight, but I want to see you at breakfast tomorrow. I don't know what you did, Richard. Not any of my business. But you're going to have to face them, face the world. You can't hide in here." She looked around and shook her head.

"One more thing. You're paid up for the next month, but unless you clean yourself up, you'll be needing to find another place to live." Lifting the corner of a shirt with her toe, she flipped it away as if she had touched a dead animal.

I started to protest, but she held up her hand. "We'll talk in a week."

After she left, I sat down on my bed, put my head in my hands, and let all the pent-up emotions of the last few weeks run down my face.

### Note from Frank
February 9, 1919

Ricardo, the last time I saw you we were in our Chemistry final exam a month ago. Since then, I've looked for you on campus and expected to see you in one of my classes. This is when I heard what happened. I led you down that path, encouraged you, and look what's happened. I asked Professor Jorgenson about you, and he wasn't happy about it. He said you would not be returning. I guess the university is really hard on students that do what you did. I didn't know. I hope you believe me, Ricardo.

I stopped by the other day, and your landlady said she didn't know where you were. She told me to come back another time. The second time, I came prepared with this note.

I asked another professor if he knew of other medical schools with possible openings. He told me the Thomas Jefferson University Medical School in Philadelphia was likely looking. With so many doctors still in the military, I bet there are other medical schools you can get into as well. I sure hope so. You'd be a darn good doctor.

I'll stop by again.

Frank

### JOURNAL ENTRY
February 9, 1919

Why did I trust Frank? I hardly knew him. He was a fish, a freshman like me, who didn't know anything. A small town white boy, he couldn't be more different than me. He has no idea what it's like to be seen as a foreigner, an outsider who is watched closely and thought to be suspect, especially when you look like me. His life goes on. He's still in medical school, and he'll be a doctor someday. And me? What will I be? Professor Jorgensen said to learn from this. What should I learn beyond the obvious? Not to trust someone I hardly know again? Me being kicked out isn't Frank's fault. It's mine. If I hadn't cheated, I would still be in medical school.

Maybe.

I try to pray, to ask for forgiveness, but never get past, "Dear Lord." Professor Jorgensen's words have sewn themselves into a blanket of loathing I've unknowingly wrapped myself in. I'm like a caged animal—caged by my own doing.

But I won't give up. I can't. I won't let this mistake define who I am. I can't change what I did, but I can commit to never cheat again. Never.

### Letter from Jaime
January 28, 1919

Friend,

We miss seeing you. We often wonder how you are, how medical school is, and if you somehow manage to find time to enjoy yourself, perhaps even dance. With the threat of influenza passing, we now venture outside of our house regularly. Like many, we are thankful for our health, especially with Esperanza's condition. If you could see her, you would find pleasure, Ricardo. Little Esperanza has rounded out. When she giggles, she now holds her protruding stomach as if to protect the baby from her rolls of laughter. I hope you come to see the sight firsthand.

Life has hardly turned back to normal, though. More soldiers have started to return, and tensions grow as most were promised jobs no longer available. Women are being sent home to make room, and many Negroes and Mexicans, too. With the war over, there are thousands who look for jobs. We're eager to have Chicago quiet down.

We're relieved the deadly influenza seems to have passed and left us healthy. Too many others did not fare as well. On our street alone, several have died: a child of the Bianchis, two sons of the Johnsons who returned healthy from the war but died at home, and the wife of Mr. Gordon. We were so worried about ourselves that we didn't find all this out until weeks after it happened. Papers say over 200,000 people died, most of them young. Ricardo, my only comfort is that you'll soon be a doctor who can help deal with diseases like this. I know of too many who weren't able to find a doctor but were sent home without receiving treatment. Hurry, Ricardo, you're needed.

With highest regards,

Jaime (and Esperanza, too)

P.S. I've also included a letter from José arriving here a week ago. I hope he is well and you are, too.

✿

## Letter from José
### Delivered February 11, 1919

Ricardo,

Perfect timing. Your letter helped me start to think more positively. I started to believe I could work my way to being more myself again. So, you say that Rose has asked about me? Funny, I find myself thinking of her sometimes. She and I had a good time. The dancing was fun, but the laughing about nothing was the best.

Did I tell you that I smoke now? We all do. I started when we were in training, and now cigarettes are a regular part of my day. But I'm eatin' and getting others to do the same. We all looked like skeletons when we first landed in the hospital. I could count all of my ribs when I first arrived. Out in the trenches, food was hard to come by. Here, we have food, but I've had little interest in it. Day by day, I guess. That is what we do here: get through one day in hopes the next will be better. At least fewer soldiers are dying from flu. Those of us who can continue to care for the ones who don't make it. You can guess we aren't sitting around telling many jokes.

I am getting better every day partly because I'm helping others with their misery instead of thinking about my own problems. I look around me here, and there is reason for all of us to be sad. When we thought of fighting for peace, none of us had this in mind. I know I didn't anyway. We all look changed, and most of us are missing pieces of our pre-war selves. Pete's missing both his legs, Antonio lost an eye and doesn't hear so well anymore, Jonathon can only move his arms, and me, well, I am missing one. I could go on and on. How will we be whole enough to go home and live normal lives? I ask myself that question a lot.

Ever since I got your letter, I think about you in medical school and shake my head. What are they thinkin', lettin' you in a school like that? Don't they know you'd rather be out havin' fun? Good thing we aren't in the same city together. I would probably drag you away from your studies like I did in Chicago. Really, Rico, I'm darn proud of you. Keep your nose in those books.

Maybe I will come visit someday. For now, write when you can. Makes me happy to think you're workin' to become a doctor. The docs here are good, work like crazy, and you can tell they really care. You'll make a fine one. You'll be the one who helps stop this crazy flu from ever striking again.

José (Lost your address, so had to send this to Jaime and Esperanza)

**JOURNAL ENTRY**
February 14, 1919

Ever since I was kicked out of medical school, all I do is think about me. Me. Me. Me. How could I have forgotten about the flu or the thousands of people who are sick and dying? Or who have already died. That first round of the flu is what pushed me forward to become a doctor. My dream was to someday help prevent viruses like this deadly influenza. No, it still is. But to think José believes I'm still in medical school makes me want to run away and hide. I won't tell him anything different for now. Not until I figure out what I can do.

I can't stop replaying the day I cheated: my desperation, and my desire to pass the test no matter what. Only this once, I told myself. If I would have gotten away with it, I wonder if once would have become twice. Even though I attacked my studies with a vengeance, I wasn't ready for medical school. I couldn't learn fast enough.

Jaime, Esperanza, Tito Juan, Tita Carmen, and José: I'm so sorry.
How will I ever tell Nena?

Papa, are you there? Don't leave me now. What should I do?

Gumagaan ang mabigat kapag nagdadamayan.

**What is heavy lightens when shared.**

# PART FOUR

# Boundaries Blurred

## JOURNAL ENTRY
February 15, 1919

I'm not sure what was worse about finding a new place to live: the Chicago hotels that turned me down because they said I wouldn't fit in, or the boardinghouses I visited that said, "Of course we have a room for you," but once I was inside, what I saw was so horrible I wanted to run out the door. In both situations, I wondered where I belong.

Some of the hotels were obviously for the rich, like the Congress Hotel. I remember how I tried to dance there once. They turned me away with a look of pity like I had committed a sin for even trying to enter. I wouldn't have been comfortable there anyway. And then the boardinghouses felt more like houses of shame. I felt like I should have immediately found the nearest Mass to attend after going through several. I couldn't imagine living there with the unmistakable smell of urine and alcohol in the hallways, people yelling from behind closed doors, women clad with painted faces while showing too much everywhere else. In each establishment, men and women's eyes seemed glazed over, lost in their moment of tragedy. My guess is they had no other choice. Walking out of each place, I found myself making the sign of the cross.

I did dare myself to step into some well-known hotels. "Why not?" I told myself. The worst they can do is turn me away. Plenty of them did. The manager at the Sisson Hotel looked aghast I had even inquired. I had almost given up when I wondered if money might sway one of these managers to rent me a room?

I walked by the Philip Manor House many times, always thinking the hotel wasn't a place I could afford. Who would have guessed all it would take was offering to pay for four months instead of one? And to find out the price really goes down as well. While the front desk clerk talked with the manager, I stood by and tried to look like I belonged. I wasn't dressed for a ball, but I knew I was dressed decently—a navy jacket over tan pleated pants. I nodded and smiled at the manager, as he looked me up and down. Finally, out of the corner of my eye, I saw a head nod. I recall

how I could finally breathe while still trying to act like I was confident by asking if I could see the room.

I shouldn't have been surprised when he led me through the kitchen to a set of stairs that led to the second floor. Although apart from all of the other residents' rooms, I couldn't be more pleased with the space. So what if the large windows face a back alleyway? I have my own fireplace, a table with two chairs, and separate sleeping quarters with a bed, drawers, and closet. So what if the furniture is christened with a line of dust?

March 1, and the room is mine. It might have taken me all day, but I have a place to live. In weeks, I'll be back in Chicago. Whenever I think of this day, though, I'll remember my aimless walk between wealth and poverty. I wandered like a ghost in between two different worlds, not knowing where I belong.

Tomorrow, I visit Dr. Webster to get his advice. Maybe he's heard of the Thomas Jefferson School of Medicine, or maybe he knows of others. Hopefully, he won't tell me no school will accept me. If he does, I don't know what I'll do.

### JOURNAL ENTRY
on the train back to Champaign
February 18, 1919

I ache to show everyone I can succeed. To show Professor Jorgenson I'm not a bungling no-nothing. To prove to my father, even though he isn't here, I can be a source of pride—not embarrassment. To prove to myself I'm more than a person who tried unfairly to pass a test. I'm much, much more. Whatever success I achieve from now on, I'll earn.

Thank the Lord that Dr. Webster said acceptance by another medical school is possible. I pray he is right. I know he was surprised by what I had done and said as much, but he didn't dwell on it. I could barely look at him when I told him the story. My voice cracked, my hands shook. For a moment, I thought I would break down. All he said was, "A grave error indeed." He got up from his desk lined with papers and began to pace. He ignored a knock on his door.

"The next time we talk, I want to hear why you want to be a doctor. I want you to think about that and why you think you'll make one of the best. I want to see your list written down." He turned to look at me.

"Yes, sir," I said. "So you will help me then?"

"On one condition. Only if you'll commit to this effort 100 percent. We don't have much time. Applications will need to be submitted soon. One more thing: From now on, you speak, read, write, and think only in English."

When I had asked Dr. Webster for his help, I thought he might say no. Instead, he offered me hope. For the first time in weeks, I no longer want to rush. Instead of scurrying around people to get to where I'm going, I want to see where I am. I no longer feel like my heart and stomach are tied in knots.

Sitting here writing in my journal, looking out at the homes of Chicago now draped in a light snow, I recall my first train ride. How spellbound I was by the countryside, the food, the passengers, even the sleeper that dropped from the ceiling. I was two years younger then and a century behind. Today that original magic has disappeared. Today I know I may not fit in, but if I keep learning and stay honest with myself, I could succeed. Today I start my journey anew.

## Letter from Nena
February 26, 1919

Dear Brother,

Another year has passed. How can this be? My letters have fallen off, but then so have yours. My days simply seem to disappear. Often I can't pinpoint what I've gotten done other than the very mundane household demands and family commitments. Then there is Pina. Not yet one year old she continues to amuse and amaze us. Were we ever this adorable, Ricardo? She has a look that reminds me of you. Although she can only sit up for short periods of time, she still manages to cock her head oh, so slightly, and grin with a mischievous purpose (a look I often saw you have, Little Brother). I laugh every time she does it, which encourages her

all the more. How can such a little being fill the whole house?

I can't wait for you to meet her. Sometimes when she is napping and the house is quiet, I think of you so far away. I try to imagine what your days are like. Your descriptions help immensely, but I still can't picture a world where people look so very different and everything, everything is not normal or what you're accustomed to. Perhaps, I will visit someday, but not for a long time. You know me, Brother. I will want more than one child in the end.

I know you are fully occupied, but if you have no time to write, do send a telegram to tell me how you are. It has been much too long, Brother. Is medical school everything you hoped it would be? I don't even know how long you will need to study; is it two years, four? Aunts and uncles always ask about you. We tell them you are well. They, like us, are so pleased with your goal to become a doctor. Today at church, we prayed for your success.

Affectionately yours,

Your sister

### TELEGRAM TO NENA
March 1, 1919

I TOO CAN'T WAIT TO MEET PINA, HOW FUNNY SHE HAS THE LOOK. I AM FINE. BUSY. NO LONGER IN MEDICAL SCHOOL. ON BREAK TO DETERMINE NEXT STEPS. PLEASE NO WORRIES. PRAYERS TO YOU. Ricardo

### *Letter from Dr. Webster*
Delivered to the Phillip Manor House—March 7, 1919

Ricardo,

I have looked into possible medical schools for you, and I am reasonably positive about your chances of being accepted by one. I trust you are settled into your new environment and have dutifully made your lists of why you want to be a doctor and why you think you could be one of the best. That is where we will start our conversation.

Please plan to meet me at my residence on Friday afternoon at 2 p.m. Here is my address: 2325 Monroe. Take the L train to Dexter, then walk east one block to Monroe. I am only five minutes from there. We will have more privacy here than at my office.

Warm regards,

Dr. Webster

### JOURNAL ENTRY
March 9, 1919

My confidence grows. How can I ever thank Dr. Webster enough? With his help, my lists sound impressive even to me.

**Why I want to be a doctor:**

1. To improve the lives of people, and medicine can do this like no other occupation.
2. To put to good use my love of science and physiology and continued fascination with medicine.
3. To be of service to the community I live in and to our country (*which country I'm unsure of*).
4, To be in a position where my actions matter, sometimes between life and death.
5. To help others address their health, especially those in greatest need, like our returning soldiers.
6. Because I am extremely determined to succeed.

**Why I think I could be one of the best:**

1. Because I am an empathetic person. From the unpaid work I have done in a hospital, I am familiar with the vast medical issues people experience and know I will care about each and every person I treat.
2. I learn quickly, work hard, and am a disciplined learner. (*I won't cheat, not ever.*)

3. I have the right mix of strong heart, soft heart—strong enough to make quick decisions and deliver difficult messages but doing so with compassion.
4. I am quiet and reserved. I listen well and make people comfortable. (*Yes, especially white men who can't see beyond what I look like.*)
5. I can speak three languages—Spanish, Tagalog, and English—and can understand Italian enough to translate.

What doesn't feel right is to leave out my quarter in medical school. Dr. Webster was adamant.

"No, Ricardo. With the way your quarter ended, your time at Champaign-Urbana can't be included," he said. "No medical school would accept you."

When he said it, I had a hard time swallowing. His words got stuck in my throat. I wanted to start saying the rosary on the spot. I wanted to argue. Honest or not, he could not have been clearer. *Lord, forgive me.*

## Letter to José
### March 11, 1919

My Friend,

I hope you didn't think I forgot about you, I know months have passed. First, I moved, so it took an extra month for your letter to reach me. When I got it, I was in a middle of my own private storm. I put the letter on top of my desk, usually a safe thing to do, but within days other papers buried it. When I found it, I had hardly remembered receiving it.

I think this is where I need to start, to tell you what a fool I am. You wrote that you thought I would make a great doctor—well, not for some time, if at all. I'm no longer in medical school as they caught me cheating on an exam. I had bought the answers, and somehow they found out. It doesn't matter how, but I did it and was caught.

My response has been to sink to a level of shame I didn't know possible. Think of a mole that never sees the light of day. That was me, José, a mole burrowing around in darkness. Believe it or not, it was the matron of the boardinghouse who dragged me out of the depths of despair by showing me not an ounce of sympathy but quite the opposite: disgust. I'm glad she did, as bit by bit I stopped wallowing in self-pity and began to see getting caught cheating didn't mean my life was over. What it meant was I needed more than ever to accept what I had done and work to forgive myself, which hasn't been easy (really, I'm not sure I have). Knowing all that you have gone through, I'm embarrassed, as what I've been through pales in comparison. But me doing something that I never thought I would do woke me up and made me realize all choices have consequences, some larger than others. Right?

I guess I lost my moral compass, José—yes, me, the person who habitually preached to you when I thought you went too far. Hopefully I've learned. Even with what's gone on, there may still be a chance for me to go to medical school. Thankfully a doctor in Chicago has come to my aid. He tells me not to give up hope, and he's helping me explore several possibilities.

Enough about me. It sounds like what you do for others is both good for them and you. I bet the doctors are glad to have you there. You're able to do as much or possibly more than they can for your fellow soldiers.

I now live at the Phillip Manor House in Chicago. You know, the place we used to walk by and wonder what lay inside. While you would call the entry posh and the interior with its marble columns and Persian rugs grandiose, my quarters are not. They gave me a room at the back of the hotel I get to by climbing a narrow stairway. It might have been where a servant once lived in the past. But it's clean and mine. Come visit. We can dine here together. Maybe Sally and Rose could join us? What do you say?

Here is my address:

Phillip Manor House

31 East Monroe Street, Room 201

Chicago, Illinois

I know Phillip Manor has a telephone, but I don't know the number or how to use the thing either. Looking forward to receiving another letter from you, José. Write, and I promise you'll hear from me much sooner.

Yours affectionately,

Ricardo

<br>

❧

## Letter to Tito Juan
### March 12, 1919

Tito Juan,

I find it hard to think I have been gone close to three years. Three years, and still I struggle—satisfied one day, filled with anxiety the next. I wonder if my father went through the same in his first years in the Philippines? I think not. He had fellow Spanish Filipinos while I do not. There are many nights I wonder why I remain here. Still, I stay. Why? Unfinished business, challenges unconquered. I still don't fully understand. Maybe because I hate to give up.

I was overjoyed to be accepted into medical school, but now realize I wasn't close to being prepared to go. I should not have been surprised my studies were short-lived. One quarter, and I failed. And so here I am in Chicago, determining what I might do next. With hopes of still pursing medicine, I have taken to studying on my own with the help of a local physician.

To be back in Chicago is good, although the city feels quite different, as if it's melody, once in harmony, is stuck in a state of discord played at full volume. The city has always had an undercurrent of nastiness toward different immigrants. I know I've written to you about this in previous letters. Today, more than ever, divisions are clearly pinpointed by a person's skin color.

The most recent enemy: Negroes, usually called colored or names too foul to write. In the six months I was away, the number here has doubled. Thousands upon thousands now live here. Many have taken over neighborhoods once considered to be white. Once we joined the war, trains, stockyards, and factories first welcomed and then became dependent on them.

This morning, I went to a park I often frequented six months ago and hardly recognized it. I used to sit on a bench overlooking a small pond. Trees filled with birds hugged its shoreline. I would spend hours mesmerized by their graceful flow from tree branch to the water's edge. Their songs were a break from Chicago's clamor. That tranquility is now absent. My park bench is no longer there. Now the space is filled with people who don't seem to want me there. Not because I am too dark but because I'm not dark enough. Today, the park is a place for Negroes only. Their cold stares and lack of friendliness made my visit short.

Tito Juan, often I wonder where I do belong. A couple of days ago, I had coffee at the Phillip Manor House where I live, like I have seen so many other residents do: in a small sunny lounge adjacent to the hotel lobby. Rather than buy a paper and retreat to my room, as is my custom, I picked up the complimentary copy of the *Chicago Times* and sat myself down in the furthest corner, away from prying eyes. I knew it was a bold act. In the weeks I have lived here, I've not seen any people who weren't fair-skinned … well, other than those who work here.

I settled in with my cup of coffee and newspaper in hand. Only one other person was nearby—an older woman, her silver hair pulled back in a tight bun with every hair in place on her refined head. A small boney creature, cultured by the outfit she wore. Her dress was of the finest cloth, with a purple jewel adorning her jacket of soft violet. She sat as if sitting on a throne, not a comfortable lounge chair. Truly, she looked ready to accept her subjects.

Periodically I would catch her looking at me, then she would nod and go back to her paper. This went on for some time until she cleared her throat. I looked up.

"Young man, what are you?"

"Pardon me?"

"From where do you come?"

"I come from the Philippine Islands."

"You do, do you?" She smoothed the front of her dress and leaned slightly forward. I found myself leaning slightly back. "At first, I thought Mexico, but you're much too tall. Then I thought perhaps a Negro, but that didn't seem right. They would never let a Negro live here. But the Philippines, you say. I don't believe I've met one before."

"I'm Spanish-Filipino, which is common in the Philippines." I started to cross my arms then took a sip of coffee instead.

"Spanish, you say, as in Spain?"

"Yes."

Part of me wanted to excuse myself, but I wasn't sure how to gracefully do so. Besides, if I was going to stay at Phillip Manor, it might benefit me to have an ally, besides the manager.

"How interesting," she continued. "Your English is quite good, although you do have a strong accent." She continued to examine me with her piercing blue eyes. They were quite disarming as if she could look into my soul.

I cleared my throat. "I came to America a few years ago with little command of English. It's a challenging language."

"How did you come to live here?"

"In the usual way a person does, I expect. I could afford it." Before she had time to comment, I arose and extended my hand, "Allow me to introduce myself. I'm Ricardo Lanuza Alvarez."

She leaned back slightly and again smoothed the front of her dress. We were like that for several seconds—me with my hand out and a smile plastered on my face, her looking like she'd wished she hadn't started this conversation—before she reached her hand out to mine.

"I'm Mrs. Fredrick Shumaker. I've been a Chicagoan for most of my life. My late husband, bless his soul, died two years ago, and rather than ramble about in our large house, I moved here."

Her hand was dry, the skin paper thin, and she withdrew it quickly.

"It is a pleasure to meet you, Mrs. Shumaker, and good to meet a long-time resident of Chicago. You are my first, also." I gestured to the seat across from her. "May I?" It was a bold move, I know.

She nodded.

As we talked, I flashed on the boardinghouses I had visited and felt a pang of guilt. Here I was sitting in the lobby of a grand hotel having coffee and making pleasant conversation while so many others were living in those warehouses.

I finally excused myself and walked away wondering how it is in a city made up of people from all over the world that this woman saw me only as white, Mexican, or Negro—black and brown, outcasts, unwanted, surrounded by whites. For Mrs. Shumaker, I was somewhere in between and, consequently, a matter of curiosity. Never have I felt more like an orphan with no orphanage in sight.

Tito Juan, these kinds of interactions make my skin crawl. Will there be a place I can be in between and accepted? Not white, not Negro, not Mexican, but me—a Spanish Filipino, unknown in this part of America. Will I find a place to be comfortable in? I could easily give in to the anger I stuff down inside me. Is it my father's spirit who tells me not to give up? I think it may be, because I refuse to live by limitations others place on me. He always said be proud of your heritage. I am.

I'm proud and thankful for relatives like you, Uncle. My letters to you always make me feel better. Your correspondence back is a pleasure to receive.

Warmly,

Ricardo

### Note to Hotel Manager, Mr. Walworth
### March 16, 1919

Sir,

As you know, I am a long-standing resident of Phillip Manor. I was away on business for the past several weeks, which as you know, is common for me. I was looking forward to returning until I found a foreigner has taken up residence in the hotel. Can it be you have altered your policies regarding whom Phillip Manor is meant to serve?

I'm not sure of the man's nationality, but I am certain he does not fit the mold that we who call Philip Manor our home desire. Although he dresses as we do, I hardly think this is reason enough to give him a room. May I assume his stay will be brief?

If you would be so kind, I would appreciate hearing your plans to alleviate the problem. Thus far, I have not discussed this with other residents. However, I'm sure there would be more than a consensus.

In earnest,

Mr. Leonard Gunderson

Mr. Walworth's response
March 17, 1919

Mr. Gunderson,

Thank you for your inquiry regarding Mr. Alvarez. He is a most recent resident, coming to us two weeks prior to your return. I imagine you have seen him in our dining room. Beyond this, he very much keeps to himself within the confines of his quarters or elsewhere. He is in the process of applying to medical schools to become a physician, which as you know we are in desperate need of. He has paid in full for an additional fourteen weeks, which we will honor.

I've changed no written policies regarding who can or cannot reside here. In fact, to be sensitive to the opinions of our current residents, he was placed in a room away from all others. Given this, your only contact, if you choose to have any, would be in the dining room.

I appreciate your concerns but believe there is no need for them. In the two weeks he has been in residence, there have been no issues. In fact, one resident has taken to conversing with him and finds him to be quite congenial, as do I. I'm quite sure he'll cause you no problems.

Respectfully,

Mr. Peter Walworth

## TELEGRAM FROM NENA
March 19, 1919

DEAR BROTHER, TITO JUAN PASSED TODAY. I SHOULD HAVE TOLD YOU HE WAS NOT WELL. HE DIDN'T WANT YOU TO WORRY. WAS BEDRIDDEN FROM STROKE. HE NO LONGER SUFFERS. FUNERAL SOON. WILL BE HONORED. GOD BLESS. Nena

## TELEGRAM TO NENA
March 20, 1919

DEAR GOD. HE NEVER MENTIONED HIS HEALTH IN LETTERS. HIS SAGE ADVICE WAS ALWAYS HELPFUL. WILL BE MISSED BY SO MANY, INCLUDING ME. PRAYERS TO HIS FAMILY. Ricardo

## JOURNAL ENTRY
March 21, 1919

Dear Lord, I sent a letter to Tito Juan only a week ago rambling on about Chicago changing and meeting Mrs. Shumaker. I should have written how much I appreciate his advice, his counsel, what a good man he was. How, of all my uncles, he was my favorite. He took the time to teach me how to use my camera, how to capture moments and people you don't want to forget. I won't forget him. But what will I do without his counsel?

## Letter to Margaret
March 25, 1919

Margaret,

We haven't communicated in a very long time. I think of you and then rush off to do something pressing, and forget to write. The cycle has repeated itself countless times.

I trust you are well. You probably have already finished Normal School and are working as a teacher. I have returned to Chicago and am no longer in medical school. There's more to the story, but for now I'll only say I wasn't ready for the rigors of the curriculum. However, I've put memories of that time in perspective, and I am once again applying for medical schools.

In previous letters, we wrote about having you and your parents visit Chicago. You seemed to think it might be possible, and I was wondering if you discussed it with them. I would very much like to see you again and introduce you to this city with all of its marvels and oddities. Let me know what you think.

Do say hello to your parents for me.

With warm regards,

Ricardo

## Letter from Margaret
April 1, 1919

Ricardo,

What a relief to hear from you. I had thought something terrible had happened. My last letter was returned to me, and when I reached out to the medical school, they said you were no longer there. I'm glad you aren't giving up on your desire to pursue medicine. We are in such desperate need for more doctors.

Ricardo, my situation has changed dramatically. I did return to Normal School and unwittingly met a young professor who has swept me off my feet. I think you would like him. He is kind, soft-spoken, and lights up every time he sees me. I find your invitation to visit tempting, but now with Peter, I'm afraid it doesn't seem right. Thank you, though. I'm so glad you are still here. You will do well, Ricardo. I always knew this. Please know I will always care about you.

Warmly,

Margaret

### JOURNAL ENTRY
April 1, 1919

What an idiot I have been. An idiot to not have written her. An idiot to think our relationship could ever be anything more than friendship. Will any American woman ever consider me?

### TELEGRAM TO JAIME
April 5,1919

JAIME, DO YOU HAVE TIME FOR AN OLD FRIEND? I'M IN CHICAGO. HOPE TO VISIT YOU. NEXT SATURDAY? AM AT THE PHILLIP MANOR HOUSE, 21 EAST MONROE STREET, ROOM 201. Ricardo

### TELEGRAM FROM JAIME
April 6, 1919

WONDERFUL, RICARDO. ALWAYS TIME FOR YOU. PLAN TO SUPPER WITH US. WE ARE SO PLEASED. MUCH TOO LONG. Jaime

## JOURNAL ENTRY
April 9, 1919

Jaime and Esperanza's house looks exactly like I remembered. The shutters still need a coat of paint, the front door is a little more worn, and the flower boxes are filled to the brim with flowers, now peppered with some weeds. I wanted to knock and let them know I'd arrived, but my hand remained suspended in the air. I was about to walk away to give myself a few more minutes to think about how I was going to tell them what I had done when the door flew open.

"Ricardo, you're here!" I about fell over as Jaime enveloped me in one of his warm embraces. The man knows how to hug. All I could do was hug back with a grin that stretched from ear to ear. Esperanza was right behind Jaime, and the three of us couldn't stop laughing. We were family reunited.

Esperanza, always a little woman, was now doubled in size. She glowed. Jaime couldn't keep his hands off her tummy. "She's amazing, isn't she?" he said with another pat. I've never seen the man so happy.

"Come in. Come in, Ricardo," Esperanza said, "Look at you. You're all grown up." I knew I didn't look any different. They simply hadn't seen me for seven months.

We talked and talked, took a stroll through the neighborhood to say hello to the few people that I knew (I'm so glad to see Mr. Vander's Bakery is still there), and then sat down to the feast prepared by Esperanza. I forgot what a good cook she is, and in my honor, the menu included my favorites: lumpia and chicken adobo. Hours later, and I still hadn't told them, always giving short answers to questions about medical school. I knew I needed to but didn't know how to start. After supper, Jaime helped me out.

"Now, Ricardo, we love your surprise visit, but tell us what troubles you. We ask you questions, and you give us half answers. You haven't told us anything about medical school. Is something wrong?"

I looked from one to the other and still nothing would come out.

"Let me get you two something to drink," Esperanza said and left us alone.

Of course, Jaime knew something was amiss. The man knows me well. I ended up blurting it out.

"I was desperate to be successful," I told him. "It was a terrible mistake, and I'm living with the consequences."

Jaime sat down in the chair across from me. "So, you'll never do something like that again." It wasn't a question.

I sat taller, made myself look him in the eyes, and nodded.

"I need to hear you say it."

"I've promised myself to never do anything like this again, and now I make that same promise to you," I said. "Can you forgive me?"

"Yes," he said reaching over to place his hand on my shoulder, "but you may have a harder time forgiving yourself."

I remember the first time he consoled me when we were coming over on the Tenyo Maru. His hand on my shoulder had the same impact now as it did then. I took another breath, this time with relief.

Later, when I told my story to Esperanza, her response surprised me.

"Oh, dis mio. I can't believe you did this."

Was I to get no compassion from her either? But what she did and said next was pure Esperanza. She gave me a big hug.

"This is not the only mistake you'll make in life, but it's a big one. Now, let's have another drink, and you can tell me what you intend to do next."

I am so lucky to have Jaime and Esperanza for my friends. How I dreaded what I thought would be their response, afraid they would be disgusted or, worse yet, never want to hear from me again. Instead, they showed me kindness, clearly expressing disappointment but also concern. What they taught me tonight was that people who care about you will accept you even when you've made mistakes, even really big ones. They have no idea how lighter I feel. They have no idea how they've helped me stop being afraid to share my mistakes, even ones you can't believe you've committed. If they care about you, they forgive you. They help you see yourself as more than the mistake.

## JOURNAL ENTRY
### April 10, 1919

I had to go see. I couldn't stop myself. I had to find out if Mr. Wojcik was still living in the same neighborhood or if anything had changed. Other than twangs of disgust, I no longer harbored any ill wishes towards him. No, others, like Professor Jorgensen, now filled that space. Although even with him, I try to set those flashes of anger aside. After all, there always seems to be another who isn't happy about having me be in their presence. This I have learned.

His house was the same, still neat and tidy, with red flowers in window boxes framing his home in color. No one was there. But the neighbors were out tending to their yards, just as Mr. Wojcik had when I passed through years ago. Today, I went unnoticed. I was simply another person passing by with many others. The only difference was the number of people who looked more like me than Mr. Wojcik. No one yelled at us, no one chased after anyone. Most had their backs to us, like they didn't care to see who was passing by. Like they knew we were there only to reach another destination.

## TELEGRAM FROM JOSÉ
### May 10, 1919

AM NOW STATIONED IN WASHINGTON, D.C. COMING TO CHICAGO. JUNE 7 FOR A WEEK. HOTEL NEAR ARMY HOSPITAL. DAYS FULL BUT NOT NIGHTS. JUNE 8 AT YOUR HOTEL? José

## TELEGRAM TO JOSÉ
### May 11, 1919

TERRIFIC. YOU ARE STATESIDE. JUNE 8, 7PM. AND THEN WHO KNOWS? LOOK FORWARD TO SEEING YOU. Ricardo

### Note from Sally
### June 3, 1919

Ricardo,

I'm still amazed you were able to track me down. From me quitting the dance hall and moving, I'm not sure how you found me. But I'm glad you did. After I got your note, my plan was to reach out to Rose, but whom do I run into? Again, uncanny! I was so surprised to see her I almost forgot to ask her about the idea of joining you and José for dinner. She shrieked when I brought up José's name. Did you know she wrote to him and she never heard back from him? I told her about his injury, I had to. I couldn't let her find out when he stood before her, could I? She couldn't stop herself from shedding some tears for his loss, but then she stopped like she had turned off a faucet and said, "Yes, yes, let's go out and have a wonderful time with the two of them."

Ricardo, even though I'm no longer at the dance hall, you know I am nervous about going. Truthfully, we both are. Of course we trust you, but Chicago has gotten worse about mixing. Where raised eyebrows were once to be expected, now a colored man with a white woman is viewed as suspect. He is often called names and even physically attacked.

But with José's return from war, we're making an exception. We can celebrate José making it home and toast to us all being here together, survivors of both war and influenza. José is a war hero, after all, and you—you'll someday be a doctor. I know it.

Warm regards,
Sally

### *Letter from Sally—thank you*
### June 11, 1919

Ricardo,

You two gentlemen certainly know how to give two girls a night to remember. Starting with our entrance to Phillip Manor. I thought the people at the front desk were about to fall over when I asked them to let you know we had arrived. "Excuse me," the young man said. "Did you say you're both here for Ricardo Alvarez?"

"Yes, that's what I said." I thought his eyes were ready to pop out. Rose and I hid our desire to turn around and walk out. We couldn't look at each other for fear we would burst into laughter—not because anything was funny, only to calm our nerves. Instead we stood trying to look nonchalant. We stepped back and turned our attention to the architecture of the lobby. Once we did, we were in awe of the detail. What a beautiful place you live in, Ricardo!

Truly the evening was wonderful from start to finish. How fun to be escorted to our table in the middle of the ornate ballroom. Was it my imagination or were we not the center of attention? Although as we had anticipated, there were lots of raised eyebrows, discerning looks, and whispers. Perhaps in part due to Joses uniform and obvious injury, but I don't think so. I'm sure you noticed as well. But as you witnessed, we relaxed, and soon paid them no heed. This time, I didn't have to worry about being told to leave.

I loved to see you have a friend at the Manor as well. Mrs. Shumaker seemed to enjoy all of the attention we were getting. So much so, I thought she might come and join us. Occasionally I found her smiling at us, and I think she might have even winked at me. Thank you for understanding our desire not to venture elsewhere and to spend the evening at your hotel. Best to stay inside with growing tensions throughout the city.

What a grand evening, Ricardo. I will remember our time together for a very long time. I do hope we stay in touch. Not sure where we might be able to dance together, but maybe someday this will change as well. Keeping my fingers crossed for you in getting into another medical school. You may have made a mistake in Champaign, but you're still one brave man.

Affectionately,
Sally

### Note from Mrs. Shumaker
June 14, 1919

Ricardo, I thought I would see you in the hotel lounge, but every morning you are absent. You must be off on business, or are you occupied with enjoyment? I hope it is the latter. I have wanted to simply say WELL DONE. Good for you for showing the folks here you belong—beautiful women at your side and a patriotic Filipino soldier to boot! I like a young man with cheek and valor, Spanish Filipino or not. You seem to have good taste in women as well.

With reserved admiration,

Mrs. Shumaker

### *Letter to Tita Carmen*
11:30 p.m., June 16, 1919

Dearest Tita Carmen,

I have to share with you what happened several nights ago as I'm still in a state of shock. If I would have been alone, I'm not sure I would be here but in the hospital or worse. My Filipino soldier friend, José, was visiting. After the war ended, he's stayed on to help injured men, like him, who suffered physical loss. Now years later, he's helped hundreds learn to better cope.

After not seeing each other for several years, we decided to celebrate at several local establishments I'd never been to and were headed back to my hotel some distance away. Nonetheless, we decided to walk, and I'm not sure what had made us laugh, but we had done so for several streets until our sides hurt. We lost track of where we were. José had to relieve himself, which was partly what we were laughing about. Apparently you did that anywhere you felt like on the battlefield. As José said, "Anywhere and in front of anyone."

I stopped him from doing the same on the streets of Chicago, convincing him to step behind a nearby building. I stood on the corner not too far away and waited. That was when I realized I wasn't sure where we were. Few streetlights were lit, and I didn't recognize the buildings. With all the nearby warehouses, I knew this wasn't a safe area. Even with a cool breeze, I began to sweat and willed José to hurry so we could be on our way.

That's when I heard voices coming closer and stepped back into the shadow of the building. They sounded like Irishmen who also had been drinking as much as we had, their voices loud and gruff. As I stepped back into the light to gauge where they were, three men, all twice my size, walked around the corner and almost ran into me.

"Well, well, well. What have we here? A nigger. Looks like he don't know where he belongs, fellas." The largest of the three got up close, took a drag off his cigarette, and blew the smoke into my face. I wanted to gag from getting too close to them; they reeked of rotting dung, whiskey, and sweat. These boys were from the stockyards.

I won't lie, Tita. I was scared.

"Look it, fellas, the boy is all decked out like he's wanting to be white or som'in. Don't ya' know you don't belong here? Come on, boys, let's teach him a lesson."

"Wait! I'm not a Negro. I'm from the Philippines. I'm Span …," I managed to get out before one of them slugged me in my gut. I doubled over in pain. One of them yanked me up by my elbows.

"From the Philippines, you say," said the man to my left. "Ever hear of that, Butch?"

The man in front of me shook his head. "I think your either a Negro or a Mexican, but it don't matter. You ain't getting out of here."

With that, Butch punched me in the face. The men at my sides let go, and I fell onto my hands and knees. I was stunned for a few seconds but pushed my way to standing and started swinging my arms. None of my punches landed as the men stepped easily out of my way. They laughed and surrounded me again. As they moved in, I thought this would be the end.

For a few minutes, I think I might have blacked out. Then I heard a voice like it came from far away. I knew it had to be José.

"Hey, what the bloody hell do you think you're doin' to my friend?" I tried to say, "José," but nothing came out.

"Let him go," José said with a force I didn't know he had.

Everything stopped for a minute, as I think they turned to see who was talking to them. José was dressed in his uniform, and he really had gotten bigger, curves of muscle from head to toe. I even think he got a little bit taller as well. I'm sure they also saw the sleeve that was pinned up showing two-thirds of a missing arm.

"You from the Philippines, too?" Butch asked

"Sure am."

There were several seconds of quiet, and I wondered if both of us would meet our maker that night.

"What division?" Butch finally asked.

"Black Hawk—eighty-sixth." José said. "You?"

"Sunset—forty-first." Butch said.

"How'd you lose it?"

"Potato masher," José said. "Are we done here?"

"I think we are, boys," Butch said.

"We can't let 'um go," the smallest one said.

"I said we're done here." Butch walked toward José. "Sorry, mate. We don't like Mexicans or niggers. They steal our jobs and take up space."

As the three wove their way down the street, I stared at José.

"The uniform. It works every time," he said with a wink. He reached out a hand as I lurched forward. "You're a mess. Let's get you home."

He draped my arm over his shoulder and put his good arm around me. My head throbbed, and I was having trouble taking a deep breath, so I gave in and let him lead me.

"Like you said, Rico, Chicago isn't the same anymore, but then neither are we. Looks like they missed your eye so you might not go black." Somehow he found that funny and started to laugh. I tried to laugh, too, but my ribs hurt too much.

"Aren't we the cat's meow?" I said which made José laugh all the harder. I joined in.

How I needed to laugh, Tita Carmen, even if it hurt.

When we got to my hotel, the boy at the front desk took one look at me and produced a bucket of ice and a bottle of whisky. We took both up to my room, and I put ice on my cheek and helped José polish off the bottle. All I could think was that José saved me—him and his one-armed bulging muscle in uniform.

Tita, to be beaten with such brutal force for the color of my skin tells me how deeply rooted this repulsion to color is here. I know I do look different. I do stand out. Having been away from Chicago for over six months and now living in a safe area of the city, I've lulled myself into thinking I was immune. I now know, I'm far from it.

My physical pain doesn't bother me as much as a longing to strike back, which I thought I had rid myself, but here it is stronger than ever. Inside, I boil and yet know these feelings aren't helping. They only keep me hidden away.

I'm ready to leave Chicago. Still determined to find a place where I can live in my own skin without fear.

Tita Carmen, send your prayers, as more than ever I need them.

With continued appreciation,

Ricardo

### Note from Dr. Webster
June 18, 1919

All of your applications were impeccable (if you don't know that word, you should; it means perfect or flawless). My insistence you write and rewrite has been grueling, but I believe the effort will soon pay off. With each application, I sent an accompanying letter to encourage the school to act affirmatively.

Now we wait. I imagine you will hear from the various medical schools in the next three to four weeks, perhaps sooner. As you know, doctors were lost during and after the war, most notably from the influenza outbreak. Schools will want to fill their seats. When you hear anything, do let me know. It has been a pleasure to assist you, Ricardo. I appreciate your tenacity (another word you should know, meaning you persist and are determined).

I don't say this often, and I now say it with great sincerity: I think you will make a fine doctor.

Respectfully,
Dr. Webster

**JOURNAL ENTRY**
June 21, 1919

While I heal from an attack from drunken fools, my applications go out to medical schools. I think of the men who thought I was a Negro or a Mexican. It didn't matter; either way, they wanted to hurt me. Now at night, I look down the street to see who is coming. I hear a sound, and I jump. My own shadow makes me stop in fear. How do I rid myself of these feelings?

**JOURNAL ENTRY**
July 7, 1919

I knew they would come—rejection letters, two so far. I can't lose hope. I have three more schools that may accept my application. Dr. Webster tells me to stay positive. I'm tired, ready to be done with the wait. I'm not sure what I will do. I can't go home, not like this.

## *Letter to Tita Carmen*
July 28, 1919

Tita Carmen,

The growing tension between black and white I wrote of in my last correspondence has gone beyond anyone's worst nightmares. It began when a group of black teenagers on a homemade floater accidentally crossed the line between the 29th Street Beach for whites and the 25th

Street Beach for Negroes. You couldn't see the line, but everyone knows the rules. They had always been abided by until two days ago.

Like many Sundays this month, it was blistery hot—hot like Philippines hot. You know, to walk outside was to sweat. I welcome it. The blanket of heat reminds me of home. But for most people, the high temperatures are unbearable. The only way for them to stay cool is to be immersed in the lake, so beaches brim with people on both sides of the invisible black and white line.

The newspaper said the Negro boys didn't know they had crossed the line. The response by nearby whites was quick. They threw rocks, and the only targets they had were the boys' heads that were above the water. Eventually they hit their mark, and one ended up drowning, which touched off a deadly brawl on the beach. Apparently dozens of men, all with fair complexions, were in hand-to-hand combat with anyone that looked different from them, mostly Negroes residing on the south end of the beach. One white and one Negro ended up dead, and dozens of others were injured.

That was bad enough, but it hasn't stopped. In two days, battles have erupted in neighborhoods all along the black belt, which is the place where most Negroes live in south Chicago.

Today, on the front page of the *Tribune*, there was an article about white mobs out to hurt any Negro they can find. John Mills, a black stockyards worker, was on his way home when a mob stopped the streetcar he was on and beat him to death. The Negroes have started to retaliate. Casmero Lazeroni, a white peddler, was pulled from his horse-drawn wagon and stabbed to death.

More men have taken to the streets to do battle. Some have guns, others pitchforks or axes. Many are using anything they can find to fight with. Hundreds of Negroes' homes have been burned to the ground, and homes of whites have now been torched. Police have lost any sense of control.

Tita, I haven't stepped outside since this craziness has started. I remain at my hotel, out of sight. Last night, I let two Mexicans who work here sleep on the floor in my quarters because they were afraid to go home. (If anyone knew, I'm sure I would be asked to leave the hotel.) Residents of the hotel are now nervous around the workers, and some no longer want to be served by anyone who looks dark. Others try to act normal, but their eyes shift between movements of one Negro to another. The tension within the walls of Phillip Manor is as thick as molasses. I'd like to be able to write that this tension doesn't impact me directly, but of course it does. I pray for the safety of everyone.

Rather than hide in my room this morning, I decided to have coffee in the parlor, which is something I had started doing regularly before the riots began. I waited until I thought few people would be there. A fellow resident, Mrs. Shumaker, arrived shortly after I did. Usually a bundle of friendliness, she stood in the doorway looking torn between returning my wave or walking in another direction. In the end, she came over to my table.

"Ricardo, Ricardo, good to see you," she said. "I have been worried for you. You aren't going out on the streets, are you? I know you are very accustomed to go to and fro at will, but with what is going on ..."

"Good morning, Mrs. Shumaker. Nice to see you this morning as well," I said. Even though the room was almost empty, I noticed how she couldn't stop looking around. "Join me for a cup of coffee?"

Her back stiffened, and she hesitated before sliding into the chair across from me and settling into her typical position of royalty. "Yes, a cup of coffee would do me fine."

I poured her a cup and handed her the sugar and creamer. "No, I don't go out these days. Like you, I'm troubled about the riots, and as you imply, I know how easy it would be to be mistaken for something I am not." I forced myself to take a sip of coffee and watched her for a reaction to my statement.

"You're a smart young man, Ricardo. This brutal heat doesn't help. Today I heard that a group of Poles attacked men they thought were Negroes, and it turns out they were Mexicans. One of the Poles is now in the hospital from a knife wound, and a Mexican is in jail."

"I didn't hear that. Has Chicago experienced anything like this before?"

"No, I can't recall anything like this ever. But then we have never had as many Mexicans or Negroes before either." She took a sip of her coffee and a small bite of a roll that had been placed before her by a young man who usually works the front desk.

"It makes me long for the old Chicago. It was simpler then. I fear where this will lead, how long the killing will go on."

I asked what it was like when she first arrived, and to hear her description, days did sound simpler, but not without strife between the different European immigrants. Maybe this proud and pompous woman does have concern for people who are different than her. As she reminisced, I noticed the curious looks from the few people in the parlor and some unable to hide their surprise. Or are they thinking something else? Are they concerned for Mrs. Shumaker? Sickened that she and I sit together?

Tita, you are well aware of my struggle to fit in. Sometimes, I'm not sure I want to anymore. When I received the rejection letter from the one medical school in Chicago, I felt relief. Even if I do have only two more possibilities, to stay here in Chicago for three or four more years would be difficult.

By the time you receive this letter, I trust these street wars will be long gone. My memory of it won't be, however. Although, Tita, little Mrs. Shumaker does give me a small bit of hope.

Yours,

Ricardo

### Note to Dr. Webster
### July 30, 1919

I received another letter of rejection today, leaving only two outstanding. I fear being Spanish-Filipino is the reason they reject my application, as my application is different from most. As promised, as soon as I hear from either Jefferson or Penn Med, I will let you know. I remain steadfast.

Ricardo

*

## TELEGRAM FROM DR. WEBSTER
August 1, 1919

RICARDO, EASY TO FOCUS ON DIFFERENCES. AS I GROW OLD I BELIEVE WE ALL NEED EACH OTHER. IF MEN ARE WISE THEY LOOK FOR A COMMON SPIRIT REGARDLESS OF COLOR. ANOTHER UNIVERSITY WILL ACCEPT YOU. Dr. Webster

## JOURNAL ENTRY
August 2, 1919

Dr. Webster writes of a common spirit. I keep repeating the words in my head, trying to understand what they mean, especially when you add "regardless of color." When I first read the phrase, I thought of angels that must be shared, spirits on high accessible to many people who need them. But no, I'm sure this can't be. Only another Filipino would think this way. José would have, and then we would have both laughed at our stupidity. Lord, I miss him.

Finding a common spirit must mean seeking out people who have similar pictures of what's important, what we as human beings should strive for. Maybe a collective view of what's right, shared with each other.

Even though I was the only one in the medical school who didn't look like everyone else, I did have moments that made me feel like we had a common spirit. We were all there to become doctors. Like me, they believed what we were doing was the most important step we could take.

I want that feeling again. If I understand what Dr. Webster says, I need to seek those out who want what I want, think the way I do whether they are red, black, brown, or yellow. I need to set aside my angst against those people who see me as something I'm not. Not bury my anger, but try to forgive. Easy to write, but I also know those who see me only as different won't be far away. I can't shed my skin—my heritage—like a costume. Nor would I want to. But I can't remain frightened I might be attacked, scared to walk down the street, or afraid I won't be seen as good enough.

## *Letter from Medical College of Thomas Jefferson University*
August 5, 1919

Ricardo Lanuza Alvarez

The Phillip Manor House

21 East Monroe Street, Room 201

Chicago, Illinois

Dear Sir,

The Medical College of Thomas Jefferson University wishes to welcome you as an upcoming student. We are pleased to offer this highly sought-after position after reading your application and accompanying materials. We believe the ultimate basis of esteem is that of personal character, and we believe you possess this. As you will discover, we also believe in experiential learning with our hospital on the campus grounds so that your exposure to latest approaches and technologies will be immediate. Copious studies and hand-on work with patients are the basic expectations for success. Both will be your barometers of success.

We trust you are able to join us this fall to occupy the rank of freshman. We are only able to make this offer due to a recent withdrawal of another who was struck down with influenza. Please inform us of your acceptance at your earliest convenience.

Respectfully,

Dr. William W. Keene

### TELEGRAM TO DR. KEENE–
to accept August 6, 1919

I AM PLEASED TO ACCEPT YOUR OFFER AND WILL GLADLY JOIN THE 1919-20 CLASS. PLAN TO ARRIVE IN THREE WEEKS. HOUSING RECOMMENDATIONS? HOPE IS TO LIVE WITH A FAMILY IF POSSIBLE. ANY GUIDANCE IS APPRECIATED. RESPECTFULLY, Ricardo Alvarez

**TELEGRAM TO DR. WEBSTER**
August 8 1919

THOMAS JEFFERSON MEDICAL SCHOOL HAS ACCEPTED ME
FOR THE FALL SEMESTER. I HOPE TO LEAVE IN THE NEXT WEEK
OR TWO. I AM INDEBTED TO YOU AND WILL NOT DISAPPOINT
YOU. MY HIGHEST REGARDS AND APPRECIATION. Ricardo

**TELEGRAM FROM DR. WEBSTER**
August 8, 1919

I KNOW YOU WILL NOT DISAPPOINT. THEY WILL DISCOVER
WHAT A WINNER THEY HAVE ACCEPTED. I PROPOSE WE
SQUEEZE IN A CELEBRATORY LUNCH AT THE PHILLIP MANOR.

**TELEGRAM TO DR. WEBSTER**
August 9, 1919

A MOST FITTING IDEA. TOMORROW AT 1PM?

**TELEGRAM FROM DR. WEBSTER**
August 9, 1919

I WOULDN'T MISS IT.

**JOURNAL ENTRY**
August 12, 1919

I don't know how long I was awake last night before my eyelids finally
gave in. My brain ran through every possible thing that could prevent
me from actually going to Philadelphia. They've sent the letter to the

wrong person. They'll see me and tell me they've made a mistake. They'll somehow find out about what I did in Champaign and dismiss me. My dishonesty in my application bothers me the most. Still, when I talked with Dr. Webster again, he simply smiled.

"Ricardo," he said, "on this matter, God probably doesn't care. He wants you to do good."

I do. I think of Mama, my baby brother and sister, and know becoming a doctor is good.

I can't question my capabilities any longer. I am enough. I have to be.

### TELEGRAM TO NENA
August 13, 1919

I HAVE BEEN ACCEPTED AT THE THOMAS JEFFERSON MEDICAL SCHOOL IN PHILADELPHIA. START IN SEPTEMBER. MORE SOON. Ricardo

### TELEGRAM FROM NENA
August 14, 1919

BRAVO, BROTHER! I CHEER YOU ON. WE NEED A DOCTOR IN THE FAMILY. Nena

### TELEGRAM TO JOSÉ
August 14, 1919

NEW ADDRESS. OFF TO A MEDICAL SCHOOL IN PHILADELPHIA. LET ME KNOW HOW YOU ARE. MY ADDRESS: WAYNE PETTERSON HOUSEHOLD, 183 FIFTEEN STREET, WARD 40, PHILADELPHIA, PENNSYLVANIA.

## JOURNAL ENTRY
Philadelphia
August 18, 1919

Pandemonium.

I like the word. It means wild and noisy disorder or confusion. Those words describe my past week, although I would also add exhausting and hectic. There are too many people to tell what I'm doing and where I'm going, especially since some thought I was still at medical school in Champaign.

I'm starting to realize that once I start as a freshman, I will have little time to stay in touch with the many people I want to: Nena, Jaime and Esperanza, Tita Carmen, José, Sally, and of course, Dr. Webster, who I am indebted to. As he has reminded me often, though, my sole purpose once the school year begins is to succeed. Nothing else matters unless it is an emergency. He said, "Tell people so they know not to expect to hear from you often." So I have. No one has been surprised, even my sister. "Write when you can, or better yet visit," Jaime said. The only one I haven't heard back from is José. He's probably too busy to respond.

Thank the Lord, the medical school helped me find a family to live with as a boarder. They're Norwegians. It turns out so is Sally. She says I'll be fine and that I might even enjoy some of the Norwegian food like lefse, made from potatoes and rolled out flat and eaten like bread. I'm not sure what Sally was talking about, but I'll find out.

In four days, I take the train to Philadelphia. This time, leaving Chicago isn't difficult. But when I think of what lies ahead, I start to eat. Doesn't matter what, I simply need to have something in hand. Food seems to calm me down. This is my second chance to feed my burning hunger to become a doctor. With enough hard work, I know I can do it. *Sé que puedo.* I know I can.

## TELEGRAM FROM JOSÉ
September 19, 1919

MY FRIEND, YOU WILL BE A DOCTOR. AND SOMEDAY I'LL BE YOUR PATIENT. PROUD OF YOU. I'M WORKING TOO MUCH. GETTING TIRED. WILL BE OKAY. José

## TELEGRAM TO NENA
October 11, 1919

I ONLY STUDY. SEE RESULTS. THINK OF YOU AND FAMILY. ALWAYS WITH AFFECTION. Ricardo

# 1920

*Letter to Nena*
January 25, 1920

Sister,

I haven't forgotten you, or Pina and Vicente. I'm only doing what I have to do, which is focus on my studies and do what needs to be done. Medical school is all-encompassing, filling my days, my nights, even my dreams, but not once have I been unprepared to take an exam.

My only companion is a medical student from Japan, Heratio. He's a serious little fellow. With round glasses framing his long and delicate face, he seems to be in a perpetual state of scorn. I remember the first time we met. We were in a building with no room numbers, both searching for the same classroom. After bumping into each other several times, I suggested we might work together. He scurried off as if he didn't hear me.

Minutes later, when I held the door open to him, he merely nodded, even as I stood there with a wide grin. Playfulness eludes him. Come to think of it, I haven't seen Heratio ever really give into a good laugh.

But he is brilliant, and we have our commonality: We are different than everyone else in our class. We are the two foreigners resolute to become doctors, willing to work hard no matter how long it takes to succeed. Daily we challenge each other. We study together and stay late, long after classes end. What was it he said after one of our first exams? Oh, yes. "Ricardo, you were lucky. I beat you next time." He did.

One Friday a month, we go to the pub where a lot of the medical students go. Heratio always orders the ham sandwich. Me, I order something different every time. You'd think we'd talk about something else besides medicine, but we don't. We are constantly readying ourselves for the next challenge, the next exam. Really, the family I live with is my only distraction. If I'm not at the university, I'm with the family of Norwegians I live with, a family who had never heard of the Philippines before I arrived.

"What is this country you speak of?" Mrs. Petterson exclaimed. "Show me, where is it?"

I showed her on a simple world map they had. She and her daughter, Aagot, squealed when I pointed out how far away it was. Young Aagot, probably fifteen years of age, asked, "How long did it take you to get here?"

"A very long time. First on a ship for three months and then three days by train."

The father jumped in: "They told us you were Spanish, not ... what do you call it? Filipino. Well, no bother. You're here now, and so it is."

As their boarder, I am treated with kindness and respect. They call me Mr. Alvarez, even though I've asked them to call me Ricardo.

"No, as our boarder, we think it important that we always call you Mr. Alvarez—to show respect, don't you know." So they do. They respect me, as I do them. I didn't know this was possible. My days and nights are full, and yet I'm content.

I pray you and your family are well and filled with happiness.

Ricardo

WE ARE WELL. YOUR SUCCESS IS NO SURPRISE. PROUD OF YOU. I CHEER YOU ON, BROTHER. Nena

## *Letter to Dr. Webster*
May 9, 1920

Dr. Webster,

My grades are acceptable, and they go up every week. My professors even understand me when I speak, although my dictionary is never far away. I do know hundreds of new medical terms as well, and I use them all: "antiphlogistine," "bronchoscopy," "Novocain," "hypodermic." Even though my studies are difficult, I am devouring the content. I am happy to be here. Again, thank you, Dr. Webster.

Next quarter, I have a class on surgery, and will assist in the surgery suite as well. I read about the procedures and think I may not be ready. Patients scream? Lose consciousness? Get sick? You are the best person to ask how I might prepare myself. Any suggestions you might have would be appreciated.

With great respect and gratitude,

Ricardo

## *Letter from Dr. Webster*
May 29, 1920

Ricardo,

How special to receive a letter from you. By now, you probably think, speak, and dream only in English. You're almost on the same level as your other classmates now who know no other language. Congratulations. Every struggle you've had, which I know have been plentiful, has been worth it. You must know how proud I am of you.

I've been a surgeon now for some twenty years. In the beginning, I found what we did to be difficult. We lacked the right tools and an understanding of how to reduce pain in an effective way. I have memories I wish I could be rid of forever. Although surgery is always an option of last choice, our practices have greatly improved. We've learned from a long string of mistakes, and we now have many physicians working hard to determine ways to lessen pain and avoid infections.

We do our best, but there is much work to be done to help more patients survive our procedures. My advice is to play close attention to everything that takes place in the suite, see what you find helpful, and think about what might improve our practices. Once you're a doctor, you'll be able to continue to improve practices even more.

Warmly,

Dr. Webster

Kapag tinapunan ka ng bato, tapunan mo ng tinapay.

**If someone throws stones at you, throw back bread.**

# PART FIVE
# Floundering In-Between

# 1921

## *Letter to Nena*
### August 22, 1921

Nena,

Today, I found the journal you gave me when I left the Philippines. It had been over a year since I'd written in it. Running my hands over the stained cover with its crumpled corners reminded me how important it was to write down my thoughts on the boat to America and those first years I was here. Writing kept me sane and helped me squash a cartload of fears I carried with me. I still collect my thoughts in a journal, a bound book I take with me everywhere.

Could I really have been that confused and scared? Some passages I've read more than once, especially the ones focused on Mother and Father. I'd forgotten how desperate I was to understand their absence and how much I missed them. I also had forgotten how many Americans looked down on me. Some still do. How I despised them. Today I only think about medicine. I stand taller knowing I will become a doctor.

So, now here I am in Milwaukee, Wisconsin, soon to be a student of the Medical School of Marquette University. If you haven't been able to keep up with where I am, I'm not surprised. I sometimes can't as well, but Milwaukee is where I've chosen to be.

This city suits me. Smaller than Chicago or Philadelphia, Milwaukee is also different. Something I learned on my very first day. Skyscrapers are absent, replaced with smoke chimneys of every size, billowing plumes of tiny black particles that land everywhere. These concrete pillars line the landscape and act as constant reminders of Milwaukee's pride—its factories.

Fresh off the train from Philadelphia, I stood alone looking at my surroundings. Although this station was smaller than the ones in Philadelphia and Chicago, it had the same masses of people who looked harried and the same smell of metal that filled your nostrils, sitting on your taste buds long after you left the station.

A middle-aged man dressed in a gray one-piece uniform stopped and said, "What you lookin' at, fella?" He stopped to see for himself. "Flock of geese up there? I can't see nothing," he said.

"The smokestacks. There's so many." I told him.

He chuckled at that, his protruding belly freely joined in, causing a cascade of jiggles.

"This is Milwaukee, son. Factories, we need 'em." He walked away, shaking his head, and turned to say, "If you're lucky, you'll git yourself a job in one of 'em."

I nodded in agreement and tipped my hat in appreciation. I imagine I'll meet many a patient who works in one. Milwaukee: smokestacks, factories, and a Catholic medical school I'm excited to attend.

I know you must wonder when I will return home, and I can only tell you I will be able to visit when I have completed my studies to become a doctor, now only years away. With our precarious status as nationalists, I need to be careful. I know of a student of science in Philadelphia from Manila who received a telegraph about his father's illness with a prognosis of five to six months to live. He caught a train west and boarded the next ship. He got to spend the last couple of months with his father but was unable to return. He hasn't been able to find out why from the Philippine government or the United States. Either way, he hasn't made his way back, and it's been over a year. He had only one year left to complete his studies.

My journey has been long, and I am fully aware of your continued support. I hope to communicate more and hope you will do the same.

I remain affectionately your brother,

Ricardo

## TELEGRAM TO TITA CARMEN
September 21, 1921

TITA, PLEASE FORGIVE ME FOR MY YEAR OF ABSENCE. NOW IN CATHOLIC MEDICAL SCHOOL. MILWAUKEE, WISCONSIN. I AM WELL. LOVE TO YOU AND YOUR FAMILY. Ricardo

## TELEGRAM FROM TITA CARMEN
September 22, 1921

RICARDO, I PRAYED FOR A TELEGRAM. FOR YOUR HEALTH. FOR YOUR HAPPINESS. CATHOLIC MEDICAL SCHOOL? WONDERFUL. I TRUST YOU ARE NOW TREATED WITH RESPECT. Carmen

### *Letter to Nena*
October 11, 1921

My dearest Sister,

Marquette Medical School is everything I imagined. In two years, I'll complete my studies. The campus is small with around 3,500 students; 200 are in the medical school, around forty in my class. What I like best about the medical program is its aim to make the best person of each and every one of us. This includes encouraging every student to have strong ties to the church. In the center of the university is a chapel that offers services every day. I plan to attend whenever I can.

Most of the students here are men from towns within a day's travel by train. Almost everyone is German, Polish, or Norwegian, and all of them are fair-skinned. But after five years and how many universities, I have grown accustomed to this fact and no longer panic or become nervous to walk into a classroom or through campus. At the university, I stand out. A block away, I blend in.

Where I live borders on a large Jewish community and growing neighborhoods of Negroes. Not far away are neighborhoods of Mexicans. I sometimes walk out of my way to hear them speak. In Philadelphia, I don't recall hearing anyone speak Spanish. Now, I linger when I hear it spoken. Sometimes I join in on the conversations, which makes me content beyond words. What does it matter that they are from Mexico and I'm from the Philippines? We're more alike than we are different.

I've decided, in fact, to become color-blind. What I mean is I'm not going to treat people any different, even if they are green, pink, or purple. This may sound preposterous, but here the color of your skin opens or closes doors and determines what you can or can't do, especially when you don't have money. As a first step, I am being friendly to all. You might be thinking, "You've always been this way," but no, I don't think I have. Growing up in the Philippines, we were the fairer-skinned people (the whites, you could say). We never felt outright rejection. Father must have when fellow Filipinos, our neighbors, stopped coming to his pharmacy. I'm sure he thought they were his friends. Or maybe he knew it didn't matter, his bloodline to Spain being stronger than anything.

I know I felt the shift when Americans took over, especially after our papa left us behind. Back then, I didn't understand, but now here, alone, I can see what I never wanted to admit—friends and strangers no longer saw a need to accept me. Here, I would need to be blind not to feel the rejection as it is tenfold. I can tell you rejection makes your heart ache. You feel a mix of hate you dare not show with a sickening sense of loss, like you've misplaced a part of you. Like you want to shout and holler, while at the same time hide in fear and shame.

So far, my attempts to be kind here in Milwaukee are surprising. This morning on my way to the trolley, I accidentally bumped into a neighbor, a Jewish father with his son of no more than six. He has never given me any notice.

"Watch where you are going," he rebuffed.

I apologized and explained I was looking to see what the time was. His son immediately craned to see Papa's pocket watch, which I held in my hand. I asked him if he'd like to see it.

"Here, let me show you how it works. That is, if you can spare a minute," I said looking to his father for approval.

His boy was obviously excited, and the father consented. I opened the watch's metal case, and the boy's eyes doubled in size. What caught his eye was the compass—you know, the one on the cover. I showed him how he could tell what direction he was going. He stood facing north, then south, then west and east, grinning the entire time.

"Where did you get this?" he asked.

I told him it was a gift from our father who wanted to know not only the time, but which way he was headed.

"Why did he want to know his direction?" he asked.

I told him about Papa coming from far away on a ship and how he wanted to know they were headed southeast because he knew that was where his new home was.

"Look," I said, "You can see we are headed north right now; this means you live directly south of downtown."

The boy grasped the watch like he had never held anything so precious. The father seemed nervous about the boy dropping it but also seemed pleased by his son's reaction.

"The watch is so big," he said turning it over in his hands.

I grabbed the moment to introduce myself.

"I'm Peter," the boy said as he handed back the watch. "Thank you for showing me your watch."

The father looked completely different when he introduced himself. His teeth glistened as he turned his lips upward into a smile. "Mr. Feinstein," he said and continued to shake my hand as he looked at me for the first time.

You have to understand. This is a man I passed every morning and sometimes again in late afternoon. He would walk by without a glance, head turned away with eyes averted. I told him it was a pleasure to meet him, especially since we were neighbors.

"Thank you, Mr. Alvarez," he said. He nodded, smile still in place as he turned to walk away. Just then, another person I have become friendly with passed us by.

"Good morning, Ethereal," I said.

Both men glanced at each other, but neither said a word. The contrast in their physiques was startling. Ethereal is a tall burly Negro with muscles that suggest he might have been a boxer sometime in his life. In contrast, Mr. Feinstein is small in stature, really a wisp of a man, with a nose like a hawk's, his mouth the size of a small bird, with eyebrows more prominent than his eyes. Ethereal didn't hesitate to respond.

"Good morning to ya', Ricardo. What, you thinkin' of runnin' for mayor or somethin'?" Ethereal said as Mr. Feinstein and Peter walked away, a small but noticeable grin escaping the corners of his mouth. I didn't have time to respond before he whispered, "You know that man has not once looked in my direction. Humph, and now look what you done, you gone and shared my name. I hope that don't bring me no trouble."

I told him good things could come of it. I do hope so. Maybe I'm doing something good, Nena. Maybe by being more myself, I'll receive kindness in return. I won't promise to write often, as I'll soon be knee-deep in my studies. Do write me when you can, and I'll be sure to write back when I am able.

With continued prayers,

Ricardo

## JOURNAL ENTRY
### November 1, 1921

I would not have guessed Dedrick and I would get along. The way he looked at me when he was assigned to be my lab partner was a look I had seen before, an "Oh, no, not with this fella" look. For a moment, I thought, here we go again, another fellow student in dread for being stuck with the foreigner. I had slogged through labs before knowing the other person felt slighted for having me as their partner. Before I knew it, I said out loud what I thought he was thinking.

"I know you're probably thinking, "Oh, no, I get stuck with the dark guy," but I'm pretty smart and know my way around a lab. You could do worse."

He seemed surprised and mumbled, "No, no, I hadn't thought that," but by the end of the lab, he turned to me and said, "Yeah, you were right about what I was thinking, but you and I will get along fine. You do know what you're doing." He also likes the fact we always finish up quicker than fellow classmates and end up quietly yukking it up about one thing or another.

Turns out he is quite the jokester. Today he surprised me when he suggested we "get a proper drink together." With raised eyebrows, he looked around to make sure no one heard. I did the same and noted only one onlooker, a person I often found to have his eye on me. I laughed and said that would be great but told him I had no idea where to go. It was his turn to chuckle.

"With a German name like Kline, you can guess this won't be a problem. How 'bout tonight?"

I was nervous and ended up showing up early, and there he was, whistling a tune, looking around like he didn't have a care to worry about.

"Ricardo, I knew you'd come a little early."

"And I knew you would, too." We both laughed.

"So what speakeasy is close by?" I asked.

"I guess you could call where we are going a speakeasy, but it's not a public place. It's a flat only friends of my family know about. We Germans pretty much laugh at Prohibition. The idea of not having good ale when you wanted is downright wrong. So we take care of ourselves." He must have seen my twitch of nervousness, because he patted me on the back. "No worries, my friend, you're with me. Let me show you a different piece of Milwaukee. If you can drink, you'll be fine."

What I remember is walking into a small room filled with people and more beer than I could ever hope to drink, the best I had in years. I have a faint memory of telling everyone this multiple times. I also remember trying to sing a German song and then Dedrick's uncle trying to show me how to do the polka, a dance I've never seen or heard of. My entrance caused people to stop talking, so much so it felt like we'd entered a library. But once Dedrick introduced me, one by one to everyone in the room, and after a couple of beers, the place was back to roaring with music and laughter. I'm not sure how I made my way home. When I woke up, I surmised I had started to undress at my bedroom door and managed to almost complete the task before I fell into my bed. I haven't had that much fun since José visited me in Chicago years ago. What a terrible friend I have been. I wrote him only once in Philadelphia, but he's never answered my telegrams.

### TELEGRAM TO JOSÉ
November 5, 1921

FRIEND, IT HAS BEEN YEARS SINCE WE SAW EACH OTHER. OVER A YEAR SINCE WE COMMUNICATED. HOW DO YOU FARE? STILL HELPING SOLDIERS OUT EAST? AM NOW IN MILWAUKEE, WISCONSIN, AT MEDICAL SCHOOL. PEN ME. BETTER YET COME VISIT. Ricardo

### *Letter to Jaime*
December 1, 1921

Jaime, my friend,

It has been much too long since my last letter, so much so you'd have difficulty finding me. I'm much closer now, in Milwaukee, Wisconsin, they tell me only an hour or two away by train. Not to worry. I am in medical school at Marquette University. I've done well. I came to this school for its reputation and its affiliation with the Catholic Church. The church is something I deeply missed while in Philadelphia—that and people like you and Esperanza.

You must think ill of me for my lack of correspondence. Has it been a year? Edgar must be two years of age now. I imagine he runs around your house chattering nonstop, while you both try to keep up with his perpetual motion. Hopefully you both pause long enough to appreciate your creation.

Are your friends happy to fill in as aunts and uncles? I know if I were there, I certainly would be. Tell me, has he transformed the room I once occupied? Surely, it is a room filled with joy.

I feel comfortable here in Milwaukee, although several recent events trouble me. My letter is, in fact, to get your opinion of what I might do. Jaime, have you heard of the Ku Klux Klan? Is it present in Chicago? I had not heard of the organization until recently, and once described, I was aghast. To think their primary goal is to attack black and other dark-skinned races ... well, I didn't want to believe such an organization could exist. They apparently have no appreciation for Catholics as well. So yes, I have two strikes against me. But I get a head of myself. I need to start from the beginning.

There are about thirty-five of us in my medical school class; most come from cities within a day's travel. I am the only person who is not fair-skinned. From the moment I walked into class, a particular fellow classmate watched my every move. Truly, at the oddest times, I would look up, and he would have his eyes fixed on me. I might be talking to a fellow student or reading in the library, and he'd be there. We had never been formally introduced, so one day after class, I took the initiative to talk to him.

"Hello. We've never formally met. I'm Ricardo Alvarez." I extended my hand.

He started to pick up his books. "I know your name. We are in the same class, after all."

When it was clear he wasn't going to shake my hand, I lowered it but pressed on. "I don't believe I know your name."

"Rufin Filkowski," he said as he shoved his way past me.

He was gone before I had a chance to say another word. Not more than ten minutes later, I saw him with his friends outside the building. They were keeled over as he was obviously mimicking my attempt to shake his hand.

"To think I would ever shake his hand," I overhead him say. "Who is he kidding? He hasn't the brains to be a doctor."

Thankfully, none of them saw me as I quickly retreated in the opposite direction. Part of me wanted to physically attack him for making fun of my attempt to be kind. Another part of me was shaken to the core. How can a fellow medical student express such contempt? I don't have the brains? I walk circles around him in the lab. And to think his friends found him funny.

Jaime, I wanted to do something, anything, to stop his ridicule of me. I knew I needed to calm myself. I went to the chapel, and even there I struggled to sit still. I wanted to believe this would be one incident. Instead, his initial rudeness turned out to be only the beginning. I would never have guessed where it would go next.

About a week later, the professor asked my lab partner and me to share with the class the results of lab tests we had completed. I stood up to address the class, and when I finished, the professor said, "Excellent. Your results are what I would expect, and I am most impressed with the speed at which you and Mr. Kline are able to produce results." At this, Rufin Filkowski raised his hand.

"Yes, Mr. Filkowski, do you have a question?"

"My question is for Mr. Alvarez. Why do you present the results rather than Mr. Kline when he is the one who leads you in the ability to produce results?"

The professor immediately protested. "This is not an appropriate question."

Dedrick—Mr. Kline—interrupted. "You are sorely mistaken. Mr. Alvarez led this experiment. I would not have been able to provide the details he recited. If there is credit to be given, he deserves it."

I searched the faces of other students to see their reactions. Most looked surprised, except for Rufin and his gang. They looked like they had swallowed a cat. I was silent, dumbfounded by Rufin's lack of civility. The professor broke the silence.

"Mr. Kline, you are kind to respond. Mr. Filkowski, I would ask you to refrain from further questions of this kind. They serve no purpose."

After class, Dedrick grabbed me and whispered, "Ricardo, we need to talk. Rufin's father is in the Ku Klux Klan."

When everyone was gone, he told me the Ku Klux Klan is a secret organization of white Protestant men promoting violence against Negroes, Jews, and others who aren't white.

"Like me." I said.

"Yeah. This organization dates back to the Civil War when Negroes were the targets for terrible attacks, especially down South."

"They were killed, weren't they?"

"They were. Here in Milwaukee, they don't kill anyone; they scare people—a way to tell them to leave. I don't know a lot about them, but I know enough to be nervous for you. Rufin's father is one of the leaders."

Jaime, the hair on my skin stood up on end. At first, I thought Dedrick was crazy. I couldn't believe Rufin's display could be tied to such an organization. However, two weeks later, something happened that changed my mind. A couple of nights ago, the landlady of the household where I live ran through the house screaming about a fire in the yard. The eight boarders woke up to a cross set on fire in our yard. The cross was small, shoddily made, but big enough to send the message Dedrick had spoken of: You're not welcome here. We stood together in silence as one of the residents, a Jewish man, threw water over the remainder of the fire.

"Who are they? How would they dare come into this neighborhood and threaten us?" one resident asked.

Others knew instantly who and what the cross was. One resident asked if anyone knew if the Ku Klux Klan had done this elsewhere in the city. Ethereal chimed in, saying he thought not, adding, "but this doesn't look like the work of the KKK. This looks like an imitation."

I immediately thought of Rufin and his gang. Had they followed me home and waited to place a pathetic cross in my yard? I think they did.

Jaime, I'm numb. I pace my room. I'm unable to eat. Years ago, in Chicago, I remember feeling this way, especially after being beaten by men from the shipyard and then witnessing the riots. When I left, I pledged to find peace within my heart for those who harbored contempt for people who have darker skin. I thought I had even found forgiveness for those who had hurt me. When I stared at the cross, I knew I hadn't.

Perhaps it is too much for me to ask for any suggestions you might have. Perhaps only prayers for my continued wellbeing are what are in order. I look forward to any ideas you may have.

Respectfully,

Ricardo

# 1922

**JOURNAL ENTRY**
January 4, 1922

I can't think about anything else. Images swirl around in my head of the cross on fire and Rufin's face twisted in a cloak of hatred, what I imagine the devil to look like. Since the incident, he makes sure to have no contact with me. I had hoped he might feel guilt. How stupid of me. When I rushed into class today and accidently bumped into him, he didn't hide his compulsion to dust off the shoulder I bumped into. For a split second, I saw his rage. No, I think Rufin is his father's son. His loathing makes me want to bump into him every day. A fire I thought gone once again burns deep in me. This man, his father make me sick to my stomach. I need to regain my composure.

*Letter from Jaime*
January 9, 1922

Ricardo,

I am glad to hear you are still in medical school but must say I found your letter to be most disturbing. Yes, sadly enough, I have heard of the Ku Klux Klan. I haven't had any contact with them but do know some recent Catholic immigrants who have.

Ricardo, I pray the Ku Klux Klan in Milwaukee is nowhere as large as the group here. Last summer, the *Tribune* published an article about the Chicago Klan and estimated their membership to be 30,000 and growing. In the article, the Klan was referred to as an invisible empire made up of men who claim to be 100 percent American. I'm not sure, but I think this means they were born here and definitely don't look like you or me. During the day, recruiters, called kleagles, travel all over the city in search of new members. You can see them handing cards to people on street corners, in parks, even in restaurants. The *Tribune* article described how recently thousands of men in white gowns piled into long lines of cars heading to a secret destination north of the city to induct hundreds more into the Klan. The newspaper photographer was allowed to take a picture, which I've enclosed. From what I know, we should not take what they are or can do lightly.

You ask what actions you might take. First, you might think of finding a different place to live, which knowing you, you probably already have or soon will. Perhaps the medical school knows of places that are close to campus where you could room with other medical students. Beyond this, I would hope you take cautionary steps. At night, walk only on well-lit streets, consider staying in rather than venturing out, and walk with others as often as you can. Most of all, I encourage you to build

friendships with others in your class. Your lab partner sounds to be a friend already. My assumption is there would be more if you opened up to them. You know this, but I will put the words to paper anyway— not everyone is like this fellow medical student and his friends (or like the others you've had to deal with).

Please refrain from doing something more forthright, daring, and bold regarding the Klansman in your class. The smallest provocation would only fuel his fire. Instead, why not show him how little effect he has on you? Think about this, my friend.

Ricardo, as you can see, my wisdom is limited. I trust you will be mindful and continue to focus on what is most important, becoming a doctor.

Always with high regard,

Jaime

## Letter from Tita Carmen
February 5, 1922

My dear boy,

I'm at loss for words. To think after years of living there, you still contend with people who don't treat you respectfully. I find the notion appalling. You didn't share details, and frankly I don't think I would be able to hear them. I'm not sure how you remain. I have no doubt you are brave, but once your medical degree is received, you might consider a permanent return to the Philippines. You have family and friends here who would welcome you. Your sister, for one, would be thrilled. Doctors are always needed here, especially with the advanced knowledge you are acquiring. The issue of your Spanish surname is less and less important, as the United States puts more Americans in charge every day. Some Filipinos now have shifted their recollections to have fond memories of Spanish rule and grow skeptical of being a nation under the thumb of United States. It is a story unfolding as each year goes by.

Consider the option to come home, Ricardo. I know this may be far from what you plan, but perchance these attacks on who you are and how you look are simply too much, with too severe consequences. Only you know if this is true or not. I trust that you will make the right decision. I look forward to the day we can discuss issues like this in person while we sip on a cool drink on your veranda.

With warmest regards,

Carmen

## TELEGRAM TO RICARDO
### February 24, 1922

MR. ALVAREZ, PLEASE CONTACT ME AT YOUR EARLIEST CONVENIENCE. THIS CONCERNS SERGEANT JOSÉ LOPEZ OF THE UNITED STATES ARMY—DIVISION OF MILITARY POST-WAR SUPPORTIVE SERVICES. I CAN BE REACHED BY TELEPHONE USING YOUR LOCAL PHONE SERVICE. REQUEST CONNECTION LAKEWOOD 2967. General William Singer

## JOURNAL ENTRY
### March 1, 1922

I huddled in the corner of the Dean of Students' office. A clerk sat several feet away from me behind her desk. Every once in a while, she'd look over to see if I was in conversation yet. She had helped me connect to General Singer's office over five minutes ago.

I hunched over with the phone gripped in my hand, my face close to the mouthpiece like she had instructed me to do. To hear the voice of a person you knew was far away in the palm of your hand didn't seem possible.

My hands shook. A phone call could mean only one thing. Something was wrong with José. While I waited, I prayed.

Outside, the sky was clear. A breeze caused the branches of birch trees near the window to sway to and fro, as if they, too, were waiting. The clerk shuffled papers. I tried to turn away from her. She was going to hear everything I said.

"Mr. Alvarez, are you there? This is General Singer."

I jumped when his voice boomed into my ear. He sounded like he was beside me, not hundreds of miles away.

"Yes, General Singer, this is Ricardo Alvarez."

"Good. I thought I might never reach you."

"General Singer, has something happened to José? Sergeant José Lopez, I mean."

"Yes, Ricardo. May I call you that? I often heard José speak of you. He thought highly of you."

"Yes, of course."

"Thank you. I will get right to what you want to know." He paused and sounded like he took a deep breath. My heart pounded—it sounded like he said *thought,* as in past tense.

"He is no longer with us. I'm sorry to inform you he died five months ago."

The room started to spin. I couldn't catch my breath and dropped the mouthpiece. I picked it up, and it was as if my voice had left me. I tried to talk, and nothing came out. The room was too bright with nothing but a clock ticking in the background. And the clerk. I tried again to speak. Nothing.

"Ricardo, are you still there? I know this is shocking. Are you all right?"

Finally I was able to speak. "No. Yes. I don't know."

I blinked my eyes to regain a semblance of vision. One tear rolled down my cheek in response. In my head, I kept repeating, *Oh my God this can't be.* I could hear myself breathing, like I had run up several flights of stairs. I needed to sit, then realized I already was.

"What happened?" I finally got out. "When we last talked, he was good, happy about what he was doing."

"When was that, do you recall?"

"We were together for about a week in June two years ago. After that, I sent telegrams and maybe a letter or two—probably a year since we last communicated.

"Ahh, yes, he came back from seeing you a happy man, and for the next year and a half, he continued to help soldiers all over the Eastern Seaboard. He helped them deal with their circumstances, life after war with a different body or mind. I should have seen the toll it was taking."

I struggled to listen. *If I could only see the man I was talking to. He knew my friend. He was responsible for the work José did.*

"What do you mean?" I managed to ask.

"He never wanted to stop. He would come back and say, 'Who else needs my help?' I tried to get him to slow down, take time for himself. Eventually he simply stopped."

"He stopped? You mean he didn't go out to help anymore, or did he stop working?

"He fell into a state of depression our physicians hadn't seen since the war. He started to relive not only his personal loss but everyone else's."

I covered my head and face as much as I could so the woman in the office couldn't witness my tears.

"No, no, no," I said. The woman handed me tissues and a glass of water. I took neither.

"Then one day, he was back, said he was all right, that he had simply needed to stop feeling all the sadness he had absorbed in the past couple of years. He laughed, joked as he liked to do. Told us not to worry, he was fine. We believed him. We let him go home, and the next morning when he didn't show up, we went to his home and found him—dead."

I dropped the phone piece and stumbled from the room. I needed air. I couldn't hear another word.

### Note from Dedrick
#### March 3, 1922

Ricardo, when you didn't show up for class or lab, I knew something must be wrong. I went to the dean's office and asked if they had heard from you. The clerk told me you had come to the office earlier to make a telephone call. I probably should not have done this, but I really pushed her to tell me what happened. She said you ran out during your call, and she picked up the phone to see if anyone was still on the line. There was, and they asked for your address and told her about your friend.

I am sorry, Ricardo. You must have been very good friends. I don't want to intrude, but if you want to talk, I am here. We don't always have to talk about maladies and medicine. I count you as a friend. I'd like to help if I can. If not, I understand. If nothing else, we could go get zozzled at a juice joint of your choice whenever you're ready.

Your friend,

Dedrick

## *Letter from General Singer*
April 7, 1922

U S Department of War
Mr. Ricardo Alvarez
630 Fifth Street
Milwaukee, Wisconsin

Mr. Alvarez (Ricardo),

Although difficult, I was heartened to be able to talk with you about the death of your dear friend, José. He was a good soldier, an even better man. I was fortunate to know him, as I know you feel the same. I thought it important you know he had attempted to communicate with you several months prior to his death.

Enclosed you will find the letter he sent on the date of May 30, 1921, to the Phillip Manor House. As you can see, it was returned many weeks later stating that there was no forwarding address available. Even then, he must have struggled, as we easily found your Milwaukee address among his papers. All of his possessions have been sent to his parents in the Philippines. I had intended to contact you months earlier; however, the demands of my office led me astray.

His letter may be difficult to read, but I thought you would want to have it. If I can be of any further assistance, please let me know. We lost many good men during the war and after, but José is one I will always remember. His kind spirit and giving nature were a special gift to behold.

Respectfully,

General Singer

## Letter from José

Rico — my friend,

I'm not sure I can continue to do what I do. I listen to these men, and I no longer feel strong. Their stories are awful. Sometimes I feel sick to my stomach. Sometimes I want to break down and cry. Other times, I want nothing more than to yell at them for being pathetic.

Look what this war has done to us. Broken, beaten, and unable to help ourselves. I ask myself all the time, how can this be? Weren't we the winners of the war? Maybe it is time for me to find something else to do, but what? I look at myself in the mirror, Rico, and I have to look away.

Did I tell you Rose came to visit me a while ago? We laughed, danced, and drank too much. I put her up in a boardinghouse nearby, one especially for women visiting their blokes. Afterwards, we stayed in touch, but then I stopped writing. What do I have to offer a beautiful woman like her? She works for the telephone company in Chicago now, connecting people to others all over the city, even to people in other parts of the country. Maybe she could connect us to talk over the tellie? But she's probably forgotten about me. I know she can do better.

What should I do? I know you always have ideas. Some of them aren't so great, but I could use some right now. Since I saw you, I have put on some weight and smoke like a chimney.

Write to me when you can. I know that medical stuff keeps you busy, but hearing from you or better yet seeing you would help. You're a good man, Rico.

José

## JOURNAL ENTRY
April 11, 1922

Dear God, he told me he would never kill himself like my father did. But he did it anyway. I might have been able to stop him. I could have tried. I didn't know. I only thought of medical school. I only thought about me. I studied, worked harder to make sure I wouldn't fail. I dreamt about medicine, about the procedures I needed to know, required terminology laced with Greek and Latin, too many names of so many different things. I let myself forget about everyone I cared about. I forgot about José.

Today I went to confession and ran out before I could admit what I had done. I wasn't there when José needed me the most.

I wish I could tell Sally and Rose, but I have no idea where they are. The last time I heard from Sally, she was soon to be married, still living in Chicago. She sounded happy. I can still feel her in my arms floating across the floor. Rose still lives in Chicago, too. Like Sally, she's probably hooked up to someone who's her own kind, not a Filipino. I'm so sorry, José.

Tears. More tears, I haven't wept like this since my father killed himself. I so badly wish I could embrace José one last time.

My tears ruined his letter. I can barely read what it says now. To think that he reached out, but I wasn't there is hard for me to come to terms with. I might have been able to help him.

## *Letter to Nena*
April 19, 1922

Sister,

I've moved. The house is only a short distance away from where I lived, although the neighborhood feels safer and calm. Mrs. Sterling, who runs the household, is a nurse at a nearby hospital. She provides rooms for university medical students. When I first visited, I instantly liked her. She had a look about her, stern and warm all wrapped up in one. She looked to be about forty years old. Tall and lean, she had the arms of someone who had worked all her life. In her eyes, I could see kindness telling me she would do anything she could for me if I respected her and everyone else living there. I knew I would.

"Medical school is difficult, and I like to think my home makes life a little easier for my boarders," she said as she walked me through the living area and dining room. In front of a large fireplace framed in mahogany are two overstuffed chairs in a blue-and-white checkered pattern. A table against one wall holds piles of books and a large bouquet of red roses.

"Picked fresh from the garden in back," she pointed out.

The dining room table is set for ten, even though with her husband there are only seven of us. "For friends and neighbors who might drop by," she said when she saw me count the number of chairs.

As I've learned in my short time here, Mr. Sterling was right. Her home is a place many people like to visit. There hasn't been one night when there have been fewer than nine people for dinner. I'm not surprised, as she has a way about her that helps you trust her. I feel I can.

My room is large with built-in wooden bookshelves and a window seat that overlooks the tree-lined street. I have a table for my studies, and my bed is soft and comfortable. Mrs. Sterling even places a vase of fresh flowers at my bedside every week.

Around the corner is a Catholic church I have started to attend. When I miss you and the family, I go there. One of the church services is done in Spanish. I close my eyes, Nena, and pretend I'm back home. The church is also the place I go to when I think too much about José. It has been months, and I still think of him, the pain he was in—alone. My heart still aches.

My studies have gone well. My grades are respectable, so respectable in fact that I would share them with Papa if he were still here. Yes, they are that good.

I have become friendly with one of my classmates. His name is Dedrick Kline, a German who loves his beer and to have a good time. The beer he introduced me to is almost as good as ours—almost. Really, many of the men in my program are friendly. There is only a handful who cause me some discomfort. I do my best to ignore them. If only they would do the same.

I'm on a path I know I should be on, Sister, as you too seem to be. Be well.

Yours in earnest,

Ricardo

## JOURNAL ENTRY
May 1, 1922

Who would have guessed scaling the City Hall Tower to watch a sunset would lead to such revelations about Dedrick, about Rufin, and about me. Dedrick and I had planned to take the tour of the tower for months. Far above all the other buildings in downtown, he always told me, it gave the best views of Milwaukee. I had doubts.

The hike up to the top surely wasn't easy. First a spiral staircase and then steep iron steps with no railing. We could have done what most people did and stop at the observation platform, but Dedrick pushed us further up another spiral staircase, "to reach the bell," he said. By this time, I wanted to call the whole thing off, but once we got to the top, I knew Dedrick was right. Both Milwaukee and Lake Michigan were splayed below us, although I didn't need to know we were over thirty-four floors above it all. With his admission, I recall holding my breath for some time, or was it the view?

To the left, we could see most of downtown with all of the department stores and shops outlined by Milwaukee's' smokestacks. To the right was the lake peppered with fisherman's boats returning with their day's catch. I don't know how long we sat there, most of the time by ourselves, save another one or two brave souls who also made the climb. Our conversation made the view even better.

"Ricardo, how are you? You've been more quiet than usual. Are you all right?"

So he noticed: I was quieter, lost in thought more often. Sometimes I found nothing to say. I had wanted to tell him about Rufin's cross burning and José, but also I didn't. School was an escape. So was he. Would he want to be my friend if he knew how others felt about me?

"I guess you're right about how quiet I am sometimes. I have been troubled by too much and haven't wanted to talk." I paused. I didn't know if what I said was true about not wanting to talk.

"Does it have something to do with Rufin and his shenanigans?"

"Why do you ask that?" I asked a bit too quickly shooting him a look, which probably told him he was right.

"Well, because about a week or so after he challenged you in front of the class, he talked to me about you."

"What do you mean? What did he say?"

"I wasn't going to tell you, but then I heard about the cross in your yard ..."

"You heard about that? Who told you? I didn't think anyone knew."

"Everyone knew, Ricardo. They, like me, didn't know what to say. They felt bad for you, but I had to say something. They didn't have the conversation I had with Rufin."

"What did he say?"

I was suddenly cold. I pulled up my coat collar and tucked my hands deeper in my pockets. I braced myself for Dedrick's answer.

"He told me to stay away from you, that you were not a worthy classmate. As he put it, 'None of them are.'" Dedrick stopped and looked at me. "You know I don't believe you are unworthy or I would never tell you." I was so deep into my own thoughts, I didn't answer.

"Ricardo, you do believe me, don't you?"

"I'm sorry, Dedrick. Yes, I do. What you say about Rufin only confirms to me what I feared: It was him who placed the burning cross on my lawn."

"I'm the one who is sorry because look how many months it's taken for me to bring this up with you. He actually tried to convince me not only to disown you but to join them. To think he will be a doctor someday."

"Well, he doesn't want me to be one."

Dedrick laughed. "You'll be ten times the doctor he is."

"I will." I paused to look out at this city I've come to know and like, in part because of the man next me. "Dedrick, do you know what it feels like when someone tells you to leave? He once whispered those words to me after class. 'Go home,' he said. 'You don't belong here.'"

As I said this, I felt heavy, old, and so very tired. My words hung in the air.

"I do know a little about being thought unworthy, less of a man as you put it. Being German, after all, although there are many of us here in Milwaukee, hasn't been a picnic in the park for the past four years." I looked at him first in disbelief and then slowly began to grasp what he said. I'd forgotten he was German.

"At first, we couldn't believe people thought we would bring the war to Milwaukee. I think some even thought we would attack them. I had friends who were told by their parents they couldn't be friends with me any longer. Some families changed their names to sound Polish or English. We went from being well liked—you know, the people you wanted to be with—to their enemy."

Memories of Chicago came flooding in: raw and unfiltered. Mr. Schmidt hanging his head rather than giving his usual good morning, his son no longer seen. Soon they were all gone, moved away in the night.

"I watched the same thing happen in Chicago." I said. "You do know what it feels like to be separated out and not trusted."

I looked out over the city again, and even though it wasn't cold out, I couldn't get warm. One by one, the buildings emerged from the growing darkness. Street lamps cast shadows as people hurried home to loved ones, families. I ached for my own.

"Only imagine, Dedrick, if you had no family to go home to, no one to talk to about the injustice. Letters and telegrams are all I have."

I knew I had said too much, but once started, I couldn't stop.

"The closest Filipino friend I had here killed himself. There are no other Filipinos in Milwaukee. I think I might be the only one."

We sat in silence for some time.

"It isn't the same. You're right," he whispered. "But I remember thinking it would never change, that no one would ever want to be my friend. I worried we may move and would always need to live separately."

He grabbed my arm. "The Ku Klux Klan are hundreds, maybe a thousand foolish men. They aren't everyone, and most people think them crazy. They do what they do in the dead of the night, hiding behind masks and sheets because they are afraid to let people know who they are."

I looked into his face, that kind freckled face I had come to appreciate. "Maybe you're right."

He took his hand away and patted me on the back. The sun had completely disappeared. Streetlights lining the downtown gave a crisscrossed pattern like a fisherman's net. To the right, Lake Michigan had disappeared.

"How many Germans are there in Milwaukee?" I finally asked.

"Thousands and thousands, I'm told. Now with Prohibition, everyone wants to be our friend."

We both laughed. Milwaukee had hardly given up drinking. Only last week, the mayor had called Prohibition a big joke. "If someone wanted to find a drink, a drink can always be found."

"How about we go get some of that good ole' German hospitality?" Dedrick asked. I chuckle now to think how quickly I said yes. We flew down the spiral stairs like we were trained athletes. We found the hospitality we were looking for at another secret speakeasy Dedrick knew of where the brew was fresh and cold. One thing I didn't share with him was the question I carried with me day and night: Should I stay here or go home? Tita Carmen's suggestion had crept into my daily consciousness, right next to José.

**Note to Jaime**
June 22, 1922

Jaime,

Finally, I have a day without looming deadlines. I thought of you immediately. Thank you for your suggestions. I did move and now live in a household for medical students. Mrs. Sterling the proprietor dotes on each of us. I continue to be harassed by Rufin, my fellow medical student, but nothing as looming as the cross-burning incident. I caught him following me home again, so this time I turned around and returned to the university to study in the library. In the classes we are in together, he now leaves me alone, but outside of class, any chance he can get, he and his gang try to cause trouble for me. Most often I am with others who help me ignore him, though.

Tell me, how is Edgar? How are you as his parents? I try to imagine the two of you and can only smile. Perhaps you'll find a free day to visit. I would truly enjoy seeing you and meeting Edgar. My very best to you both.

Fondly,
Ricardo

## Letter to Nena
July 15, 1922

Nena,

How often I intend to write to you of my events only to find at day's end I haven't written a thing. I tell you this so you at least know I have good intentions and do think of you. I assume your days and evenings are as full as mine with your busy household. When you can, do send me pictures.

Today, I was inducted into the Pi Beta Phi fraternity, a fraternity for medical students here at Marquette. My friend Dedrick is a member and encouraged me to apply. Turns out I'm the first Filipino to be accepted, and actually the first from another country. To show my appreciation, I purchased a Victrola. I presented it to them today at the ceremony.

"Ricardo, the gift is wonderful! Cheers to our new brother!" the president of the chapter said.

Everyone in the room broke into applause. A couple of my new brothers said they had never seen a Victrola, so I put on a record, and soon music and laughter filled the room. To be welcomed by a fraternity of medical students is something I'll hold dear for the rest of my life.

I've not told you much about Dedrick. Or if I have, I'm sure I haven't told you enough. He is from Milwaukee, from a large clan like ours—all Germans settled in the area a generation ago. He reminds me of Mario, not in looks but in personality. He's tall, a good five inches taller than me, with freckles and golden blond hair. Like Mario, one minute he can be serious and sincere, and the next you're not quite sure what he might say. Sometimes he throws in a word or phrase only to see if I'm paying attention or not. Today when we were on our way to the induction ceremony he said, "Do you have underclothes on? I might have forgot to tell you it's a requirement to show them at this event." I looked at him as we both fell into laughter.

He has shown me the German side of Milwaukee, which of course involves sampling homemade brews. Germans do love their beer. I've discovered that I do, too. I hope you meet him someday. I think he would get you to laugh about the silliest of things.

There are still those in the medical world that don't appreciate me here. One was at the ceremony today. I had heard he was the one dissenting vote to let me join. He stood in the background with his arms crossed. He never smiled or laughed with the others, and after the Victrola was unveiled, he left.

Someday I will tell you more about him, but not today. Today I'm happy. Today his voice was drowned out, and kindness prevailed. Today I belong.

Warm regards to Vicente, prayers to you and your blessed children always,

Ricardo

## Letter from Jaime
August 27, 1922

My dear friend,

I'm glad to hear no further incidents have occurred and of your move as well. Esperanza would like nothing more than to take a train ride to visit, but this may take us some time to do. Life with a three-year-old has been overflowing and full of surprises.

Edgar was born healthy, his first year a time of long dizzying days. I went to work, ready to turn around and come home as quickly as I could. Esperanza, a mother more marvelous than I can describe, would always greet me at the door, usually looking like the day was anything but restful but would still be aglow even though he had kept her busy all day long. Refusing to take naps, he would rather be entertained.

But I didn't know how tired we would be. We don't go to bed, Ricardo; we shuffle, we stumble, and we sometimes are barely able to walk to our bedroom. We may be the oldest parents in our neighborhood, but we miss nothing. This little boy is our constant, and somehow or another, we have remained specimens of patience.

When Edgar turned two his health turned as well. One day he was walking, and the next he'd rather sit. I would ask him, "Edgar, does anything hurt?" He would shake his head back and forth, but then he would take naps three to four hours long. This went on for several days, and on the third morning, his neck was swollen. As you can imagine, we panicked and rushed to Saint Agnes Hospital. With your experience there, we thought it the best choice.

A doctor who had only been there for a year or so saw us. He immediately knew what needed to be done. He asked Edgar to open his mouth as wide as he could, which brought tears the size of raindrops but showed him what he needed to see: a thick grayish white mass deep in his throat. He told us Edgar had a bacterial infection called diphtheria. We had heard there was a disease killing people, healthy people— men, women, and especially children. Esperanza who had Edgar on her lap began to cry. She wasn't alone. I couldn't imagine life without Edgar.

The doctor told us that recently a new vaccine was made available showing positive results. We didn't hesitate to have him give it to Edgar. He stayed in the hospital for several days, but we eventually got our bundle of energy back. If we hadn't gone to St. Agnes where they were using this new vaccine, we may have lost Edgar. Others we know went elsewhere and were not given the option. Some came home. Others didn't. Oh, and while we were at St. Agnes, we inquired about the doctor who helped you, Dr. Webster. We learned he was still there but will soon retire.

I knew your studies were important but now, after all we've been through, I think you couldn't do anything more valuable. Wherever you end up living, the people living there will be glad to have you.

We are so very thankful you sent your correspondence and you are well. You know you are always welcome here. Come meet our impressive little boy. We would like him to know you as we do.

Warmest regards,

Jaime and Esperanza (who at this moment chases after Edgar giggling in delight)

### TELEGRAM TO JAIME AND ESPERANZA
September 8, 1922

WONDERFUL TO RECEIVE LETTER. THANK GOD EDGAR RECOVERED FROM DIPHTHERIA. THERE ARE GOOD DOCTORS. HOPE TO BE ONE SOMEDAY. WILL TRY TO VISIT SOON. Ricardo

### *Letter to Tita Carmen*
September 14, 1922

Tita Carmen,

I appreciate you concern about my welfare. I do wonder what I may do at the end of my studies. At one time, the end seemed far away. Now in less than a year, being a doctor will become a reality.

I know our correspondence has always focused on the problems I've encountered. Never have I written to you of anything trivial. No, I reserve only the monumental for you, my friend. Before I plunge into my latest concern, I want you to know how much I appreciate your unwavering guidance.

Three weeks ago, I started an internship at the Mount Sinai Hospital near the university here in Milwaukee. Most days, I jump out of bed ready to be at the hospital and meet the patients.

This week, however, I started to feel something I haven't felt since my first failed attempt at medical school. My heart races, I start to perspire, and I can't focus. I feel like I'm in a tunnel growing narrower every step I take. I felt this way when I tried to talk with my professor in Champaign-Urbana, struggling to understand the principles of chemistry, really trying to understand the information that flew out of his mouth. Especially when he became irate when I didn't understand what he said, I think I sort of froze on the inside and overheated on the outside. I couldn't reason. I couldn't take in what he said.

Since then, I have had varying degrees of success working through it. Up until this week, it only happened a couple of times at the hospital, and both times I wasn't seeing a patient. Today, however, I wasn't prepared at all. I was in the middle of a conversation with a young boy, helping him calm down. Not surprising, there he was lying in a strange bed with instruments all around him. His eyes darted from me to the nurse, and he clung onto the bedsheet as if it was his lifeline. He father stood several feet away. I was surprised he wasn't at his son's side, but I've learned people have different ways of dealing with stress. Perhaps, I thought, he thinks he will be in the way if he comes closer to calm his son down.

I asked the boy if he wanted to listen to his heartbeat. His eyes widened with surprise, and he immediately stopped fidgeting. His father had said the boy was six years old, but he looked smaller: thin and pale as if sunlight had not been a part of his life for some time.

"I could listen to my heart?" he said, pushing himself up so he could sit.

Suddenly, his father stepped forward. He extended his arm to prevent me from placing my laparoscope over his son's ears.

"That's enough," he said. "Where is the other doctor?"

"Sir, he was called to another patient," I said as calmly as I could. "He asked me to examine your son and ..."

"Get the other doctor."

Tita, my heart began to beat faster. I knew what was about to happen. I stepped back and motioned the man to a corner of the room away from the bed.

"I think you know what the problem is. Get the other doctor before I make a bloody scene you won't forget." His fists were clenched, and I didn't doubt for a minute he would follow through on his threat. "They may have let you into this country, but I don't have to let you treat my son."

A light spray of spit landed on my face. At that moment, I was there physically but mentally somewhere else—in the tunnel with little light or air. He may have said more, but I turned away and immediately went to find Dr. Winhold. I could barely get out what the father had said without completely being swallowed in my tunnel. Dr. Winhold's response was more than I had hoped for, helping me stop the spinning I was beginning to feel.

"This will happen from time to time, Mr. Alvarez. He's probably never seen a Filipino before. Some people haven't accepted Italians, and they've been here for twenty some years."

He asked me to finish bandaging his patient. He looked at her, she nodded, and he skirted away to deal with my patient. All I could think was, *I hope change will come sooner than twenty years* as I managed to introduce myself to his patient.

But Tita, as I reflect on what happened this morning, I can't help but ask when? When will people stop being afraid of someone who looks different? Who sounds different? Will it take years or—as Dr. Winhold implied— decades? Why can't they imagine what it feels like to see disdain, to feel it deep down, that aching that tells you they don't want you near them? They don't trust you.

I know if I stay here, I will need to learn to accept that not everyone will be comfortable with me. In my head, I know this, but in my heart, I still struggle to accept it. I hope for so much more—that my color, my accent, my differences won't matter. How simple. Such a simple idea, to see beyond small differences yet seemingly impossible for some to grasp.

I don't expect you to have the answers, but to write to you helps immensely. Prayers to you, dear Tita. Do write to me of your family affairs, I know too little.

Ricardo

## Letter from Nena
October 21, 1922

My dearest Brother,

How nice once again to be hearing of your many escapades, especially when I know you are happy. You are a fraternity brother with a German friend who enjoys your company. I believe you have become an American. So there are those that stand in the background and frown, but they are nothing more than that, individuals who are in the shadows of many other people.

But of course, you would award the fraternity with a Victrola. You have always been a man of music. Is there such a thing as a dancing doctor? If so, I am sure you should sign up right away.

When I received your letter, we were in our hottest season—you know those days when fanning yourself was the task of the day. Do you recall when we were children we begged Mama and Papa to take us to Lake Taal so we could play in its cool water? We went there several weeks ago, and I was flooded with childhood memories. How Mama loved to spend time with us in the water, even when we splashed and threw things at each other while she searched for shaded areas so we wouldn't become too dark. How she worked to keep us out of the sun. Sitting on the shoreline, Papa would move along with us, looking up to see how far away we had traveled. He always seemed to have something to read in hand.

Our time with Pina and Mario at the lake is much the same, only I don't try as hard to find shade. Instead, I clothe them in long sleeves to which they loudly protest. Vicente, too, joins us for a time in the water, as I'm sure you would if you were here.

I do think of you, Brother, but as you guessed, my days are full with these two disorderly children. I can't recall either of us being this way. If it is not me they call after, it is Eleanora, my new live-in housekeeper and helper. I know I would be lost without her by my side. By the end of the day, she looks even more exhausted than me.

Vicente, like our papa, is often gone late into the evening, and I continue to be much too involved with the church. At the church, they still speak of Lola Brigida. Some think she is a saint for all she gave and did for them. I do less than she did, but what I do, I know is appreciated.

Ricardo, write again. Write more often as you used to. Your letters remind me you are still there thinking of us. Stay positive, Brother. Can you not still hear Father? He would tell you to keep your head held high and at the same time tell you to be the best man you can be. I know you are. His pride shines down on you.

Your devoted sister,
Nena

### JOURNAL ENTRY
December 4, 1922

Last night's dream made me wish this Christmas Eve I could be at Nena and Vicente's for midnight supper. I was never good at making all eight Masses the week leading up to Christmas Eve. In the dream, as it was in real life, Uncle Vince wasn't happy about that.

"You boys show up for maybe two of the services the past week and think you'll be rewarded with this feast like the rest of us loyal parishioners? I think not."

"No, they can hardly think this, but we are Christians, so perhaps we should allow them to partake in the feast we are about to have. What do you say, Vicente? After all, it is your home," Uncle Carlito added.

"How devilishly heathen of them," Vicente said with a twinkle in his eye, looking at the sizeable group of young and unmarried men.

"I think it best we feed them, or who knows what might happen? But us devotees will serve ourselves first." He walked by me and whispered,

"They think I, too, made all of the Masses, but let's not let them know otherwise."

"I'd never think of it," I whispered back.

The feast was exactly that. Plates of all sizes filled with my favorites: queso de bola, tsokalate, noodles and pasta, pandesal, relleno, ham, with platters of fruit of every kind, including mango slices as large as my hand.

In the dream, I ate until my stomach started to complain. I walked away from the tables of food and found a place to sit near Fredrico, a cousin I hadn't seen for some time. He wanted to know how my studies in Manila were going. I told him well, but I wanted more, something I haven't experienced. I was tired of the big and noisy city full of people. I asked him about what he was doing. He said that he was planning a coup against the government. We both laughed because, like me, he didn't know what he wanted.

I looked out over the room, and I could feel my heartbeat slow down. My sister stood by her husband and glowed. She caught me looking at her and made a face so silly I laughed out loud, as did she. Everyone was in conversation, giving toasts to each other and to the year ahead. My heart felt full.

I woke up feeling blanketed by family. Alone.

I miss them. I miss them all.

# 1923

## Letter to Nena
### January 2, 1923

My dearest Nena,

It is a new year, and I send the best of wishes for a happy and prosperous year ahead. I trust your Christmas was filled with family, food, church, and your two children. How easy it is for me to picture you wrapped up in all of the holiday doings, your children and Vincente beaming at you. How I wish I could have been a part of your celebrations.

Perhaps I will soon.

Winter's wrath is upon us again. With the lake so nearby, wind is ever present, sometimes blinding you with snow, other times with tiny particles of ice. My daily ploy is to run from building to building in search of a warm fire to sit by. This probably sounds absurd as you deal with unbearable heat. Sometimes I think it absurd as well.

You'll be happy to know I no longer spend every night indoors, locked away from the blasts of cold in wait for spring. I venture out with a handful of friends who encourage me to do so. Several nights ago, however, I needed to be convinced.

"Ricardo, join us. We'll come and get you, for heaven's sake. We'll have a jolly good time. Antonio is taking us to his uncle's nightclub on Detroit Street," Paul said.

"Yeah, come on," Jonathon added. "They have a show that's supposed to be the best, and there'll be dancing. You tell us you're a good dancer. Let's see it!"

I knew they would only continue on until I said yes, so to stop it from going any further, I said all right, "but if I go and there's a dance floor, you'll join me!"

I knew a couple of them weren't keen to dance and said it half-kidding.

The place we went to was The Monte Carlo, usually a place only Italians frequent, but Antonio asked if he could bring some of his doctor friends. When we arrived, we all had doubts. From the outside, it looked like a condemned warehouse. "To keep the police away" is what Antonio told us as we were about to enter. The last thing any of us needed was to be hauled in drunk to the police station as a "wet."

"Forgetaboutit," Antonio said. "The Monte Carlo has a system alerting them when the police are on their way, and everything is put away. No worries."

Once inside, we did forget. The place was packed with people, almost all Italians who looked like they didn't have a care in the world. The favorite drink was raisin wine that turned out to be drinkable, and better yet, there was a jazz band perfect for dancing.

So, of course, Sister, I did dance. Young Italian women were more than willing. I danced, but not too much to avoid upsetting the many Italian men who watched—still enough to put a permanent grin on my face.

"Well, jumping jackknives, you really do know how to dance, don't you?" said one of my non-dancing friends who I could not convince to give it a try.

"Where'd you learn how to do that anyway?"

"In the Philippines, everyone dances as much as we can."

"Well, dang it all, you might have to teach me a step or two. Those girls like it."

Sister, I flashed on the two women I've known since the start of this journey. Only two. One now married and the other, Margaret, I've lost touch with when she announced she had a special someone. Even when I was in Philadelphia and Virginia, not far from her, I let her go. I fear she would have been a distraction from what was most important: medical school. How far I've come, though, now out with friends at an Italian nightclub.

We laughed and drank a lot that night, oohing and awing about the entertainment, the place, the lovely girls. Later in the evening, I'm not sure what we drank, but after several rounds, it didn't matter. We even played a few friendly hands of cards far into the night. Times like this make me think I belong. Next month, I meet with the head of the medical school to discuss my future. I know you want me to come home. I think of it, I do. Right now, though, studies and the hospital demand my attention. Time to bundle up and make my way to the hospital.

Warmest regards,

Your brother, Ricardo

## *Letter from Tita Carmen*
### January 15, 1923

My dear boy,

Once again, I have found myself in a state of anger. Anger and disbelief at the level of rudeness you have had to face. Your story of the father and his son in the hospital, who you were simply trying to help, makes my blood curse through my veins. My body shakes in disgust when I think of you being talked to in such a fashion. I can't quite grasp the lack of civility you speak of.

The Americans I have encountered here seem refined. As you can imagine, more and more Americans continue to be placed in positions of authority on all levels in government. Given our family's involvement in local affairs, we are often invited to one of their social events. Father would request I attend, I think, in hopes of finding me a suitor, but he never admitted it. I accept, being the good daughter that I am. And since his passing, God bless his soul, I continue on.

Most often, they are quite delightful. Usually, I find myself having polite conversation with one of the many officials' wives, more often now in English (yes, I have worked to improve my skills in this area as well). Different than what you describe, the women are polite and congenial, but perhaps they are of a particular class that has been raised to be so.

In the hospitals there, I imagine you must take care of all kinds of people. I only wish you wouldn't have to be battered by them. The tunnel you speak of sounds like the only plausible way for you to escape what you must feel, your private place to escape the situation. But Ricardo, you know staying present and calm is best for you and your patients. I pray you find a way to rise above the situation. I like your fellow doctor who tells you it will change. It must. They simply don't know there is world of people different than themselves.

Yes, there has been considerable time since our last correspondence. You mustn't concern yourself. I know you have been hard at work, and time does have a way of disappearing.

I have little news to share. I remain without a partner, surrounded by my loving family. I am content—something I hope you find.

Your father, bless his soul, would be so very proud of what you are becoming. Come home soon.

Tita Carmen

### JOURNAL ENTRY
January 19, 1923

Rufin and his gang don't play by the rules of the Ku Klux Klan. No, Rufin likes an audience. Any opportunity he can find, he tries to shame me, even at a fraternity gathering I had planned with a special speaker we were all excited to hear. Rufin raised one question after another about club protocol. Fellow fraternity brothers chose to ignore him, even when he raised his voice. "Mr. Alvarez, why haven't you introduced the speaker you invited for tonight's program? How reprehensible." I didn't know what the word meant but knew it was an insult. The doctor I had invited had asked me not to introduce him and quickly spoke up.

"Young man," he said. "I hardly need an introduction. Most of the people in this room know me, as I'm sure you should. After all, I'm quoted in many of the textbooks you have supposedly read." Everyone laughed, including me.

Rufin turned at least two shades darker. His display of loathing—or what someone called "showing his power"—isn't working so well these days. I looked around to see a crowd around me, shaking my hand, telling me how much they liked the program. Some even mentioned how they liked seeing Rufin finally being put in his place. Rufin stood alone, looking noticeably uncomfortable. Could the winds be shifting? Maybe I simply have to continue to do what I do: remain calm and make the appearance I'm not upset. Can it be that simple?

How many times have I walked by my neighborhood pharmacy? Fifty times? One hundred? Today, I stopped. The pharmacist, an older man, his back permanently stooped from his many hours of mixing one thing or another, asked how he might assist me.

"Do you have something that might ease my aching neck that doesn't have alcohol or cocaine in it?" From my studies, I knew most remedies included one or both. Aspirin was the only thing he had.

As he wrapped the bottle in paper, I looked around. The place reminded me of my father's pharmacy in Santa Cruz. The only difference was in my father's pharmacia, men in white jackets stood ready to serve you. Here, the pharmacist was in street clothes, alone behind a long counter of cures.

Rows of concoctions in bottles of every shape and size were laid out as if this were a candy store. Some of the bottles had labels to entice like Dr. Miles Tonic, Fruitola, or St. Joseph's Laxative Syrup, as if a saint's name would encourage you to buy. Other bottled remedies took on a more serious tone: Heroin Hydrochloride, a sedative for the serious cough; Dr. Hobson's Nerve and Bone Liniment; or Swamp Root, a diuretic for the kidneys.

The mixtures were more advanced than my father's, but like his, they were potions invented to help ease pain. This was my father's world, a world I have entered without fully realizing what a similar path I chose. He wasn't a doctor, but in his time, he was regarded as the person who knew the most.

For a moment, I was back there in his shop, as he called it. Oh, how he loved to please every one of his customers. He knew them all—what they needed for their ailments, who their children were, what they should never take. Standing there in the pharmacy, blocks from where I live, I inhaled my memories. With closed eyes, I was there, my father steps away helping a customer make the right choices. I could hear my father asking Mrs. Pingahoy how her parents were, if they were able to move about given their advanced years. I could hear my father's voice, kind and consoling. I could smell what I always thought were traces of cinnamon, mixed with garlic and something woody. As a boy, I loved how the mixture tickled my nose. The aroma was my father, his shop. I breathed in the smell of his many concoctions, trying to hold on to that moment. My childhood, before I lost so much.

When the pharmacist handed me my package, I jumped and leapt back to where I was, wishing I could have stayed back with Papa a little longer.

※

## Letter to Jaime and Esperanza
March 12, 1923

My dear friends,

Again, months have gone by, and I haven't written. Please know I often think of you especially when I see a small boy chased by his father. I have been known to laugh out loud to the surprise of people near me. I must meet Edgar before he no longer sees the humor of you chasing him. I trust the three of you are well and, like me, wait with growing impatience for winter to surrender its blistering cold winds—although I no longer groan or sniffle as much about these winter months … well, not like I did the first several years. I know you remember, as you often witnessed my behaviors firsthand.

Next week, I meet with the medical director to discuss my future. I have been exposed to many different areas of medicine and will need to make decisions regarding what I want to do, as well as where I would do my residency.

The science of medicine is changing rapidly, and it seems like every day we learn of new discoveries. This past week, we were instructed about a new drug that will help people with diabetes live better and longer lives, a concoction discovered by testing dogs, of all things. The discovery is quite miraculous. With this new medicine, people won't waste away from an imbalance of sugar in their blood, but will be able to live quite normally. I'll stop now, as I am sure my medical ramblings can easily bore. I may have fought the idea of being a student when I lived with you, but now I may be one the rest of my life, all to be the better doctor.

Jaime, I still deal with the fellow medical student who seems to loathe my every move. One night, I was walking home and got the feeling like someone was watching me. You know … when you get a sort of a prickly feeling that starts at the base of you back and flies up to your neck. I readied myself for an attack but then thought better. Instead, I turned a corner and waited, hiding behind some overgrowth. Sure enough, there he was. He didn't see me and quickened his pace, thinking he'd lost me. In his hand was a club the size of a small tree. As he walked forward, he swung it to and fro.

This time, he apparently wanted to do me harm. I crept out and headed in the right direction. I'm realizing I can't change the way this man thinks, but I can stand up to him. The next morning in class, I walked up to him and told him I saw him following me. He immediately said, "I don't know what you're talking about," loud enough for his friends to hear. I quietly said, "Don't think about doing it again. Next time, I will tell others: the woman who runs our household and the other medical students I live with. Especially about the club you carried. Next time, everyone in this room will hear what I have to say."

He laughed and shoved his way past me, but you know what, Jaime? He looked uncomfortable. Good enough for me. Enough about him.

I graduate in June and then hope to have time to visit you. It may have taken me three different medical schools and six years, but I will soon be done with school and begin practicing. Seeing you and your family is something I look forward to.

Indebted with warm regards,
Ricardo

## JOURNAL ENTRY
March 26, 1923

Surgery is a bloody mess. I thought I would hate it, but I don't.

To be successful requires calm steady hands while being witness to a storm of pain. I'm drawn to its unpredictability. I think of my first time in a surgery. The act of cutting left me cold. I was dizzy and sickened. I can still picture the theater at Jefferson Medical. A single light bulb hung from the ceiling over a large wooden table covered with a white sheet. The walls were bare, and the floor spotless, the room designed only to be efficient to save a person's life.

An elderly man lay on top of the table, motionless except for his hands that quivered uncontrollably. He talked nonstop. The doctor told him to calm down, and asked the nurse to give him more Novocain. He allowed him one more sip of whiskey as well.

Every crevice in the man's face was filled with fear, his eyes were wild, and although it was cool in the room, he was covered with sweat. He looked from person to person imploringly, as much to say, "Please, is there no other way? How will I live without my leg?" He had injured it while plowing his fields; his horse bolted and ran him over. His leg had broken in several places with an open infected wound. The best answer was to amputate; the only way to ensure he survives, the doctor had said. The patient understood but was terrified regardless.

My job was to hold him down. He eventually passed out, which made the process to saw and sew him up much easier. We left a small opening to allow pustules a place to escape and freely applied alcohol to safeguard against infection. At least the patient didn't scream or become violent. The doctor had performed this surgery enough that he was quick and proficient.

Here at Marquette, surgeries seem more humane. The theater has more light, isn't as cold, and tools are within arm's reach. Doctors and nurses are more diligent in their attempts to minimize fear and pain. Both talk quietly to the person much longer before the surgery. Often the nurse joins them in prayer while holding their hand. I'm thankful to have witnessed people who are often in dire situations treated with such kindness. I think back to José losing his arm and wonder if he experienced the same kind of kindness. I don't imagine he did. I shudder to think of how much pain he endured, then and later.

I want to be a doctor who places kindness right next to proficiency. I want to not only be a doctor but a surgeon as well.

### Letter from Jaime
April 2, 1923

Friend,

Sometimes I'm simply staggered by the number of obstacles you've faced, all in effort to become a doctor. As to this latest one with Rufin, all options to address the situation are less than perfect.

I'm afraid I have little advice to give other than what I've suggested before—be cautious and courteous. Your confrontation with him seems bold to me, and yet I applaud you for speaking up. I would hate to think of you becoming comfortable with his antics. No, Ricardo, I hope you never become comfortable with the notion that others can treat you without respect.

Once you're a full-fledged doctor perhaps, color will matter less to others. Ricardo, don't underestimate your friendly nature and contagious full-face smile. Combined with your skills and knowledge, you'll not be mistaken for being stupid. You have shown you have a capacity to find people who support you. Remember, good people far outnumber bad. Continue to surround yourself with them.

With warm regards,

Jaime

### JOURNAL ENTRY
April 4, 1923

Jaime is right. Good people do far outnumber the bad. I have managed to collect a good number of friends here in Milwaukee, none of them

Filipino or Spanish. Yet all of them are kind and trustworthy. And like myself, they are all soon to be doctors. Why do I continue to think about going home? What would my father say? Would he tell me I have already made my decision, I simply haven't fully accepted it? Perhaps.

## Letter to Nena
### April 12, 1923

Dearest Sister,

Today I left Milwaukee and got to see more of Wisconsin with my friend Dedrick. Taking most of a day, we went by motorcar to pick up medical supplies in a small city named Marshfield, located somewhere in the middle of the state. Normally our supplies are delivered by train, but they were accidentally left behind, so we offered to pick them up.

Blue skies escorted us on our way, as well as cows who had little interest in getting out of the way. I can't count the number of times we used our voices and horn to convince them to move. Sometimes the roads were quite good; other times, I held on to my seat. Dedrick drove. He is the one who manages to see humor in almost everything, including pot holes the size of rickshaws that he enjoyed flying through at speeds Lola Brigida would faint over.

At one point, we needed to pull the car over and stop because tears filled our eyes we had laughed so hard, silly as I can't even recall what about. We were both giddy about our escape from the stresses of our last months of medical school. For a day, we were free.

When we quieted down, all I could think about was the unplanned automobile ride you and I took weeks prior to my voyage. Do you remember, Nena? We were in Manila, and it was a hot, windless day. The sun was hidden behind plumes of grayish-white clouds hanging low above the city. The possibility of rain lingered, pressing against our skin like a heavy wet blanket. The palm trees stood still as statues, and people moved as if their feet were stuck in mud. Do you remember how the streets of Manila reeked of slow-baked garbage, instead of the usual aromas of spicy foods and burning wood? You held your nose closed as we drove through the streets until you couldn't stand it any longer.

"Ricardo, let's get out of Manila to get some fresh air," you said.

"Disappear without telling others where we are going?" I didn't think it wise, but you were very convincing, so off we went. Whose auto had we borrowed anyway—Uncle Victor's?

When we finally reached country roads, we looked at each other and beamed as we could finally see the sky of deep blue that had been invisible in Manila. Roads usually clogged with horse carts, wagons, and autos were open. We flew down the road, like two caged birds set free.

Sister, do you remember how we drove and drove, often with no idea where we were? It didn't matter; we were happy to be free to go where we pleased. Thank you, Nena. This memory I hold dearly.

My ride today wasn't quite as pleasurable, but it came close. Dedrick drove most of the way. I kept commenting about the hills of green, some covered with towering pines, others barren. "Ready for planting," Dedrick said. When we reached rock croppings that shot out of nowhere and I had to know all about them, he stopped the motorcar.

"Well, I'm not sure, but I think millions of years ago, all of this was underwater." I started to ask another question, but he held up his hand.

"You know, it's about time you tell me more about where you come from. You talk of banana plantations, rice paddies, and sand beach islands upon islands? Sure isn't what we have here. And you can drive."

As I drove, I told him about our island, Luzon. How not only are there rice fields in the north but mountainous jungles in the south, followed by beaches that people live on. I told him how I never had been to the thousands of islands called the Philippines, but what I knew was there were many different dialects depending upon where you lived. He was baffled by that. I enjoyed trying to describe all that is unique about the Philippines, but in the end, he concluded the only way he would ever be able to imagine it would be to go there. I told him he must come with me so he could meet my family. I also suggested I teach him some Spanish and Tagalog, telling him he's a fast learner so it would be no problem.

Sister, you would have thought I'd suggested he cross the ocean in a rowboat. He snorted, as I once again tried to teach him a few words with little success.

"How do you do it?" he said, "I mean, you haven't seen your family now in how many years?"

"Almost seven," I said. "I try not to think about how long it's been. I still picture them the way they looked when I left, and yet I know how much I have changed. I'm sure they've changed as well. My sister has had two children I've never met."

I pulled off the road to look at a small lake we were passing by. The shoreline was filled with people. Some were in boats, others meandered along paths not far from the water's edge. They looked content, like they wouldn't want to be anywhere else in the world. I thought of you, Nena, knowing you could very well be picnicking with your children a world away.

"I miss them," I whispered.

"I bet they miss you as well. Do you think about going back?"

"More now than ever. I'm torn. Go home, or is my home now here?"

I hadn't said this out loud to anyone, and the words sounded odd to me. I wanted to take them back, pretend I didn't say them. Their reality was too harsh even for my own ears. We were both silent for a long time. There wasn't anything that could have been said. We both knew it. I had a decision to make, plain and simple.

I hope whatever I decide, you will accept. Whatever I decide, I promise we will see each other.

With warmest regards always,

Ricardo

### JOURNAL ENTRY
April 23, 1923

Today I had the dreaded meeting with Dr. Wilber to find out where I was going to be placed for my internship and residency. This morning, when I came down for breakfast, Mrs. Sterling knew instantly what was going on.

"Ricardo, you have your meeting today, don't you?"

"What?" I said. "You can tell?"

"Well, sometimes it's hard for me to know, but son, you have the look of a man either going to his execution or wedding. Goodness, have you had yourself some coffee yet?"

"Um, no. I thought it might not be a good idea. Not sure about food either," I said.

"Sit down. I am going to get you both. For heaven sakes, I know Dr. Wilbur. And I've seen quite a few students like yourself come back from the meeting you are about to have happy and relieved." She could see I wasn't convinced.

"He's done his homework about what you want, and nothing is engraved in stone. He wants you to be happy with the decisions."

I heard what she said, but she didn't know one of the options I was considering was to return to the Philippines for my final steps to become a physician. Still unable to decide where my home should be. She brought me a heaping plate of eggs and potatoes, and I gobbled them down.

I could breathe again.

She was right about Dr. Wilbur. He was there to steer me in the right direction. For such a short man with easily the widest smile I've ever seen, he also had a commandingly serious side that made you afraid you'd said something wrong. I bounced between being relaxed and nervous as a cat on a hot tin roof.

"Ricardo, I've been hearing such good things about you. Your professors think you're quite capable." Looking up at me, he added, "A person with great tenacity."

"Thank you, sir. I have enjoyed my studies immensely. They have all been excellent instructors—the professors, I mean."

"So, tell me, what kind of internship would you like to have? I have suggestions, of course. With your grades, you do have some choice."

"Well, I am very curious about additional experience in the field of surgery, although I want to do general practice as well. You know, some kind of family practice."

"What I've heard is you're not afraid of adversity and work hard to develop rapport with patients, no matter the circumstances."

I nodded but couldn't stop from wondering if he knew. Had he heard of Rufin's continual challenges? The incident with the cross? Or the patients who have struggled to have me as their doctor? To hear his compliment, it didn't matter.

Maybe I am better prepared to deal with difficulties, with people who would rather spit on me than have me touch their loved one, who'd rather walk out than deal with a person who looks and sounds different from them. I've come to accept those who struggle with who I am, what I look like, what I sound like, and no longer lose myself or even feel much anger anymore. Papa would say I'm forgiving them. Not yet, Papa, not yet. I hope to someday, but for now I accept and continue on.

For the rest of the meeting, I relaxed. He heard me about my interest in surgery and said he would place me accordingly. Same with the residency, adding he could see me in a larger city. I agreed and never thought to bring up the idea of anything else.

### TELEGRAM TO JAIME & ESPERANZA
May 16, 1923

DEAREST FRIENDS, BE MY GUESTS AT MY GRADUATION CEREMONY ON JUNE 10. THEN TO MRS. STERLING'S HOUSE FOR FOOD DELIGHTS. Ricardo

### TELEGRAM FROM JAIME
May 21, 1923

RICARDO, WISH WE COULD. REGRETTABLY CANNOT. MUST ATTEND SALVADORE'S BAPTISM. A BABY GIRL. CONGRATULATIONS. WE WILL CELEBRATE WITH YOU SOON AFTER. Jaime

## TELEGRAM TO JAIME
May 24, 1923

I UNDERSTAND. WILL MISS YOUR EXUBERANCE. WILL TAKE TRAIN TO VISIT IN SEVERAL WEEKS. HAVE OTHER NEWS TO SHARE. Ricardo

## JOURNAL ENTRY
June 9, 1923

I woke up this morning, and my heart immediately started beating faster. Today is the day I graduate and go forward as a medical intern and resident. Now my classroom will be completely in the hospital. How often I have doubted myself, wondered if I would ever reach this day. By the grace of God, I prevailed.

All of my classmates will have family and friends at the ceremony this afternoon. No one will be in the audience for me. Last night, my fellow fraternity brothers asked what my plans were to celebrate. I didn't want to tell them I would be returning to my boarding home to dine with Mrs. Sterling—alone, but I ended up spilling the beans. The invitations I got were kind. Antonio's offer to stop by his family's restaurant where they were going to celebrate and Derrick's insistence for me to come home with him. "You've met my family. They would welcome you," he said. To be with his family and friends would only make me miss my own. Instead, I told him Mrs. Sterling promised she would have something special for me at her home. "I wouldn't want to disappoint her," I said.

How I wish there would be people, my people, here to help me celebrate. Surrounded by those who know me, who know about this journey I've been on, who would shake my hand and be happy for me. Is this what I lost along the way?

## Letter to Nena
June 11, 1923

Dearest Sister,

If I had known better, I would have thought you had your hands in yesterday's events. Turns out, Esperanza has a similar trait to you. She loves to surprise people who think surprises are impossible. I am even more convinced you two would become best of friends.

Let me start at the beginning, the beginning of my day that is. I admit I was sad there would be no one in the audience to witness my receipt of a medical degree. I'm sure I looked like a man headed out to a funeral, not an important graduation ceremony where I knew at least a hundred or more would be in attendance.

For the thirty-five of us graduates, there was a sense of relief, all of us anxious to step out of the classroom into the hospital and excited about some recognition. As we sat on the stage, I became acutely aware of my aloneness. Everyone around me pointed to the people there in their honor. I studied the program. I tried my best to be happy. I visited with classmates but wished only to have the ceremony start and be done.

Dedrick chided me with his elbow to look up and see his family who were waving with their thumbs up. I grinned and flipped my thumb into position in response. Inside, I felt as if my stomach had attached itself to my heart, pounding my breakfast into tiny pieces. I wanted to somehow become invisible.

This is when I thought I heard a voice I knew, and then another. Three rows back from the stage, sitting close to Dedrick's family was a group of people I had never seen together before, and they were all waving at me. I thought I was in the middle of a dream, seeing friends who weren't there. But they were real, Nena, a whole group of them.

Dr. Webster stood and yelled for the entire room to hear, "Bravo, Ricardo! Bravo!" I wanted to run to him like a small boy to his father. Without him, I would not have made my way to that stage. Next to him were several of the nurses from Saint Agnes Hospital in Chicago. They were the ones who continually encouraged me to study to become a doctor and not worry about people who didn't want me to examine them. And next to them were several nurses from the nearby hospital where I was a medical student. Of course they would come, not only for me but several other men on stage.

What took my breath away were who sat in the middle of them all—Jaime, Esperanza, and their bouncing happy boy, Edgar. Edgar looked like a miniature Esperanza in Jaime's body.

They were all there for me, Nena.

"Ricardo, I thought you said no one would be here! Who are they all?" Dedrick asked.

"Friends," I said. "Some who I thought I had lost years ago. I want you to meet them all afterwards."

Dedrick smiled. "I wouldn't miss it."

My eyes began to water while my lips were placed in a permanent grin plastered across my face. To add to the surprise, there sat Mrs. Sterling, chatting away with Esperanza. Those two women had obviously been in cahoots.

The ceremony seemed to go on forever with the president of the medical school and professors who needed to share their wisdom with the captured audience. Finally, each of us was called to cross the stage to receive our diploma. When I stood to receive mine, my cheering crowd matched the volume of any other. Here I thought I would scurry across the stage with my head down, sure no one would lift their hands in applause. Instead, I walked deliberately, chest out with my head held high.

Afterwards, we all gathered at Mrs. Sterling's home for a wonderful mix of American and Filipino cuisine. Esperanza brought mouth-watering pieces of my homeland to me when I needed them the most. As I attacked another lumpia, I paused to drink in the room with all the people who chose to be there for me. Most were Americans; others were like me, hoping to become a permanent part of this country's fabric. The nurses from Saint Agnes Hospital wanted to know what I was going to do next.

"Come back to Chicago. We need Spanish-speaking doctors!" they said.

I remember those days: new immigrants unable to tell someone what they needed, the doctors and nurses who depended on my translations for anything remotely similar to Spanish. They were kind to want me back.

"I never doubted you, Ricardo, but it sure took some work to get you to do the same," Dr. Webster said while he helped himself to another serving of chicken adobe.

And Jaime and Esperanza. Oh, how I wish you could meet them. Although one or both of them spent much of their time chasing after Edgar, we managed to find time for a hug and quiet conversation.

"We hated to send the message we were unable to attend. We were afraid something might happen to have it come true," Esperanza shared.

"But we are here, and the look on your face, Ricardo, made it all worthwhile," Jaime chimed in.

"How did you find Dr. Webster?"

"Nurses know everything," Esperanza said with a wink.

They, like everyone else, wanted to know what my plans were. So, Sister, I told them what I want to tell you. I'll be leaving for an internship at Saint Francis Hospital in Peoria, Illinois, in a couple of weeks, and then I'll be doing a residency at Saint Mary's Hospital in Madison, Wisconsin. Both will be helping me explore surgery, which is something I'm excited about.

I had said to myself, if I can't find experience in the operating room, then perhaps I'd return to the Philippines. But even as I write this, I think I've always known my place is here, just as your place is there. You are doing exactly what you love, and so am I. How can we not be happy for each other?

I'll come to visit, Nena. I will. I will stay so long you'll want to be rid of me. And someday you'll visit me as well. I'll make sure of it.

Ricardo

Tularan ang tangkay ng palay, kapag dumarami

ang bunga, lalo siyang yumuyuko.

**Imitate the rice stalk: The more grains it bears, the lower it bows.**

Three Years Later
## PART SIX

# Garden of Eden

I'm sitting here in a state of shock. How did I let Dedrick talk me into leaving Madison tomorrow for a town I've never heard of? Maybe because he begged or maybe I simply wore out, I don't know. He certainly talked his head off until I couldn't take another word.

"Ricardo, it's a small town called Galesville, a town of about 800. Friendly, quaint and desperately in need of a second doctor."

"A village then," I said. "Where everyone knows each other."

"Yes, the town is small. The clinic is right in the center of town and steps from the city square where musicians play once a week and everyone gathers. Two blocks in the other direction is a lake enclosed by hills covered with trees. Locals call the town the Garden of Eden."

"Like in the Bible?"

"I suppose that's right."

I know I must have looked dazed. I hadn't once thought about the possibility of going to a small town to practice. Especially one called the Garden of Eden.

"Tell me again, what kind of medicine would I practice?" Before he could answer, I blurted out, "And where is this town?"

"You would practice all kinds. The clinic does everything from house calls to surgeries right at the clinic."

My mind began to race. I so liked the idea of continuing to do surgeries.

"The town is on the western side of the state, close to the Mississippi River. To go by motorcar would probably take around three and a half hours. By train, it would be several hours to La Crosse, where the hospital is that you would have access to for more complicated surgeries. Galesville a short drive further by motorcar."

I stood up. I needed to stretch my legs.

"Even if you go for six months, it would give them time to find someone else," he said.

I listened intently as he went on and on about how much they would appreciate me, and how thankful he would be as well. At first, I was intrigued only because I'd never seen Dedrick as passionate, begging me to change my plans to return to Peoria.

I thought he had given up when he started digging through his briefcase, mumbling to himself. I looked at my watch. It was past midnight. Lord, he arrived over six hours ago. I was about to say, "No more," when he handed me a postcard. "She's lovely, isn't she? They are in true need of another doctor, Ricardo. They really are. We can't let them down."

"We?" I said. I couldn't stomach much more of this. I didn't want to say yes, but by then, I knew it would be the only way to get rid of him. The picture did grab me. No skyscrapers, no tall buildings, no chimneys shooting out never-ending plumes of smoke. Instead, friendly brick buildings all connected to each other, with people strolling around an open structure I could imagine filled with musicians. This was the picture of America I had in my head before I arrived. I handed the picture back to him, trying not to show interest. He was right. Peoria would wait six months for me. I know they would.

"Like I said, Ricardo, I'll help you get done tomorrow what you need to get done. I'll go with you to the docs here and explain why it's important to leave right away. You won't be sorry. I know you won't. Dr. Powell, he's a good man ..."

"Enough," I said. "I'll go, but only for six months, and if the place is horrible, I'll leave sooner. You have to tell this to Dr. Powell before I go tomorrow."

His embrace, more like a bear hug without the claws, told me he was ecstatic.

What have I done?

## *Letter to Nena*
### June 6, 1926, Galesville, Wisconsin

Sister,

My plans have changed. I know I wrote about returning to Peoria, the place I interned at before coming to Madison. Well, I haven't. Instead I'm in a small town in Wisconsin, filling in for my friend Dedrick for the next six months at the town's clinic. The locals actually refer to it as "the Garden of Eden," like in the Bible. If you saw it, you might think it even possible, although the town's real name is Galesville.

Imagine crossing an ornate iron bridge to arrive in a town smaller than Santa Cruz. There are only about 800 people here. On the right, there is a swinging footpath that crosses over a river to a park bordered by cliffs. Drive a little further, and you are in the town's center with cobblestone streets surrounding a gazebo where musicians often entertain. Horse carts and automobiles line its border with storefronts forming a perfect square. People aren't rushing to and fro but greet each other as if they've known one another their whole lives, which they may very well have. Having lived only in larger cities for the past seven years, this place feels peaceful, like I've wondered into the American version of a Filipino village—although I don't have much time to enjoy the setting as I often work from dawn until nightfall.

The clinic is a short walk away from the apartment I've been provided, and the place never seems to be without people waiting to see the doctor—either me or Dr. Powell, who has been here for over twenty years. People don't seem troubled to wait. They lounge in the clinic's parlor, most chatting with each other or content to look at the local newspaper.

My first day was the worst. I arrived in the clinic, met Dr. Powell, and was handed Dr. Powell's keys as he ran next door to get someone to drive me to a nearby town. That's when I noticed the sign in the waiting room, "Emergencies Anytime." As I was soon to find out, the sign was accurate.

We left right away because a ten-year-old boy about nine miles away in Ettrick was near death from pneumonia. I didn't even need my stethoscope to hear the crackling sound in his lungs to confirm this, plus he was burning up with fever. I gave him aspirin, propped him up to help him breathe easier and had his mother boil water to place at his bedside. As I encouraged him to drink one glass of water after another, he started breathing easier. His mother's cousin couldn't stop thanking me.

I really like Dr. Powell, but he's asked me the same question three different times this first week.

"Tell me again where you are from."

"The Philippine Islands."

"Yes, yes, but where in the Philippine Islands?"

When I tell him, he shakes his head. "It might take people a little time to warm up to you. You're probably the first Filipino they've ever seen, but I think you being here is going to work out just fine."

I think about correcting him and saying that I'm a Filipino-Spaniard, but I let it go.

People here do look at me with caution. No Negroes or Mexicans live here, and I've no doubt I'm the first Filipino-Spaniard they've ever seen. To me, the townspeople look like the people I treated in Madison—fair-skinned and well groomed, but their dress is simpler and less formal. Most of the men look accustomed to physical labor, and the women, regardless of their age, are a mix of blond- and dark-haired beauties.

Today, I explored the swinging bridge and discovered it really does swing. As I stood gripping onto the rope swaying back and forth, I realized how easily I was breathing. I wasn't nervous or worried. I was conscious of everything around me. The river below flowed downstream over rocks, over logs long ago swallowed by the current. Birds were everywhere, with coats of brown, blue, and yellow flying back and forth, singing tunes unfamiliar to me. I breathed in the country fresh air. I felt full, content, something I haven't felt for such a long time.

Down deep, Sister, there is something alluring about this village. Perhaps this little town too could swallow me up.

Prayers to you, Sister,

Ricardo

## *Letter from Mr. Severson-hand-delivered*
June 7, 1926

Dr. Powell,

I'm writing this letter even though my wife tells me I'm sticking my nose in somebody else's business. I guess that would be your business. But you know me. How long have my family and me been coming to you? I think some twenty years. You, more than most, know I have a hard time keeping my mouth shut about things I think important.

So, I'll get to the point. A couple of days ago, I guess on Monday, I offered to take the wife to town since I had gotten the fields plowed, ready for planting. I stopped by your office to pay my bill, and what do I see but a man, a doctor they tell me, darker than I've set eyes on before, coming out of your office? It didn't take me long to figure out you done brought him on in your clinic. It better not mean you're planning on going somewhere, or I'll have a lot to say about that for sure.

This new doctor is the talk of the town. Most everyone thinks he's a friendly sort of fellow but don't know where he comes from (well, along with some other things you might not appreciate hearing).

I'm writing because there's a group of us who would like to meet him so we can answer some of the questions folks are having.

You know I throw out the idea only to be useful. I'm going to be in town again in a couple of days and will stop by to see what you think. I'd be happy to pull some of us together if you think it's a good idea.

Thanks, Doc.

Ralph Severson

## JOURNAL ENTRY
June 9, 1926

He told me not to worry, that the meeting would be in his office and last no more than half hour. When I asked how many people he was talking about, he said a handful, maybe a dozen at most. I was not reassured. When I walked in the room, I knew I would be there for more than a half hour. There sat five men and one woman. I didn't recognize any of them. They sat in a circle around Dr. Powell's overflowing desk. Across from them was a metal chair pulled out from my small office, my designated place to sit facing them all.

They came ready with questions, most about where I was from and why I wanted to come to their city. I think one of them believes the town really is the actual Garden of Eden. What was his name? Mr. Severson. He reminded me of the four-minute men in Chicago. When he talked, his face got flushed, and by the time he was done, he was bellowing. I'm sure someone down the road would be able to hear every word he said. He wanted to know what my religion was. When I answered Catholic, he nodded, while several others rolled their eyes. One whispered, "Lord, not another one.

The woman, who on several occasions tried to ask a question, finally raised her hand and asked how I might handle someone who might not want to be touched by someone like me. "You know, looking so different and all," she said. I didn't see hatred, only concern. Her face helped me stay calm and not retreat into my tunnel. I told her there might be some who would need time to adjust to my differences, but with kindness, the difference would become less important, invisible.

During the hour I spent with these folks, I found myself thinking of Santa Cruz. This very thing could happen if a person who looked like them were to become their doctor. I relaxed. Sometimes I could even feel myself grinning, especially when someone asked me if I hoped to marry someday and how many children I hoped to have. Have I really only been here a week?

*Letter from Nena*
October 23, 1926

Brother,

The description you've given of Galesville reminds me of Santa Cruz before it outgrew its smallness. Tell me, is the church also nearby? The

Garden of Eden must have a Catholic church, or I know you wouldn't be there. Maybe you'll want to stay even longer.

I'm so very proud of you. Everyone is here. They now talk about you as if you are a hero, how you bring good fortune to the family name. I'm also happy for you because you are doing exactly what you set out to do years ago. I know I expressed concern about you becoming an American. *One of those,* is the way I put it. You haven't; you've only become who you were destined to be.

So have I. Mother of two, with hopefully another soon. I'm content, grateful for what I have. And I don't feel like I have lost you. If anything, I feel at peace because I know you too are content, maybe even ready to settle down and find a wife? One can only hope. I try to imagine who that might be and can only guess she'll be an American with a big heart. Mariposa still asks of you, waiting for your return. I think she would welcome you with open arms. But then, there are plenty of women there who I'm sure will do the same. I look forward to that day. Then I will visit.

Nena

### Letter to Nena
December 9, 1926

Your letter arrived, and all I could do was smile. So you wait for me to meet someone? I use to think I never would, or better said, no American woman would have me. Today, I have more faith. In fact, I may have already met her. There is a young woman, a nurse who I can't stop thinking about: Hazel, with gray-green eyes and a laugh you can't resist. Our eyes met, and my heart jumped. Since then, we've had short conversations, mostly about the patients we are tending to or the hospital we work in. I've always wanted to have them last longer, away from prying eyes and the bustle of the hospital. They're probably only moments of folly, but they've lifted my spirits.

Still, I'm weeks away from leaving to go back to St. Francis Hospital in Peoria, some six hours away. Once I leave, I'll probably never see her again. My letter is short, as there is seldom a time when a patient or two aren't waiting to see me.

Blessing as always,
Ricardo

# 1927

**TELEGRAM FROM THE MAYOR OF GALESVILLE**
January 23, 1927

DR. POWELL HAS PASSED. TOWN IS IN MOURNING. WOULD YOU CONSIDER COMING BACK? YOU WERE NOT REPLACED. PLEASE CONSIDER.

**JOURNAL ENTRY**
February 8, 1927

My bed is covered with piles of letters from Galesville and nearby towns—all with pleas for my return. Some I don't even recall meeting. There's even one from Mr. Severson saying, "Doc, we need you. For crying out loud, first I have to drag my wife to see you, and now she tells me she won't go to nobody else. Lordy, come back and be our doctor!"

Mrs. Olsen can't sleep at night, worrying about her four little ones. Ester Johnson says, "Get on back here. We can't survive without you." Mr. Saboda says it hasn't been the same since I left. I've even gotten a handwritten note from Chief Elkhorn saying the tribe needs me to return. I was shocked to learn I had been the first doctor they ever allowed into their tiny community of cabins a couple of miles out of town.

As I opened one letter after another, I started to shake. Is this what I'm meant to do? I thought I would someday be back in a large city like Milwaukee or Chicago, not in a small town near the Mississippi.

## Letter to Nena
### March 4, 1927

Sister,

I've returned to Galesville. Dr. Powell, the doctor I was helping, passed away in January, and they were left without a doctor. A week later I received a letter from the mayor asking me to come back, telling me he was barraged with folks coming to his home and office with one thing in mind—getting me back. In his letter, he said, "I couldn't walk down the street or have my morning coffee without someone bringing up your name." His was the first letter I received, followed by dozens more. That was in February.

When I returned several days ago, a large crowd gathered in the town square to welcome me back. A small troop of musicians broke into play as I pulled into the town square in my new motorcar I purchased knowing full well how many house calls I would be making. Mrs. Severson handed me a bouquet of flowers; the Johnsons, owners of the bakery, presented me with a loaf of bread straight out of their oven. I couldn't stop myself from lifting the loaf to my face, inhaling cinnamon and brown sugar. The mayor handed me keys to my old apartment nearby, saying, "Until you find a house you might want." With hands full, men and women patted me on the back as they escorted me to the doorstep of the clinic. Mayor Gale unlocked the door and held the door open for me, as the crowd broke into cheer.

Nena, my heart is telling me more and more that America will be my home, my second home, something I sensed you've suspected for some time. The sounds and voices of this country have captured me. I no longer reminisce of our old neighborhood; now I wait to hear the quiet cooing of mourning doves and the chimes of nearby churches announcing early Mass services are about to begin. I no longer miss the scent of sampaguita flowers; now I look forward to smelling the springtime buds of the black locust tree, a sweetness that lingers as you pass by, causing you to stop and inhale deeply—not once, but several times. And the fall colors making you feel like you're in the middle of a portrait. Or snow blanketing homes and streets for months on end, which now I no longer dread. Even the children calling to each other on their way to the nearby park—I listen as they chatter about nothing important, although huge in their minds. Here in Galesville, I've discovered pheasants: birds two feet tall with red faces, green necks with long tails of copper. They sound like they could be related to macaws. Every morning, they wake me with their piercing cackle. They are better than my watch, telling me it's time to rise. They ground me, help me realize where I am, who I have become, who I am still becoming.

Yesterday, I went for a drive around Lake Marinuka, the lake that Galesville is built around. Outside of town, I stopped as the sun was beginning its slow decent, and a herd of deer stood in a nearby field. There were dozens of them. Larger than those in the Philippines, they're lovely with coats the color of sand, short white tails, and eyes the size of saucers. I watched as they grazed, immune to my presence and the beauty surrounding them. When I started my motor, they were startled and in mass sprang into a leaping frenzy. In minutes, they were hidden from my view. Deer are apparently masters at hiding.

Perhaps this is what I've been doing, Sister. Hiding. Afraid to show more of me, the me you grew up with and grasp like few others. What I know is I've come to breathe easier, offer and accept a helping hand more often. In Galesville, I know I will find my way. I accept there will be many times I feel alone, different from those around me. But I've also learned with kindness this can be changed. And, too, accepting some may never come to know me or me, them.

In your first letter to me, the one you hid within my trunk when I left the Philippines, you gave me such wise and sage advice. You wrote: *Patience and prudence need be posts for you to lean on.* They have been, and will continue to be. Especially as I now bear the name of doctor.

I think of our dear father. He had so much, and yet it wasn't enough. I have found the beginnings of my enough. I no longer doubt I will find more. This morning as I write to you feels like the beginning of my story. My hope it is a long one between people and places I can't yet even imagine.

God bless you, Sister, for your acceptance and continued love.

Ricardo

# Near My End

# 1973

## High School Gymnasium, Galesville, Wisconsin

Sitting here on the stage takes me back to the only other stage I've been on, so many years ago. I think of it, and suddenly I'm there, a young man about to become a doctor with no one to celebrate with. Then I remember. Oh, to think of the many friends who showed up to bask in my success. I had never been as surprised.

Until today.

I had known the city had wanted to recognize me for the many years I've been their doctor. What has it been—forty-five? Can that be right? I had no idea this is what they had planned. Hazel grabs my hand; she squeezes and pulls me back to the here and now. I automatically cup my hand in hers. When I look up, she has a radiant glow, warmth I'm accustomed to and never tire of.

On this stage, we're not alone. Our eight children, their wives and husbands, their children and our grandchildren, encircle us. And like most Alvarez gatherings, they are all talking, pulling on the hands of their kids who aren't used to sitting in front of hundreds and hundreds of people. I've never seen the high school gymnasium as packed. The floor, usually reserved for basketball players, is filled; so are the bleachers.

One of my youngest catches my eye, she raises the large button she has pinned to her chest. Besides Hazel and me, everyone on the stage has them on. They all say the same thing: "I'm a Doctor Alvarez baby." In the audience, the buttons are like beacons shining from every corner, every row. Judge Twesme is trying to get everyone to sit down to start the program. I feel such a strong feeling of pride mixed with humility I fight back tears.

I'm content beyond my dreams.

# Acknowledgments

Thank you…

To the Ordoveza clan, who have diligently preserved our family history dating back to the sixteenth century, stories of who we were, and are still striving to become. Special thanks to our clan's history recorder, Dr. Luciano P/R. (Chito) Santiago, whom I met in the Philippines before he passed away, and who grounded me in family details. I credit him for setting me on the right track and Rena Tobias, my sister Diane, and brother Mario for keeping me there.

To the University of Wisconsin Continuing Educational Programs and the fabulous historical novel author and instructor, Kathy Steffens, who cheered me on as I tackled telling a story in the epistolary format.

To Tim Storm, another instructor, editor, and short story author, for his kind and spot-on developmental assessment of my first completed draft (or was it my second? Truly I can't remember, as they do all blend together.).

To Jody Whelden, my writing partner, whom I met in my first writing class, and who, over the past three years, has been so generous with her observations, advice, and encouragement.

To the early readers, Teresa Wolbers, Paula Huff, and Barb Robson who gave me hope that I might indeed be able to write the story.

To my twin brother, Marcos, who helped me relax a bit and believe our dad was guiding my writing of his story.

To friends Eileen Schein and Linda Preysz, who gave me much-needed reality checks in the eleventh hour, leading to one more rewrite.

To Kristin Mitchell of Little Creek Press and Diane Franklin, her trusted editor, who made a world of difference by believing in me and skillfully helping me through the publication process.

And finally to Ritchey Stroud, who with little complaint and notable patience, put up with what must have seemed like incessant rewrites in every hour and place imaginable. Thanks for hanging in there with me, Hon.

Truly, writing a novel is not one person's effort but involves many people's hearts and minds. I'm grateful to all.

# About the Author

Maria Alvarez Stroud lives in Madison, Wisconsin, with her husband, Ritchey. This is her debut novel, although she has an extensive writing background within public broadcasting. An avid reader and lover of historical fiction, she also writes short stories and essays.

# Discussion Questions

1. What do you think were the biggest struggles Ricardo had in assimilating to America?

2. Do you think Ricardo's life of privilege in the Philippines helped or hindered his adjustment?

3. Do you believe there are more or fewer people today, who like Mr. Stein and Mr. Filkowski, believe certain people do not belong in America?

4. What was different about Ricardo's journey in comparison to today? Do you think it was more or less difficult?

5. In the end, what helped Ricardo reach his goal?

CPSIA information can be obtained
at www.ICGtesting.com
Printed in the USA
BVHW040930230721
612715BV00019B/459

9 781955 656016